A Case For Salvation

RW Nelson

A Case For Salvation

Copyright© 2025 Richard W. Nelson (RW Nelson)

All Scripture quotations are taken from the New American Standard Bible (NASB). Copyright© 1960, 1962, 1963, 1968, 1971, 1972, 1973, 1975, 1977, 1995, 2020, by The Lockman Foundation. Used by permission. www.Lockman.org

Italics and underlines added to direct Scripture quotations are the author's emphasis.

This work is a revised and expanded edition of the author's previously published book, originally copyrighted in 1981 entitled: *A Case for Salvation: A Scriptural Study for Maturing in Christ,* by Richard W. Nelson.

The new version includes original commentary, updated chapters, and newly created topics. The copyright claim is a new expression of the original material.

Any internet addresses, phone numbers, or company or product information printed in this book are offered as a resource.

Associated with Layman Bible College Institute. www.laymanbiblecollege.institute

ISBN 979-8-9934384-0-5 (Hardcover)
ISBN 979-8-9934384-1-2 (Paperback)
ISBN 979-8-9934384-3-6 (ePub)
ISBN 979-8-9934384-2-9 (audiobook)

Pax Veritas Media LLC

Printed in the United States of America

A note from the author

This novel is an enhanced edition from the original book written more than four decades prior to the current copyright date. I assure you, as a young minister (back then) the original book was much less than two hundred forty pages.

According to Hebrews 4:12, "… the Word of God is living and active and sharper than any double-edged sword, even penetrating as far as the division of soul and spirit, of both joints and marrow, and able to judge the thoughts and intentions of the heart."

This verse beautifully captures how Scripture is not just ink on a page – it is dynamic, piercing, and deeply personal. It speaks to the living nature of God's Word, always relevant and transformative. Just as Jesus is the eternal living Word of God, the Bible is the eternal written Word of God.

Those who know Jesus should continue to grow and learn from Scripture each day. That is the way it should always be. Always learning, always hungry to grasp the "*mind of Christ*," (1 Corinthians 2:16), which is a reminder that believers (through the Holy Spirit) are given insight into God's will and character by studying the Bible and aligning our thoughts, values, and decisions with those of Christ.

For readers who are searching for answers or seem to have a deep void in your life, allow these Bible verses to systematically speak to your heart concerning the depths of what salvation in Christ is all about. The readers may notice that there are parts of this new edition that appear to be repetitious with certain verses being used repeatedly. I assure you it is not due to clerical errors or a lapse in writing judgement or penmanship skills.

When I was a young boy growing up in Texas, the pastor of the Baptist church my family attended, preached the same message two weeks in a row. I approached the pastor saying, "Pastor, I think you preached this same message last week." He turned towards me smiling and replied, "Yes, I did. And if the congregation does not listen and apply the lessons from this week's sermon, I will preach it again next week."

It is my heartfelt prayer that as you read '*A Case For Salvation*,' you will be open to hear from the Holy Spirit, learn things you never knew before concerning the Word, and formulate Biblically based thoughts and ideas in order to grow in your own spiritual walk and be able to share these truths of the Bible with others.

'A Case For Salvation'
Workbook

A 16 Lesson workbook complete with questions, answers, and chapter summaries are available in pdf form at:

www.laymanbiblecollege.institute
and
www.rwnelson-author.com

Contents

1. Finding God In A Confused World — 1
2. How We Got Separated from God — 14
3. The Holy One – Who Came To Us — 27
4. Reconciliation and the Power of the Blood — 39
5. The Tabernacle: A Blueprint for Redemption — 51
6. The Blood That Speaks — 66
7. The Permanent Sacrifice and Our Living High Priest — 80
8. "Behold the Lamb" — 96
9. Your Life: Living Evidence of Resurrection — 112
10. The 'I AM' – Said So (1) — 128
11. The 'I AM' – Said So (2) — 146
12. Your Certificate of Debt Canceled — 163
13. The Early Church and the Question of Salvation — 178
14. The Honor Roll of Faith — 191
15. Salvation and the Holy Spirit — 212
16. The Crowns, Rewards, and Heaven — 228

Finding God In A Confused World

Back in the 1960s, two Soviet astronauts - Yuri Gagarin and Gherman Titov - made headlines not just for orbiting Earth, but for what they said about God. Gagarin reportedly said, *"I did not see God in space,"* and Titov added that he saw no sign of a higher power. Their comments reflected a growing belief at the time: maybe God was not real after all.

That decade was full of chaos. People marched for civil rights, protested wars, and watched cities erupt in riots - all broadcasted on television. Some people even carried signs that said, *"God is dead,"* quoting the philosopher Friedrich Nietzsche. It was a way of saying that traditional faith did not seem to fit in a world full of pain and confusion. Many turned instead to human ideas and personal freedom, questioning whether religion had any answers.

But here is the twist: while many rejected Christianity, others were desperately searching for something spiritual. Eastern religions like Hinduism and Buddhism became popular in the U.S., offering peace and purpose through meditation and mantras. Gurus like Maharishi Mahesh Yogi taught Transcendental Meditation, claiming it could connect people to the divine within themselves.

By the 1970s, the spiritual scene exploded. Scientology promised mental freedom. Astrology and witchcraft showed up in magazines and TV shows. Some people even followed charismatic leaders who claimed to be prophets - but many of these groups turned into dangerous cults. One of the most tragic examples was the Jonestown massacre in 1978, where over 900 followers of Jim Jones died in a mass suicide-murder.

The 1980s brought a new wave of spiritual interest - but this time, it was often mixed with materialism. Televangelists filled the airwaves, preaching prosperity and healing in Jesus' name. Numerous ministries grew exponentially, while others collapsed under scandal. Some began to ask: was faith becoming business and entertainment?

At the same time, the Cold War and fears of nuclear disaster made many wonder about the end of the world. Books like *The Late Great Planet Earth* stirred up interest in biblical prophecy, and movies about the apocalypse (i.e. *The Day After*, ABC Circle Films, 1983) stirred up 'troubling and uncertain hearts'. Christian television personalities pointed to verses like Matthew 24:6, *"You will be hearing of wars and rumors of wars. See that you are not alarmed, for those things must take place, but that is not yet the end,"* and seemed to speak directly to the chaos people saw around them.

In the 1990s, spirituality became more personalized. The rise of the internet gave people access to every belief system imaginable. "New Age" ideas - like crystals, energy healing, and spirit guides - grew in popularity. Many people said they were "spiritual but not religious," choosing bits and pieces from different traditions. But this mix-and-match approach often lacked depth or truth. As Proverbs 14:12 warns, *"There is a way which seems right to a person, but its end is the way of death."*

The 2000s were shaped by global tragedy. After the 9/11 attacks, churches filled with people seeking comfort and answers. But over time, attendance dropped again. Some began to question how a good God could allow such evil. Others turned to politics or activism as their new source of hope. Yet the Bible reminds us in Psalm 33:17, *"A horse is a false hope for victory; nor does it rescue anyone by its great strength."* Human solutions cannot replace divine truth.

In the 2010s, social media changed everything. People curated their identities online, chasing likes and followers. Mental health struggles rose, especially among teens. Many felt isolated, anxious, and unsure of their worth. Some found comfort in mindfulness apps or self-care routines, but others sank into despair. The longing for purpose though remained strong. Psalms 63:1 states, *"... I shall be watching for You; my soul thirsts for You, my flesh yearns for You, in a dry and exhausted land where there is no water."* Deep down, people still yearned for something eternal and genuine.

In the 2020s, the search continues. The COVID-19 pandemic shook the world, forcing people to face death, loneliness, and uncertainty. Some returned to faith. Others turned to conspiracy theories or digital escapism. The rise of AI and virtual reality has raised new questions: What does it mean to be human? Is there more to life than algorithms and screens?

These mixed-up ideas raise big questions: Who's right? Is God gone, like the astronauts said, or is He in temples, self-help books, or apps promising happiness? Can money, popularity, or a good GPA fill the emptiness inside? Many today feel the same confusion. You might say, "I believe in God, but He feels far away," or "I hear about being 'saved,' but what does that even mean?" Or maybe you wonder, "Saved from what?"

Through all these decades, one truth remains: people are hungry for meaning. They may reject religion, but they cannot escape the need for hope, love, and purpose. As Jesus said in John 6:35, *"I am the bread of life; the one who comes to Me will not be hungry, and the one who believes in Me will never be thirsty."* The world keeps changing, but the answer stays the same.

A Living Guide for a Broken World

The answer to life's biggest questions is not found in the latest TikTok trend, a new self-help book, or a viral life hack - it is in the Bible, God's unchanging Word, written by ordinary people who were guided by the Holy Spirit.

Two key verses explain why we can trust the Bible: 2 Timothy 3:16 and 2 Peter 1:21.

In 2 Timothy 3:16–17, Paul writes to Timothy, a young pastor serving in the spiritually complex and morally chaotic city of Ephesus around A.D. 62–64. Christians were under pressure - mocked, marginalized, and persecuted. Paul himself was imprisoned, possibly awaiting execution. His words carry the weight of urgency and legacy.

He tells Timothy, *"All Scripture is <u>inspired by God</u> and beneficial for teaching, for rebuke, for correction, for training in righteousness; so that the man or woman of God may be fully capable, equipped for every good work."* (2 Timothy 3:16–17)

The Greek word translated *"inspired by God"* is *theopneustos* (θεόπνευστος) - a compound of *theos* (God) and *pneō* (to breathe out). It is a rare and potent term, possibly coined by Paul himself. It does not mean God breathed *into* the Bible, as if animating something already written. It means Scripture was **breathed out by God** - it originated in His very being. Just as God breathed life into Adam in Genesis 2:7 -

"Then the Lord God formed the man of dust from the ground, and breathed into his nostrils the breath of life; and the man became a living person" - so He breathed truth into Scripture. It is alive, powerful, and divine in origin. This breath is not mere air - it is essence. It carries the weight of eternity, the wisdom of heaven, and the love of a Father who longs to guide His children.

Hebrews 4:12 affirms this: *"For the word of God is living and active, and sharper than any two-edged sword... able to judge the thoughts and intentions of the heart."*

Paul (from 2 Timothy 3:16,17) then outlines four transformative functions of Scripture:

Teaching. Scripture reveals what is true - about God's nature, our identity, and the purpose of life. It answers the deepest questions: Who am I? Why am I here? What is good? What is eternal? Psalm 119:105 says, *"Your word is a lamp to my feet and a light to my path."* It does not just illuminate facts - it reveals meaning.

Rebuking. God's Word confronts us when we stray. It exposes sin not to shame us, but to awaken us. Like a mirror, it reflects the places we have distorted truth or ignored love. Proverbs 3:11–12 reminds us, *"My son, do not reject the discipline of the Lord or loathe His rebuke, for whom the Lord loves He disciplines."* Rebuke is a form of grace - it calls us back to life.

Correcting. Correction is not condemnation - it is restoration. Scripture does not just say, "You're wrong." It says, "Here's how to make it right." It is like a skilled surgeon removing what is harmful and healing what is broken.

James 1:21–22 urges, *"Therefore, rid yourselves of all filthiness and all that remains of wickedness, and in humility receive the word implanted, which is able to save your souls. But prove yourselves doers of the word..."*

Training in Righteousness. This is spiritual conditioning. Just as athletes train their bodies, believers train their souls. Scripture shapes our habits, attitudes, and choices so we reflect God's character. 1 Timothy 4:8 says, *"For bodily training is just slightly beneficial, but godliness is beneficial for all things..."* Righteousness is not just about rules - it is about becoming who we were created to be.

Think of Scripture like a divine GPS. It does not just alert you when you have taken a wrong turn - it recalculates your route and guides you back to the path of life. But unlike a GPS that relies on satellites, this guidance comes from heaven itself. Proverbs 3:5–6 says, *"Trust in the Lord with all your heart and do not lean on your own understanding. In all your ways acknowledge Him, and He will make your paths straight."*

Because Scripture is *God-breathed*, **it is not just advice - it is revelation.** It is not just helpful - it is holy. **It is not just informative - it is transformative**. In a world full of noise, confusion, and counterfeit truths, the Word of God remains the one voice that is trustworthy, timeless, and true.

How the Holy Spirit Guided Scripture

In **2 Peter 1:21**, the apostle Peter - one of Jesus' closest friends and eyewitnesses to His transfiguration, resurrection, and ascension - writes to Christians who were facing a crisis of truth. False teachers had infiltrated the church, twisting Scripture to suit their own agendas. Peter's words are both a warning and a reassurance.

He writes: *"For no prophecy was ever made by an act of human will, but men <u>moved</u> by the Holy Spirit spoke from God."* (2 Peter 1:21)

The Greek word translated *"moved"* is *pheromenoi* (φερόμενοι), which means "**carried along**." It is the same word used to describe a ship driven by the wind. Picture a sailboat on open water - not powered by engines or oars, but by the invisible force of the wind filling its sails and directing its course. That is how Peter describes the process of divine inspiration. The authors of Scripture were not inventing ideas or pushing their own opinions. They were vessels - lifted, steered, and propelled by the Holy Spirit.

This metaphor is powerful. It tells us that the Bible is not a human invention - it is a divine transmission. The writers retained their personalities, styles, and experiences, but the message came from God. Just as the wind is unseen but undeniable, the Spirit influenced and shaped every word, every truth, every prophecy.

Even When People Doubt

Peter's assurance matters, especially in a world where skepticism is common. Think of astronauts again – such as floating in space, staring into the vastness of the universe, and wondering if God is real. Some have returned to Earth with faith deepened; others have come back with doubts. But Scripture remains trustworthy - not because it aligns with human opinion, but because it originates from divine authority.

Isaiah 55:8–9 reminds us: *"For My thoughts are not your thoughts, nor are your ways My ways," declares the Lord. "For as the heavens are higher than the earth, so are My ways higher than your ways..."*

The Bible does not depend on human validation. It stands firm because its source is eternal. The Spirit who hovered over the waters in Genesis 1:2 - *"And the Spirit of God was hovering over the surface of the waters"* - is the same Spirit who hovered over the hearts and minds of the prophets and apostles, guiding them to write what God intended.

A Compass in the Storm

In a world full of misinformation, shifting values, and spiritual confusion, Scripture is like a compass in a storm. It does not change with the winds of culture - it points to true north. And because it was *carried along* by the Holy Spirit, it remains reliable, even when everything else feels uncertain.

John 16:13 says, *"But when He, the Spirit of truth, comes, He will guide you into all the truth..."* The same Spirit who inspired the Bible now helps us understand it. We are not left alone to interpret ancient words - we are invited into a living conversation with the Author Himself.

The Bible says God is not dead - it is people who are spiritually lost because of sin, which is choosing to do wrong. The astronauts did not see God because their hearts were not open to Him, not because He was not there. And when people worship things like nature, money, or themselves, they miss the God who made them and can fill their hearts. This book will dive into the Bible to explore why people feel empty, how sin separates us from God, and how Jesus offers a way back to Him. We will study key verses to understand God's plan and how it can change your life.

The Empty Space Inside: Why We Long for Something More

Have you ever felt a quiet ache inside - like something is missing, but you cannot quite name it? It is not just sadness or boredom. It is deeper than that. It is like a hollow space in your soul that no achievement, relationship, or distraction can fill. People have felt this for thousands of years. Ancient kings felt it. Modern teenagers feel it. It is the same longing, just dressed in different clothes.

Today, that ache might look like chasing likes on social media, obsessing over image, or striving for perfection. In Solomon's day, it looked like palaces, wealth, and endless pleasures. But underneath it all is the same question: *Is there more than this?*

In Ecclesiastes 3:11, Solomon - one of the wisest men who ever lived - wrote:

"He has made everything appropriate in its time. He has also set <u>eternity</u> in their heart, without the possibility that mankind will find out the work which God has done from the beginning even to the end."

The Hebrew word for *"eternity"* is *olam* (עוֹלָם). It does not just mean "forever" in a calendar sense. It means **something vast**, **veiled**, and **beyond human grasp**. It is the sense of the infinite - the mysterious reality that stretches beyond time and space. It is as if God planted a divine echo inside us, a whisper of something eternal. We carry it like a compass that always points beyond the horizon.

The God-Shaped Vacuum

This longing is not a flaw - it is a feature. It is part of our design. Blaise Pascal, a 17th-century mathematician and theologian, once said:

"There is a God-shaped vacuum in the heart of each man which cannot be satisfied by any created thing, but only by God the Creator."

That is why money, fame, romance, or success cannot fill the void. They are finite. And we were made for the infinite. Psalm 42:1–2 captures this beautifully: *"As the deer pants for the water brooks, so my soul pants for You, God. My soul thirsts for God, for the living God..."*

We thirst - not just for meaning, but for *presence*. For connection with the One who made us.

When we try to fill the emptiness with temporary things, we end up more lost than before. But when we turn toward God, something shifts. The ache becomes a doorway. The longing becomes a signal. We begin to understand who we are - not just as consumers or performers, but as *image-bearers* of the eternal.

Colossians 1:16 says, *"For by Him all things were created... all things have been created through Him and for Him."* We were not made to orbit around ourselves. We were made to orbit around God.

A Soul That Reaches Beyond

Think of your soul like a telescope - not meant to stare at the ground, but to gaze into the heavens. That is what *olam* is. It is the built-in desire to reach beyond what we can see, touch, or control. It is the hunger for transcendence - for something that does not fade, break, or disappoint.

Romans 8:22–23 describes this longing as part of creation itself: *"For we know that the whole creation groans and suffers... and not only that, but also we ourselves... groan within ourselves, waiting eagerly for our adoption as sons and daughters..."* Even the universe is waiting. Even our bodies groan. Because we were made for more.

The good news is that the empty space inside us is not a curse - it is an invitation. It is God's way of drawing us toward Himself. And when we respond, we do not just find answers - we find *relationship*. We find the One who fills the void not with stuff, but with Himself. The ache becomes peace. The longing becomes love. The hole becomes whole.

Chasing the Wind: Solomon and the Search for Meaning

In the 1960s and 1970s, people were searching – desperately - for something to fill the emptiness inside. At music festivals like Woodstock, they chased freedom through parties, psychedelic drugs, and rebellion against tradition. Scientology offered self-improvement through mysterious tests and spiritual hierarchies. Charismatic leaders claimed to have all the answers, drawing crowds hungry for purpose. Others turned to more familiar pursuits: money, grades, popularity, or romance. But none of it fully satisfied. The thrill faded. The emptiness remained.

This hunger is not new. It is ancient. Nearly 3,000 years ago, King Solomon - the wealthiest, wisest ruler of his time - embarked on the same quest. But unlike most people, Solomon had unlimited resources. He did not just dream about pleasure, power, or success - he lived it.

He writes in Ecclesiastes 2:10–11: *"All that my eyes desired I did not refuse them. I did not restrain my heart from any pleasure... When I considered all that I had done and the labor I had expended... behold, it was futility and striving after wind, and there was no benefit under the sun."*

Solomon had it all - palaces, vineyards, entertainers, gold, wisdom, fame. Yet when he stepped back and looked at his life, he saw a mirage. It was like chasing the wind: exhausting, elusive, and ultimately empty.

Solomon's Mirror: A Reflection of Our Age

Solomon's story is eerily modern. His words echo the disillusionment of every generation that tries to fill the soul with things that do not last.

He became a mirror for humanity's restless heart. Ecclesiastes is not just a journal - it is a diagnosis.

In Ecclesiastes 1:2, he opens with a haunting refrain: *"Futility of futilities," says the Preacher, "Futility of futilities! Everything is futility."*

The Hebrew word for *"futility"* is *hebel* (הֶבֶל) - a word that means **vapor**, **breath**, or **smoke**. It is not just meaningless - it is *fleeting*. It vanishes when you try to grasp it. Solomon is not saying life has no meaning; he is saying that meaning cannot be found in the things we often chase.

Solomon's insight is echoed across history. Civilizations built empires through military conquest, hoping power would bring peace. Philosophers like Plato sought truth through reason, hoping logic could unlock the mysteries of existence. Religions devised rituals and sacrifices, hoping to bridge the gap between humanity and the divine.

But the ache remained. The vacuum persisted.

Romans 1:21–23 describes this universal drift: *"For even though they knew God, they did not honor Him as God... but they became futile in their reasonings... and exchanged the glory of the incorruptible God for images..."*

Humanity has always traded the eternal for the temporary. We build idols - whether golden statues or glowing screens - and hope they will satisfy. But they never do.

Solomon's Wisdom: A Call to Look Higher

Solomon's journey was not just about despair - it was about awakening. He realized that life *"under the sun"* - life without God - is hollow. But life *with* God is full of meaning, even in its mysteries.

In **Ecclesiastes 12:13,** he concludes: *"The conclusion, when everything has been heard, is: fear God and keep His commandments, because this applies to every person."*

Solomon does not offer a formula - he offers a relationship. Meaning is not found in possessions or achievements. It is found in reverence, in surrender, in walking with the One who made us.

The world still chases the wind. But Scripture invites us to chase wonder - to seek the eternal, the unseen, the divine. That is what Solomon discovered after a lifetime of searching. And it is what every heart still longs for.

Jeremiah 29:13 says, *"And you will seek Me and find Me when you search for Me with all your heart."* The hole inside us is not a flaw - it is a homing signal. It is God's way of drawing us back to Himself.

The Promise of Living Water

In John 4:13–14, Jesus meets a Samaritan woman at a well - a moment that seems ordinary but unfolds into one of the most profound conversations in Scripture. He says:

"Everyone who drinks of this water will be thirsty again, but whoever drinks of the water that I will give him will never be thirsty; but the water that I will give him will become in him a fountain of water springing up to eternal life."

At first, the woman thinks He is talking about physical water. After all, they are standing beside a well, and "she is come to draw water" in the heat of the day. But Jesus is offering something far deeper - *spiritual life*. The "water" He speaks of is a symbol of the Holy Spirit, who fills the soul with God's love, peace, and purpose.

The Greek phrase Jesus uses - *ou mē dipsēsei* (οὐ μὴ διψήσει) - is emphatic. It is not just "you will not be thirsty." It is "you will *never ever* thirst again." It is a promise of **permanent satisfaction** - not in the body, but in the soul. Jesus is saying, *"If you receive what I give, the emptiness inside you will be replaced with a spring that never runs dry."*

This moment is even more powerful because of *who* Jesus is talking to. The woman is a Samaritan - part of a group Jews typically avoided. She is also carrying deep personal shame. She has had five husbands, and the man she is with now is not her husband. She comes to the well alone, in the hottest part of the day, likely to avoid the judgmental stares of others.

But Jesus does not reject her. He does not shame her. He *sees* her. He speaks to her. He offers her *living water* - a new life, a fresh start, a relationship that heals what is broken. This is the heart of the gospel: God meets us in our mess, not after we have cleaned it up.

Romans 5:8 says, *"But God demonstrates His own love toward us, in that while we were still sinners, Christ died for us."* Jesus does not wait for perfection. He offers grace in the middle of our imperfection.

The Good Shepherd and the Abundant Life

Later, in John 10:10, Jesus expands on this idea: *"The thief comes only to steal and kill and destroy; I came so that they would have life and have it abundantly."*

Here, Jesus compares Himself to a *Good Shepherd* - one who knows His sheep, protects them, and leads them to safety. The *"thief"* represents anything (not just Satan) that tries to pull us away from God: lies, fear, addiction, shame, even the pressure to be perfect. These things promise happiness but leave us feeling empty.

Jesus does not promise a life without problems. **He promises a life with purpose.** A life that is full - not of stuff, but of *substance*. Not of ease, but of *eternal significance*.

"Abundant life" is not about having more - it is about *being more*. It is the difference between just surviving and truly living. It is waking up with peace, walking through pain with hope, and knowing you are deeply loved by the One who made you.

Isaiah 58:11 captures this beautifully: *"And the Lord will continually guide you, and satisfy your desire in scorched places, and give strength to your bones; and you will be like a watered garden, and like a spring of water whose waters do not fail."*

Jesus does not just quench our thirst - He transforms us into fountains. We become sources of life, healing, and hope for others. In a culture that offers endless distractions but little depth, Jesus offers *living water*. Not temporary relief, but eternal renewal. Not surface-level fixes, but soul-level restoration.

The Samaritan woman came to the well thirsty. She left transformed. And her story reminds us: no matter who we are, where we have been, or what we have done, Jesus meets us at the well - and offers us life that never runs dry.

Why does this matter? Many people feel like life has no point. You might hear about Jesus' promises and wonder, *"If He came to give us abundant life, why does mine feel so hard?"* That is a fair question - and it points to something deeper. The reason life feels broken is because of sin - the moment humanity turned away from God. Ever since, we have been trying to fill that emptiness with things that do not last.

But Jesus came to fix that. He offers living water that satisfies our deepest thirst and abundant life that gives us hope, even in the middle of pain. He does not just patch up our problems – He transforms our hearts.

"*Abundant life*" does not mean tons of money or no problems. It is about having peace and purpose with God, even when things are tough. To understand why that feels 'out of reach', we need to look at where it all went wrong.

2
How We Got Separated from God

The Bible opens not with chaos, but with beauty. Genesis 1 paints a picture of a world in perfect harmony - light and land, stars and seas, animals and humans, all declared *"very good"* by their Creator. At the center of this masterpiece is humanity.

In Genesis 1:26–27, God says: *"Let Us make mankind in Our image, according to Our likeness... So, God created man in His own <u>image</u>, in the image of God He created him; male and female He created them."*

The Hebrew word for *"image"* is *tselem* (צֶלֶם). It does not just mean a physical copy - it comes from a root that implies a *shadow* or *reflection*. In ancient Hebrew thought, to be made in God's *tselem* meant we were designed to **mirror His character** - to love as He loves, to be unique as He is Unique, to reason, to choose, and most importantly, to live in relationship with Him.

Imagine standing in front of a mirror - not just to see your face, but to reflect something greater. That is what Adam and Eve were meant to be: living mirrors of God's goodness on earth. They walked with Him in the Garden of Eden, unashamed and unafraid. Genesis 2:25 says, *"And the man and his wife were both naked, but they were not ashamed."* There was no guilt, no hiding - just pure communion with God.

The Fall: Missing the Mark

But in Genesis 3, everything changed. The harmony of Eden was pierced by a voice that sowed doubt. A serpent - Satan in disguise - walked into the garden and whispered a question that would echo through history: *"Did God really say...?"* He tempted Eve to eat from the one tree God had forbidden - the Tree of the Knowledge of Good and Evil. The fruit looked desirable, the promise enticing. Eve took and ate. Adam did the same. In that moment, they chose to trust their own judgment over God's wisdom. They reached for autonomy instead of intimacy. That choice is what Scripture calls *sin*.

The Hebrew word for sin is *chata* (חָטָא), which means **"to miss the mark"**. It is not just about breaking a rule - it is about aiming at the target of God's design and shooting wide. Imagine an archer drawing back a bow, eyes fixed on the bullseye, but the arrow veers off course. That is *chata*. It is failing to live up to the purpose we were made for. It is choosing distortion over reflection, self over surrender. Sin is a fracture in the mirror we were meant to be - a crack that distorts the image of God in us.

Adam and Eve's decision did not just affect them - it sent shockwaves through all of creation. First, it brought **spiritual death**, a severing of the intimate connection they had with God. Where once they walked with Him in the cool of the day, now they hid in shame, covered in fig leaves and fear. The bond was broken. They were exiled from Eden, cut off from the presence that gave them life.

Second, it introduced **physical death** into the human story. Mortality began. The dust from which they were formed would one day reclaim them. The eternal became temporary. The breath of life was now shadowed by the reality of decay.

Third, their sin unleashed **brokenness into creation itself**. The world that had once responded in harmony to God's voice now groaned under the weight of curse. Pain, toil, and suffering entered the human experience. As God said in Genesis 3:17–18: *"Cursed is the ground because of you; With hard labor you will eat from it all the days of your life. Both thorns and thistles it shall grow for you…"*

The soil would resist. The body would ache. Relationships would strain. The mirror was not only cracked - it was surrounded by a world that reflected that brokenness. And yet, even in this moment of loss, God's voice did not vanish. His judgment was laced with mercy. The story was not over. The image could still be restored.

Thanatos: The Death That Divides

Paul, writing centuries after Eden's gates closed, traces the effect of Adam's choice in Romans 5:12: *"Therefore, just as through one man sin entered the world, and death through sin, so <u>death</u> spread to all mankind, because all sinned."*

The Greek word for "*death*" here is *thanatos* (θάνατος). It is a word that carries more weight than just the end of breathing or the stillness of a body. *Thanatos* means **separation** - a severing from the source of life itself. In biblical thought, life is not just existence; it is connection. To live is to be plugged into God, the One who breathes, sustains, and empowers. So, when Paul says death spread to all, he is describing a spiritual unplugging. The soul's power cord is yanked from the outlet. The light goes out. The warmth fades. The connection is lost.

This was not just Adam's tragedy - it became ours. His sin did not stay contained in Eden; it spilled into every generation like a toxin in the bloodstream. Humanity inherited a broken nature, a spiritual condition that Biblical teachers call *original sin*. It is like a disease passed down through the family tree - not one we chose, but one we carry. We are born with a longing we cannot name, a hunger we cannot satisfy, a homesickness for a place we have never seen. Deep down, we sense that something is missing. That we were made for more.

A Spiritual Inheritance of Disconnection

This inherited brokenness is not just about behavior - it is about identity. We were created to reflect God, but the mirror is cracked. We were designed to walk with Him, but we are born wandering. Even our best efforts - kindness, creativity, love - are shadows of what they were meant to be. *Thanatos* means we are spiritually adrift, like a boat cut loose from its anchor, drifting farther from the shore of God's presence.

And yet, even in this bleak diagnosis, Paul is preparing us for hope. Romans 5 does not end with death - it leads us toward life. The story of humanity is not just about the fall; **it is about the rescue**. The same passage that names Adam as the source of sin will soon name Jesus as the source of salvation.

The gospel does not leave us in the shadow of *thanatos*. Romans does not stop at death - it pivots toward life. Paul continues in Romans 5:17: *"For if by the offense of the one, death reigned through the one, much more will those who receive the abundance of grace and of the gift of righteousness reign in life through the One, Jesus Christ."*

Just as death entered through one man – Adam - *life* now enters through another - *Jesus*. But Jesus did not come merely to cancel sin like erasing a mistake from a chalkboard. He came to **restore the image**, to reconnect us to the source, to breathe life back into what was lost. Where Adam fractured the mirror, Jesus begins the work of repair. Where Adam unplugged the soul from its power source, Jesus reconnects the cord.

In Colossians 1:15, Paul describes Jesus as: *"The image of the invisible God..."*

The Greek word here for *"image"* is *eikōn* (εἰκών), meaning a visible representation of **something unseen**. The word "icon" in modern English is derived from *eikōn*. Jesus is the perfect *tselem* - the flawless reflection of God's character, love, and holiness. He is what Adam was meant to be, and more. Through Him, we are invited to become mirrors again - not cracked and distorted, but whole and radiant.

Through Jesus, the power cord is plugged back in. The light returns. The soul flickers to life. The relationship that was severed in Eden is restored - not by our effort, but by His grace. We are no longer defined by *chata* - missing the mark - but by **grace**, which hits the target we could never reach on our own.

Paul proclaims this transformation in 2 Corinthians 5:17: *"Therefore if anyone is in Christ, this person is a new creation; the old things passed away; behold, new things have come."*

This is not just a fresh start - **it is a new identity**. The old story of separation is rewritten with restoration. We were made to reflect God. Sin cracked the mirror. But Jesus came to restore the reflection - and to walk with us again, just like in Eden.

In Christ, we do not just return to Eden - we move toward something even greater. Revelation 21 describes a new heaven and new earth, where God dwells with His people, and death is no more. The mirror is not just repaired - it is glorified. The reflection becomes radiant. The story that began with *tselem* ends with transformation.

Humanity's Universal Need for Grace

After the fall in Genesis, the rest of Scripture becomes a long, honest reckoning with human nature. The Bible does not sugarcoat our condition - it exposes it with clarity and compassion. In Romans 3:10, Paul quotes Psalm 14 to make the point unmistakable: *"There is none righteous, no, not one."*

The Greek word for *"righteous"* is *dikaios* (δίκαιος). It does not just mean someone who behaves well or follows the rules. It means someone who is in **right standing with God** - someone whose life is fully aligned with God's character, justice, and holiness. It is about being in sync with the Creator, like a musical instrument perfectly tuned to the divine melody. But Paul says no one - whether Jew or Gentile, religious or irreligious - can claim that status on their own. The human condition is universally out of tune.

This is not just about breaking commandments - it is about **falling short of the image** we were created to reflect. We were designed to shine with God's glory, but sin has dimmed the light. We were meant to walk in step with Him, but we all stumbled off the path.

Paul continues in Romans 3:23: *"For all have sinned and fall short of the glory of God."*

The phrase *"fall short"* comes from the Greek word *hystereō* (ὑστερέω), which means **to be lacking, to miss out, to be inferior or depleted**. It is the image of someone climbing a mountain, straining toward the summit, only to realize they are still miles below the peak. No matter how hard we try - through good deeds, religious rituals, or moral effort - we cannot reach the top. The gap is too wide. The summit is too high.

The *"glory"* we fall short of is *doxa* (δόξα) - God's radiant perfection, His holiness, His breathtaking beauty. It is the brilliance of His presence, the purity of His love, the majesty of His justice. And it is the very thing we were meant to reflect. But sin has fogged the mirror. The image is blurred. The light is dimmed.

This universal falling short is not just a theological statement - it is a lived experience. We feel it in our failures, our regrets, our insecurities. We sense it in the ache for meaning, the hunger for love, the longing to be whole. Deep down, we know we were made for more - but we cannot reach it on our own.

And that is exactly where grace enters the story. Grace is not just a divine favor it is God reaching down from the summit to lift us up. It is the light piercing the fog. It is the mirror being cleaned, not by our effort, but by His mercy.

Sin's Consequences

Sin is not just a slip-up or a bad habit - it is a **spiritual transaction**. Paul makes this crystal clear in Romans 6:23: *"For the wages of sin is death, but the gift of God is eternal life in Christ Jesus our Lord."*

The word Paul uses for *"wages"* is *opsōnia* (ὀψώνια), a term that originally referred to the **payment a soldier received for his service**. It is earned. It is deserved. It is the result of labor. In this context, Paul is saying that sin pays out a salary - and that salary is *death*. Not just physical death, but spiritual death - a severing from the source of life, from God Himself. The Greek word *thanatos* again emphasizes this kind of deep, soul-level separation. It is like being paid in darkness. The paycheck comes, but it bankrupts the soul.

This is the grim reality of sin: it compensates us with isolation, emptiness, and eventual destruction. It is not just about punishment - it is about consequence. Sin leads us away from life, and the further we go, the more we earn what we were never meant to receive.

But Paul does not leave us in despair. He follows the word *wages* with a radical contrast:

"But the gift of God is eternal life..."

The Greek word for *"gift"* is *charisma* (χάρισμα), which comes from *charis* - grace. It means a **freely given favor**, something **unearned**, **undeserved**, and overflowing. It is not a paycheck - it is a present. And this gift is not just a better alternative to death - it is **eternal life**. Not just endless existence, but a restored connection to God, the source of all joy, beauty, and meaning.

This sets up one of the most important themes in Romans - and in the entire gospel: **salvation is by grace, not works.** We do not climb our way back to God. We do not earn our way into heaven. We receive. We open our hands. We say yes to the gift.

Two Roads, Two Outcomes

Romans 6:23 lays out two paths like a fork in the road. One is the path of *opsōnia* – *'the wages of sin'*. It is paved with self-reliance, pride, and rebellion. It leads to *Thanatos* - spiritual death. The other is the path of *charisma* - the gift of grace. It is offered through Jesus Christ, and it leads to *eternal life*.

The choice is not about being good enough - it is about being willing to receive. It is about trusting the One who earned what we could not and offers what we do not deserve.

Sin writes a paycheck we cannot afford to cash. But Jesus tears it up and hands us a gift instead - a new identity, a restored relationship, a life that begins now and stretches into eternity. The mirror is no longer cracked by wages - it is healed by grace.

Judgment: The Final Reckoning

The Bible does not shy away from the reality of judgment - it presents it as a moment of ultimate truth. In Hebrews 9:27, we read: *"It is appointed for men to die once, and after this comes judgment."*

The Greek word for *"judgment"* is *krisis* (κρίσις), which means a **decisive verdict** - a **final ruling** based on what is real, not what is hidden. It is not just a courtroom drama; it is the moment when every life is laid bare before God. There are no retakes, no appeals, no hiding behind excuses or appearances. It is like a final exam where the only passing grade is perfection - and none of us, by our own merit, can achieve that.

In Revelation 20:12, John gives us a vivid image: *"And I saw the dead, great and small, standing before the throne, and books were opened... and the dead were judged according to their works."*

These "books" contain the record of every person's deeds - every thought, word, and action. It is a sobering picture: nothing forgotten, nothing omitted. But then another book is mentioned - the Book of Life. **This book does not record deeds - it records names**. If your name is written there, it means you have received God's gift of salvation through Jesus. It is not about what you have done - it is about who you belong to.

Without that gift, the verdict is devastating. Matthew 25:41 describes the outcome for those who reject God's grace: *"Depart from Me, you accursed people, into the everlasting fire which has been prepared for the devil and his angels."*

This is not meant to scare - it is meant to **wake us up**. The Bible's message is clear: we all fall short, but God offers a way back. Judgment is real, but so is mercy. Through Jesus, we do not just escape condemnation - we are invited into eternal life, restored to the glory we were meant to reflect.

The Barrier Between Us and God

The biggest obstacle between us and God is not physical distance - it is **spiritual distortion**.

In Isaiah 59:1–2, the prophet writes: *"Behold, the Lord's hand is not so short that it cannot save; nor is His ear so dull that it cannot hear. But your wrongdoings have caused a separation between you and your God, and your sins have hidden His face from you so that He does not hear."*

God is not weak or distracted. His arm is strong enough to rescue. His ear is attentive enough to hear. The problem is not His ability - it is our condition.

The Hebrew word for "*wrongdoings* (iniquity, guilt, perversity)" is *avon* (עָוֹן), which refers to **twisted, crooked behavior** - not just accidental mistakes, but deliberate choices that bend away from God's design. It is like taking a detour off a straight path and ending up lost in a maze of our own making. These twisted choices do not just make life harder - they create a spiritual wall between us and God. They distort the image we were meant to reflect. They dim the light. They sever the connection.

But even here, in the stark reality of judgment and separation, the gospel whispers hope. The same God who judges is the God who saves. The same hand that holds the verdict also offers the gift. The wall built by sin can be torn down by grace.

From Verdict to Victory

Judgment is coming - but so is redemption. The cross of Christ is where justice and mercy meet. It is where the record of our sins is nailed and canceled. It is where the twisted path is straightened, and the name is written in the Book of Life.

Faced with the gap between ourselves and God, many people instinctively try to build a bridge with good deeds. They go to church, volunteer, try to be kind, and hope that being "good enough" will tip the scales in their favor. But Scripture offers a radically different solution - one that does not rely on human effort, but on divine mercy.

In Ephesians 2:8–9, Paul writes: *"For by grace you have been saved through faith, and that not of yourselves; it is the gift of God, not of works, so that no one may boast."*

This passage flips the script. It does not say we climb a ladder to reach God - it says God came down to us.

Imagine being caught in a riptide, unable to swim, sinking fast. Then someone dives in, pulls you out, and saves your life. You did not earn the rescue. You did not contribute to it. You simply received it. That is *charis* – *that is grace*. It is God diving into our brokenness and pulling us out - not because we are worthy, but because He is loving.

The word *"gift"* in this passage is either *dōron* (δῶρον) or *dōrea* (δωρεὰ), depending on the context. Both mean a **present freely given**, not a wage or a prize. Salvation is not payment for good behavior - it is a gift from God's heart. It is not something we achieve; it is something we accept. Like a wrapped present handed to you on your worst day, it comes not because you earned it, but because the Giver delights in giving.

Paul emphasizes that this salvation is *"not of works."* That means no amount of effort, rule-following, or religious performance can earn it. You cannot rack up enough spiritual points to unlock heaven. You cannot boast about your goodness, because the whole point is that it is *not about you*. It is about God's mercy. It is about His initiative, His love, His grace.

This passage dismantles the myth of spiritual self-improvement. Instead of climbing a ladder to reach God, we realize He descended the ladder to reach us. Jesus came down into our world, into our sin, into our death - and lifted us up. The only thing we can do is receive that grace through faith - trusting Him, not ourselves.

Faith is not just belief - it is surrender. It is letting go of the rope we have been trying to climb and allowing God to carry us. It is saying, "I cannot fix this - but You can."

When we receive grace, everything shifts. We stop striving and start resting. We stop performing and start trusting. We stop boasting and start worshiping. **Grace does not just save us - it transforms us**. It restores the image we were meant to reflect. It reconnects us to the source of life. It writes our name in the Book of Life.

God's Nature: Why Sin Keeps Us Out and Hope Lets Us In

To understand why sin separates us from God - and why we cannot fix that separation ourselves - we first need to understand who God is. The problem is not just that we have failed; it is that we have failed in the presence of someone who is utterly flawless.

In Deuteronomy 32:4–5, Moses sings a poetic reflection on God's character and Israel's rebellion: *"He is the Rock, His work is perfect; for all His ways are justice, a God of truth and without injustice; righteous and upright is He. They have corrupted themselves."*

This passage draws a sharp contrast between the nature of God and the condition of humanity. Let us unpack the key Hebrew terms and what they reveal:

God is called the Rock - tsur (צוּר) - a symbol of **stability, strength, and faithfulness**. In a world of shifting values and fragile foundations, God is unshakable. He does not change with culture or compromise under pressure. He is the immovable center of truth and justice.

His work is described as perfect - tamim (תָּמִים) - meaning **complete, whole, without flaw.** God does not make mistakes. His actions are never random or reckless. Every decision He makes flows from perfect wisdom and love. He is the standard of what is good.

All His ways are marked by justice - mishpat (מִשְׁפָּט) - a word that refers to **fairness, legal judgment, and moral order.** God does not bend the rules or play favorites. He does not overlook wrongdoing or redefine righteousness. His justice is pure and impartial.

But then comes the contrast: *"They have corrupted themselves."* The Hebrew word for *"corrupted"* is *shachat* (שָׁחַת), which means **ruined, spoiled, or morally decayed**. Humanity has not just made a few mistakes - we have twisted what was meant to be good. The image we were created to reflect has been distorted. Like a mirror left out in the rain, the surface is warped, and the reflection is no longer clear.

Imagine trying to climb a mountain made of polished glass. At the summit is God - perfect, radiant, unchanging. But every time we take a step, the surface cracks beneath us. Our sin makes the climb impossible. Not because God is cruel, but because He is holy. His perfection is like the peak of a mountain that no human can reach on their own. And our corrupted nature is like muddy boots trying to scale a flawless surface - we slip, we fall, we stain what was meant to shine.

This is why sin keeps us out. It is not just about guilt - it is about incompatibility. A corrupted soul cannot dwell with a perfect God. His justice demands holiness. His love desires restoration. But He cannot compromise His nature to accommodate ours.

And yet, this is where hope lets us in.

Hope Through Holiness

God does not lower the mountain - He sends a Savior to lift us up. Jesus, the flawless reflection of God, walks the path we could not. He climbs the mountain in our place. He takes our corruption and offers His perfection. Through Him, the mirror is restored. The muddy boots are washed. The climb becomes possible - not because we are strong, but because He is gracious.

This is the heart of the gospel: God is holy, and we are not. But through Jesus, holiness is given as a gift. The Rock remains unshaken, but the door is opened. The justice of God is satisfied, and the mercy of God is poured out.

God's holiness is not just about moral purity - it is about absolute otherness. It is the blazing perfection of a Being who is completely set apart from anything corrupt, twisted, or impure. Holiness is not just one of God's attributes - it is the atmosphere of His presence. It is the fire that surrounds His throne, the light that exposes all shadows, the purity that makes even angels cover their faces.

In Habakkuk 1:13, the prophet cries out in confusion over injustice yet still affirms a foundational truth: *"Your eyes are too pure to look on evil; You cannot tolerate wrongdoing."*

God's purity is so intense, so radiant, that He cannot even gaze upon sin without judgment. It is not that He is squeamish - it is that His nature is incompatible with evil. Like light and darkness, they cannot coexist. Where holiness is present, sin is undone.

Psalm 5:4 echoes this reality: *"You are not a God who takes pleasure in wickedness; evil cannot dwell with You."*

This is not about God being picky or distant - it is about spiritual reality. Sin is not just a bad habit - it is a contaminant. It is like mud in a sterile operating room. No matter how small the stain is, it threatens the integrity of the whole space. Holiness is like surgical sterility - perfect, precise, life-giving. Sin is the infection that cannot survive in that environment. It must be removed, or the patient dies.

Imagine trying to hold a snowflake in the heart of a furnace. The snowflake does not survive - not because the furnace is cruel, but because it is hot. That is what holiness does to sin. It consumes it. It exposes it. It cannot tolerate it. And that is why sin separates us from God. It is not just a rule violation - it is a **relational rupture**. It is the snowflake trying to live in the fire. It is the mud trying to cling to the clean.

This is why we cannot simply "be better" or "try harder" to get close to God. To repeat - our sin is not just a surface issue - it is a spiritual incompatibility. We were made to dwell with Him, but our corruption makes that impossible. The mirror is cracked. The boots are muddy. The snowflake is melting.

And yet, this is where the gospel becomes breathtaking.

3

The Holy One Who Came To Us

Instead of banishing us forever, God sent Jesus, the Holy One, into our contaminated world. He did not compromise His holiness - He carried it into the mud. He walked among sinners, touched the unclean, and absorbed the infection of sin into Himself. On the cross, He became the snowflake that melted so we could be refined. He took the filth so we could be made clean.

Through Jesus, we are **not just forgiven - we are declared holy.** The sterile room is reopened. The fire no longer consumes - it purifies. The relational rupture is healed. We are invited back into the presence we were made for.

Here is the miracle at the heart of the gospel: the same God who **is** perfectly holy - blazing in purity, unable to coexist with sin - is also perfectly loving. He does not just tolerate us. He pursues us.

In 1 John 4:8, the apostle writes: *"God is love."*

The Greek word used here is *agape* (ἀγάπη) - a word that describes **selfless, sacrificial, unconditional love.** It is not based on emotion or attraction. It is not earned by performance or reputation. *Agape* chooses to care even when the other person does not deserve it. It is the kind of love that sees the broken mirror and still reaches out to restore it. It is the kind of love that sent Jesus to the cross.

John 3:16 declares: *"For God so loved the world, that He gave His only Son, so that everyone who believes in Him will not perish, but have eternal life."*

This is *agape* in action. God did not wait for us to clean ourselves up. He came while we were still covered in mud, still running away, still lost. His love is not passive - it is **pursuing**. It is the shepherd leaving the ninety-nine to find the one. It is the father running to embrace the prodigal son. It is the holy God making a way for unholy people to come home.

Why Hell Exists - and Why Love Still Wins

Sometimes people ask, *"If God loves us, why would He send anyone to hell?"* It is a fair question - and the answer is layered with truth and tenderness.

Hell was not made for people. In Matthew 25:41, Jesus says it was *"prepared for the devil and his angels."* It was created as a place of judgment for spiritual rebellion - not as a destination for humanity. God's desire is not condemnation - it is **restoration**.

But Revelation 20:15 offers a sober warning: *"If anyone's name was not found written in the Book of Life, he was thrown into the lake of fire."*

This is not about God being cruel - it is about **honoring human freedom**. God does not force anyone into separation. He offers grace, forgiveness, and eternal life - but He does not coerce. If someone refuses His gift, they are choosing to remain disconnected. Hell is not a punishment imposed - it is a **condition chosen**. It is the soul saying, "I do not want You," and God, in love, saying, "I won't force You."

Imagine a warm house on a freezing night. Inside, there is light, laughter, and life. Outside, there is cold and darkness. The door is open. Anyone can come in. But if someone chooses to stay outside, they are not being thrown into the cold - they are choosing it. God's love is the open door. Hell is the cold that comes from refusing to enter.

This is why the gospel is urgent. It is not just about avoiding judgment - it is about **embracing love**. God's holiness demands separation from sin. But His love offers a way back. Through Jesus, the door is open. The mirror can be restored. The connection can be healed. All we have to do is say yes.

God's Justice and Love Work Together

In Isaiah 45:9, the prophet offers a sobering caution: *"Woe to him who strives with his Maker!"*

The Hebrew word for "*strives*" is *rib* (רִיב), which means **to argue, contend, or bring a legal case against.** It is the image of a creature challenging its Creator - like clay talking back to the potter, questioning the shape it is given. It is a warning against accusing God of unfairness, especially when we do not see the full picture.

We may not understand everything about suffering, judgment, or salvation - but Scripture assures us that **God's justice is never random,** and **His love is never absent**. These two attributes - justice and love – are not in conflict. They are in perfect harmony, like two notes in a divine chord that resonates through all of history.

God's justice means He must deal with sin. He cannot ignore it, excuse it, or sweep it under the rug. His holiness demands accountability. Sin is rebellion, distortion, and destruction - and justice insists that it be addressed.

But God's love means He offers a way out. He does not leave us condemned. He does not abandon us to our brokenness. Instead, He steps into the courtroom Himself - not as the judge, but as the one who takes the penalty.

The Cross: Where Justice and Mercy Meet

The cross of Jesus is the place where justice and mercy collide. It is where the full weight of sin is punished - and the full depth of love is revealed. Jesus did not die to cancel justice - He died to fulfill it. He took the verdict we deserved so we could receive the grace we never earned.

Imagine a courtroom where the judge pronounces a guilty verdict - and then steps down, removes his robe, and offers to serve the sentence in your place. That is the gospel. That is the cross. It is not the absence of justice - it is justice satisfied by love.

Sin keeps us out. It builds walls, breaks mirrors, and severs the connection. But hope - through Christ - lets us in. The door is opened. The record is cleared. The relationship is restored. God's justice builds the wall. His love breaks it down. Through Jesus, we are no longer clay contending with the potter - we are vessels of mercy, shaped by grace, filled with purpose.

How Jesus Bridges the Gap

When Jesus' disciples began to grasp the weight of God's holiness and the depth of human sin, they asked a question that echoes through every generation: *"Who then can be saved?"* (Matthew 19:25)

It is a question born from desperation. If perfection is the standard, and corruption is our condition, then who has any hope? Jesus' answer is both sobering and stunning: *"With man this is <u>impossible</u>, but with God all things are <u>possible</u>."* (Matthew 19:26)

The Greek word for *"impossible"* is *adynatos* (ἀδύνατος), which means **utterly incapable**. It is not just hard - it is **beyond human ability**. Salvation is not something we can earn through effort, achieve through discipline, or manipulate through religion. The gap between sinful humanity and holy God is too wide, too deep, too absolute.

But then comes the word that is the opposite of impossible, the word *'possible'* - *dynatos* (δυνατός) - **powerful, capable, able to accomplish**. It is the word used throughout the New Testament to describe God's miraculous power - the kind that raises the dead, heals the broken, and parts the sea. Jesus is saying: *what you cannot do, God can.* The bridge you cannot build, He has already constructed.

Imagine standing on the edge of a vast canyon. On one side is humanity - flawed, broken, reaching. On the other side is God - holy, radiant, unreachable. The canyon is sin. The walls are steep. The bottom is dark. No amount of jumping, climbing, or building can get you across.

But then, a bridge appears. Not built from human effort, but from divine sacrifice. It is shaped like a cross. It stretches from our side to God's, anchored in grace and paved with mercy. That bridge is Jesus**.** He did not just point the way - He became the way.

In John 14:6**,** He says: *"I am the way, and the truth, and the life; no one comes to the Father except through Me."* Jesus is the only one who could span the gap. Fully God, fully man, He carried our sin and offered His righteousness. He took the impossibility of salvation and made it possible - not by lowering the standard, but by meeting it Himself.

This is God's fix. Not a patch, not a workaround, but a complete restoration. Jesus does not just help us reach God - He brings God to us.

God's Plan Is Jesus: Love in Action

Focusing on John 3:16 again, its depth deserves more than a passing glance, especially the meaning of "*believe*". It is not just a slogan - it is a summary of the gospel's heartbeat:

"For God so loved the world, that He gave His only Son, so that everyone who __believes__ in Him will not perish, but have eternal life."

The Greek word for "*believes*" is *pisteuō* (πιστεύω), and it carries far more weight than mere intellectual agreement. It is not just saying, "I think Jesus is real." *It means* **to commit, to entrust, to have faith in, to believe**. It is about entrusting your life to Him, like a drowning person grabbing a lifeline. It is the kind of belief that clings, not just considers.

And the verb is in the present tense, which means it is not a one-time decision - it is **ongoing faith**. It is waking up each day and choosing to trust, to follow, to surrender. It is not just a moment - it is a movement. To believe in Jesus also means submission - recognizing Him not just as Savior, but as Lord. It is laying down your own crown and bowing to His. It is saying, "You lead, I follow."

Even more, the phrase "*believes in Him*" in Greek is *eis auton* (εἰς αὐτὸν), which literally means into Him. It is not just belief *about* Jesus - it is a movement *into* relationship with Him. It is union. It is connection. It is stepping into the life, love, and presence of Christ.

This is why Romans 5:8 is so powerful: *"But God __demonstrates__ His own love toward us, in that while we were still sinners, Christ died for us."*

The Greek word for '*demonstrates*' is *synistēmi* (συνίστημι) meaning **to present, prove, establish, or commend**. It is not just a statement - it is evidence. God did not wait for us to clean up our act. He did not demand perfection before offering grace. He proved His love by sending

Jesus while we were still in rebellion. While we were still running. While we were still broken.

This is **love that acts**. Love that **sacrifices**. Love that **pursues**.

Imagine falling into deep water, unable to swim. Panic sets in. You flail, sink, gasp. Then someone throws you a rope. That rope is Jesus. But it is not enough to know the rope is there - you have to grab it. You have to trust it. You have to let it pull you to safety.

That is *pisteuō*. That is belief that saves. God's plan is not just an idea - it is a rescue mission. Jesus is the lifeline. The cross is the proof. And faith is the leap that brings us home.

The Prophets Saw It Coming

But He was pierced through for our transgressions, He was crushed for our iniquities; The chastening for our well-being fell upon Him, and by His scourging we are healed. All of us like sheep have gone astray. Each of us has turned to his own way; but the LORD has caused the iniquity of us all to fall on Him. Isaiah 53:5,6

Isaiah (seven hundred years before Christ) did not just predict a Messiah - he painted a portrait of **a suffering servant**, one who would step into the chaos of human sin and absorb its full weight. This is not abstract theology - it is personal substitution. Jesus did not just die - He **died in our place**.

"*Pierced (wounded) for our transgressions*" - The Hebrew word for transgressions is *pesha* (פֶּשַׁע) refers to **rebellious acts** - not just mistakes, but deliberate defiance. It is the clenched fist, the turned back, the "I'll do it my way." And Jesus was pierced for that. The nails in His hands and feet were not just Roman instruments - they were the visible cost of our rebellion.

"*Crushed (bruised) for our iniquities*" – here again the Hebrew word *Avon* (עָוֹן) is used - meaning **twisted, perverse sin** - the kind that warps what is good, that bends truth into self-serving lies. Jesus was crushed under the weight of that distortion. He did not just carry our guilt -He bore the twistedness of our hearts.

"Chastisement for our well-being (peace)" - The word *shalom* (שָׁלוֹם) is more than peace - it is **wholeness, restoration, harmony**. Jesus took the punishment so we could be made whole. He absorbed the chaos so we could live in calm. He was rejected so we could be reconciled.

"By His scourging (stripes) we are healed." The word "stripes" refers to the lashes He received - each one tearing flesh, each one a mark of suffering. But through those wounds, we are restored. Not just physically, but spiritually. Our souls, fractured by sin, are stitched back together by His sacrifice.

"All of us like sheep have gone astray, each of us has turned to his own way." This compares people to sheep wandering off, ignoring the shepherd. We have all chosen our own path - thinking we know better - whether it is chasing popularity, ignoring morals, or prioritizing ourselves over others. This verse is honest about human nature - we all mess up and wander off. But it sets up the next part: someone else paid the price for our wandering

"But the LORD has caused the iniquity of us all to fall on Him." All the sin, rebellion, and twistedness - God placed it all on Jesus. He did not just suffer randomly; He carried our wrongs so we would not have to bear the ultimate consequences. This is the heart of the passage. It is not just that Jesus suffered – it is that He suffered for us. It is personal, showing God's love in letting Jesus take our place.

This passage might feel heavy, but it is really about love and hope. Isaiah 53:5-6 is not just an old prophecy; it is a message about someone who saw all the ways we mess up - our rebellion, our selfishness, our brokenness - and chose to take the consequences so we could be forgiven and restored. It is like Jesus saying, "I've got you," even when you have messed up big time.

Think about your own life: the times you have felt guilty, made bad choices, or hurt someone. This passage says those things do not have to define you. Jesus' suffering - His piercing, crushing, and scourging – was not just a historical event; it was a way to make you whole again. It is about second chances, forgiveness, and a relationship with God that is possible because of what Jesus did.

Victory Over Death: The Resurrection

Paul's words in 1 Corinthians 15 are not quiet reflections - they are a shout of triumph. He is standing on the battlefield after the war, looking at the defeated enemy and declaring: *"You lost."*

"But when this perishable will have put on the imperishable, and this mortal will have put on immortality, then will come about the saying that is written, "DEATH IS SWALLOWED UP in victory. O DEATH, WHERE IS YOUR VICTORY? O DEATH, WHERE IS YOUR STING?" The sting of death is sin, and the power of sin is the law; but thanks be to God, who gives us the victory through our Lord Jesus Christ." 1 Corinthians 15:54-57

He is quoting Hosea 13:14, but he is reframing it through the lens of the empty tomb. Death once had a sting - a venomous bite powered by sin. And sin had power because the law exposed it, like a spotlight revealing every hidden fault. But Jesus fulfilled the law, absorbed the sting, and rose again. Now, for those who belong to Christ, death is not the end. It is a doorway. A defeated enemy. A shadow that cannot hold us.

This passage, a blazing anthem of triumph, unveils the profound truth of Jesus' resurrection, redefining death not as a final curtain but as a fleeting veil, torn apart by divine power. This is a call to see beyond life's fears and uncertainties, to grasp the hope of a victory already won through Christ.

Paul, writing to the early Christian church in Corinth around 55 A.D., is addressing a community wrestling with doubts about the resurrection. Some questioned whether the dead could rise, a skepticism that threatened the core of their faith.

Think of this passage as Paul standing atop a mountain, holding the broken chains of death in his hands, shouting to the world that the impossible has happened. Jesus' resurrection is not just a miracle; it is the pivotal moment when the universe's rules were rewritten. Death, once an unconquerable fortress, is now a crumbling ruin. This passage invites you to see your life as part of this victory, to live with courage knowing that even the darkest fears - failure, loss, or death itself - have no ultimate power over you.

"But when this perishable will have put on the imperishable, and this mortal will have put on immortality." Our bodies, like fragile clay jars, are perishable - subject to decay, weakness, and time's relentless march. But Paul envisions a divine transformation, a moment when these frail vessels are clothed in the radiant armor of immortality. Through Jesus' resurrection, believers are promised new, eternal bodies that will never fade, like stars that burn forever in the heavens. Picture yourself shedding an old, tattered coat - your mortal body - and stepping into a shimmering robe woven from eternity itself. This is the promise of resurrection: your temporary, breakable self will be transformed into something unbreakable, radiant, and forever alive.

"Then will come about the saying that is written, 'DEATH IS SWALLOWED UP in victory'". Jesus' resurrection is like a cosmic black hole, swallowing death's power whole and leaving nothing but victory in its wake. Death is no longer the endgame; it is a defeated foe, stripped of its terror. Imagine death as a roaring lion, feared by all, its jaws dripping with menace. But in the resurrection, Jesus steps into its den, breaks its teeth, and leaves it powerless - a mere shadow of its former self. The grave is now an empty cage, its bars shattered. Or think about the scariest thing in your life - maybe it is failing, losing a friend, or facing the unknown future. Now imagine that fear being swallowed up, its power drained, leaving only the light of hope. That is what Jesus' victory over death means for you. This is a game-changer. The things that scare you most - loss, endings, death – do not have the final word. Jesus' victory means you are part of a story that ends in triumph, not tragedy.

"O DEATH, WHERE IS YOUR VICTORY? O DEATH, WHERE IS YOUR STING? "The sting of death is sin, and the power of sin is the law". Paul taunts death, mocking its once-invincible power. The "sting" of death - its ability to terrify and destroy - has been ripped out like a venomous fang. Jesus' resurrection disarmed death, turning its dreaded finality into a mere pause before eternity. The law (God's moral standards) reveals sin's depth, like a mirror exposing every flaw. The law shows us how far we fall short, making sin's consequences – death - feel inescapable. But Jesus fulfilled the law's demands and took sin's punishment, draining death's sting dry.

"But thanks be to God, who gives us the victory through our Lord Jesus Christ." The victory over death is not something we earn; it is a gift

from God through Jesus. His resurrection is the cornerstone of this triumph, shared with all who trust in Him. This is the heart of the Christian hope - a victory won by Jesus and freely given to us. Imagine a war hero returning from battle, having defeated an enemy no one else could face. He hands you the flag of victory, not because you fought, but because he fought for you. That is Jesus, handing you the victory over death through His resurrection. This is about gratitude and purpose. Knowing that Jesus won this victory for you frees you to live with joy, not fear. It is a call to say *"thanks be to God"* by living a life that reflects His love and victory.

Think of death as a dark, locked gate that once stood between you and eternity. Jesus did not just unlock it - He tore it off its hinges, leaving a wide-open path to eternal life. This passage invites you to see your life as part of a victorious story, where sin's poison and death's shadow have no ultimate power. Paul's triumphant shout is your invitation to live fearlessly, knowing that Christ's victory is yours.

Picture yourself standing at the edge of a great chasm, the shadow of death looming large. Across the gap shines a radiant city, filled with life and hope. Jesus, the victorious king, builds a bridge with His own body - His cross and empty tomb - spanning the chasm. He takes your hand and says, "Walk with Me. The path is secure, and the victory is yours." That is the heart of 1 Corinthians 15:54-57 - a triumphant call to cross the bridge, leaving death's shadow behind, and step into the eternal light of God's love.

Repentance: Our Response to the Gift

As mentioned, the resurrection is a gift - but gifts must be **received**. That is why Acts 3:19 calls us to respond: *"Repent therefore and be converted, that your sins may be blotted out."*

The Greek word for 'repent' is *metanoeō* (μετανοέω) meaning more than regret - it means **a change of mind and direction**. It is a spiritual U-turn. Imagine driving full speed toward a cliff, then slamming the brakes, turning around, and heading toward safety. That is repentance.

It involves: Recognition – seeing your sin for what it is. Not minimizing it. Not blaming others. Just naming it honestly. It involves: Remorse – feeling the weight of it. Not shame that crushes, but sorrow that leads to healing. And it involves: Redirection – turning toward God. Not just away from sin, but **toward trust, obedience, and relationship**.

Repentance and faith are inseparable. You cannot turn from sin without turning toward Christ. And when you do, something miraculous happens: *"Your sins are blotted out."* The image here is stunning. In ancient times, ink did not soak into parchment - it sat on the surface. So, to *"blot out"* meant to **wipe it clean, leaving no trace**. That is what God does with your sin. He does not just forgive - He erases. **He does not just pardon - He purifies.**

Imagine your life as a scroll, filled with every wrong thought, word, and deed. Now imagine Jesus taking that scroll, dipping His hand in grace, and wiping it clean. Not a smudge remains. That is the power of repentance and faith.

Your Move: What Will You Do With Jesus?

You have now heard the story - from prophecy to resurrection, from rebellion to redemption. But now it is not just a story. It is your story. God is not asking you to be perfect before coming to Him. He is asking you to come. To trust. To turn. To let Him fill the hole in your heart that nothing else can.

Romans 10:9 says: *"If you confess with your mouth the Lord Jesus and believe in your heart that God has raised Him from the dead, you will be saved."* This is not a magic formula - it is a **heart decision.** It is saying, "Jesus, I believe You died for me. I want to follow You. I want You to lead my life."

Imagine standing at a fork in the road. One path is familiar - it is your way, your rules, your control. But it is also filled with emptiness, anxiety, and guilt. The other path is Jesus' way. It is harder sometimes, but it is filled with peace, purpose, and love that never quits.

Which path will you take?

When you look at your life, what do you see? Mistakes? Regrets? Questions? Jesus sees all of that - and still says, *"Come."* He does not flinch. He does not walk away. He reaches out and says, *"Let Me carry that. Let Me heal that. Let Me lead you."*

We have shown that you do not earn a gift - you receive it. Jesus offers forgiveness, eternal life, and a relationship with God. But you have to **open your hands**. You have to open your heart. You have to say yes.

You can pray something like this - not as a script, but as a starting point:

"Lord Jesus, I need You. Thank You for dying on the cross for my sins. I open the door of my life and receive You as my Savior and Lord. Thank you for forgiving my sins and giving me eternal life. Take control of my life and make me the kind of person You want me to be. Amen."

If you mean that from your heart, God hears you. And He responds - not with judgment, but with grace.

4

Reconciliation and the Power of the Blood

In the previous chapter, we saw how humanity's quest for God is often veiled in despair, as sin does not just dim our sight; it cuts our lifeline. Like a ship adrift after its anchor chain snaps, sin severs the vital connection we were created to have with our Creator. But the story does not end in aimless drifting. The Bible shines a light of hope: God Himself takes the helm to guide us back. He does not wait for us to find our way - He sails into our brokenness to bring us home.

This restoration is called <u>reconciliation</u>, and it is made possible through the sacrificial death of Jesus Christ. But what does reconciliation truly mean? Why is it necessary? And how does the shedding of blood become the key to unlocking it?

Reconciliation: Restoring What Was Lost

At its core, reconciliation is about repairing a relationship that has been torn apart. It is not just a truce - it is a transformation. Because of sin - our rebellion, our turning away - humanity became estranged from God. We were like prodigal children who left home, convinced we could thrive on our own, only to find ourselves starving in a distant land. Reconciliation is the moment the Father runs to meet us, arms wide, heart full.

The New Testament uses the Greek word *katallassō* (καταλλάσσω) to describe this process. It means **"to change thoroughly"** or **"to exchange hostility for friendship."** It is the movement from alienation to intimacy, from being enemies of God to being embraced as His beloved. Romans 5:10 captures this beautifully: *"For if while we were enemies we were reconciled to God through the death of His Son, much more, having been reconciled, we shall be saved by His life."*

This is not just a legal transaction - it is a relational resurrection. Reconciliation removes the root cause of separation (sin) and restores the possibility of communion. It is like a bridge rebuilt over a canyon of guilt, allowing us to walk back into the presence of God.

The Blood: The Cost of Restoration

Reconciliation is not cheap. It comes at a cost - one that we could never afford. Hebrews 9:22 reminds us: *"Without the shedding of blood there is no forgiveness."*

Why blood?

Because Scripture declares with piercing clarity: *"For the life of the flesh is in the blood, and I have given it to you on the altar to make atonement for your souls; for it is the blood by reason of the life that makes atonement"* (Leviticus 17:11).

Blood is not just a symbol - it is the essence of life. It pulses through every vein, carrying oxygen, nutrients, and vitality. To shed blood is to pour out life. And in the divine economy, life is the only currency that can pay for sin.

In God's justice, sin demands death. *"For the wages of sin is death..."* (Romans 6:23a).

But in His mercy, God allows a substitute. The animal's life stands in for the sinners. The altar becomes a place of divine exchange - death for life, guilt for grace. Imagine a courtroom where the guilty stand condemned. Then, a substitute steps forward - not to argue the case, but to absorb the sentence. That is what blood does. It does not plead - it pays.

The Altar: A Place of Exchange

In the Tabernacle, the altar was the first stop - the place where sin was confronted and covered. The worshiper would bring a spotless animal, lay hands on its head, and watch it being slain. The blood was collected, sprinkled, poured out. It was messy, costly, and sacred.

"Then he shall slaughter the bull before the Lord; and Aaron's sons... shall offer up the blood and sprinkle the blood around on the altar" (Leviticus 1:5).

This was not ritual for ritual's sake. It was a vivid reminder that sin is serious, and that forgiveness is costly. The altar was not a place of sentiment - it was a place of substitution.

But even this system had limits. *"For it is impossible for the blood of bulls and goats to take away sins"* (Hebrews 10:4).

The sacrifices of the Tabernacle were temporary. They covered sin like a tarp over a broken roof - effective for a season, but unable to repair the damage. They pointed forward to something greater.

Blood in Scripture is not just a symbol of life - it is the price of redemption. In the Old Testament, sacrifices were offered to cover sin temporarily. But Jesus, the Lamb of God, offered Himself once for all. His blood does not just cover - it cleanses. It does not just delay judgment - it defeats it.

Colossians 1:19–20 declares: *"For it was the Father's good pleasure for all the fullness to dwell in Him, and through Him to reconcile all things to Himself, whether things on earth or things in heaven, having made peace through the blood of His cross."*

Think of reconciliation like restoring a priceless painting that has been vandalized. The damage is deep, the canvas torn. You cannot just tape it back together - you need a master artist who knows every brushstroke, who is willing to pour out their own resources to restore what was lost. That is what Jesus did. His blood is the ink of restoration, rewriting our story with grace.

From Enemies to Friends

The shift from enmity to fellowship is radical. It is not just that God tolerates us now - He delights in us. 2 Corinthians 5:18–19 says: *"Now all these things are from God, who reconciled us to Himself through Christ and gave us the ministry of reconciliation, namely, that God was in Christ reconciling the world to Himself, not counting their wrongdoings against them…"*

God does not just forgive - He entrusts. He hands us the ministry of reconciliation, inviting us to become bridge-builders in a world full of walls. We are not just recipients of grace; We are ambassadors of it.

Imagine a courtroom where the guilty are not only pardoned but invited to sit at the judge's table as honored guests. That is the scandal of grace. That is the power of the blood.

Reconciliation and the Power of Transformation

Let us return once again to one of the most sweeping and intimate declarations of the gospel's power to transform - a passage that does not just explain reconciliation, but invites us to experience it:

2 Corinthians 5:17–21: *"Therefore, if anyone is in Christ, this person is a new creation; the old things passed away; behold, new things have come. Now all these things are from God, who reconciled us to Himself through Christ and gave us the ministry of reconciliation, namely, that God was in Christ reconciling the world to Himself, not counting their wrongdoings against them, and He has committed to us the word of reconciliation. Therefore, we are ambassadors for Christ, as though God were making an appeal through us; we beg you on behalf of Christ, be reconciled to God. He made Him who knew no sin to be sin in our behalf, so that we might become the righteousness of God in Him."*

A New Creation: More Than a Metaphor

Paul begins with a bold claim: *"If anyone is in Christ, this person is a new creation."* This is not just a metaphor - it is a spiritual reality. To be *"in Christ"* means to be **united** with Him through faith, to be **grafted** into His life, death, and resurrection. It is not about adopting a new set of rules or behaviors; it is about undergoing a divine rebirth.

Imagine a caterpillar entering a cocoon. What emerges is not a slightly improved caterpillar - it is a butterfly. The old form is gone; something entirely new has come. That is the kind of transformation Paul is describing. The *"old things"* - our guilt, shame, and spiritual separation - have passed away. In their place is a new identity, shaped by grace, filled with purpose, and rooted in sonship.

Paul's language echoes Genesis, where God spoke creation into being. Now, through Christ, He speaks *re-creation* into the hearts of those who believe.

Reconciliation: God's Initiative, Not Ours

But this transformation is not something we achieve - it is something we receive. Paul makes it clear: *"Now all these things are from God."* Reconciliation is God's initiative. We did not 'climb our way back' to Him; He descended into our brokenness to bring us home.

And how did God accomplish this? *"God was in Christ reconciling the world to Himself, not counting their wrongdoings against them."* The divine ledger, once filled with the debts of our sin, has been wiped clean - not because we earned it, but because Jesus paid it.

This reconciliation **is not a private transaction - it is a global invitation**. Paul emphasizes that God's offer is for *"the world."* That includes the religious and the rebellious, the privileged and the forgotten. No one is excluded. The cross casts a wide shadow, and under it, all are welcome.

And those who have received this gift are now entrusted with its message. *"He has committed to us the word of reconciliation."* We become messengers of the very grace that saved us.

Paul calls us *"ambassadors for Christ."* An ambassador does not speak on their own behalf - they represent the heart of their king in a foreign land. That is our role. We carry the message of heaven into the noise of earth. And we do so not with cold detachment, but with passionate urgency: *"We beg you on behalf of Christ, be reconciled to God."*

The Great Exchange

The passage reaches its theological summit with a breathtaking exchange: *"He made Him who knew no sin to be sin in our behalf, so that we might become the righteousness of God in Him."*

This is the heart of reconciliation. Jesus, utterly sinless, took upon Himself the full weight of human guilt. He did not just sympathize with our brokenness - He absorbed it. He became the embodiment of sin - not in action, but in judgment - so that we could be clothed in His righteousness.

Imagine a prisoner on death row, guilty and condemned. Then, a royal figure steps in - not just to pardon, but to take the prisoner's place. The innocent is punished; the guilty goes free. But more than that - the prisoner is adopted into the royal family. That is the gospel. That is reconciliation.

We do not merely escape punishment - we are welcomed into divine favor. We do not just receive forgiveness - we are transformed into righteousness.

Living as Agents of Reconciliation

In these few verses, Paul captures the entire arc of the Christian faith:

- A God who pursues
- A Christ who redeems
- A Spirit who transforms
- A people who proclaims

To be reconciled is to be remade. And to be 'remade' is to be sent. We are not just recipients of grace - we are agents of reconciliation, called to bear witness to the love that makes all things new.

Paul's words in **Colossians 1:21–22** open with a stark diagnosis of the human condition: *"And although you were previously alienated and hostile in attitude, engaged in evil deeds…"*

This is not exaggeration - it is spiritual reality. To be *alienated* means to be estranged, cut off, like a branch severed from the tree that once gave it life. We were not just wandering - we were willfully resistant. Our thoughts, desires, and actions were shaped by rebellion. We were spiritual exiles, not just lost but opposed to the One who made us.

But then comes the turning point, the divine interruption:

"Yet He has now reconciled you..."

The contrast is breathtaking. From hostility to harmony. From estrangement to embrace. And this reconciliation did not come through vague spiritual sentiment - it came through something tangible, costly, and physical:

"...in His body of flesh through death..."

Paul emphasizes the incarnation - God taking on human flesh. Jesus did not just walk among us; He died for us. His body was pierced, His blood poured out. This was not symbolic - it was sacrificial. The cross was not a metaphor; it was a method. A brutal, beautiful method of redemption.

Why was this necessary? Because sin is not just a mistake - it is a violation of divine justice. And justice, by its nature, demands satisfaction. Always remember: *"Without the shedding of blood there is no forgiveness."* Hebrews 9:22

If there had been another way - a cleaner, less painful path - God would have taken it. But only the death of the sinless One could absorb the full weight of humanity's guilt and restore what was broken.

The Result: Holy, Blameless, Beyond Reproach

And what is the outcome of this costly reconciliation? Paul writes: *"...in order to present you before Him holy and blameless and beyond reproach."* These are not just lofty adjectives – they are declarations of identity.

Holy - means set apart, consecrated, belonging to God.

Blameless - evokes the image of a spotless lamb - pure, acceptable, without flaw.

Beyond reproach - means no accusation can stick, no condemnation can stand.

Reconciliation: A Word Forged in Blood

The word *reconciliation* should spark awe, gratitude, and joy. It is not soft or sentimental - it is forged in suffering, sacrifice, and blood. It tells the story of a God who refused to let sin have the final word. A God who stepped into our alienation and bore its cost so that we could stand before Him not as strangers, but as sons and daughters.

Think of a broken violin, discarded and forgotten. Then a master musician finds it, repairs it, and plays a melody so beautiful it silences the room. That is reconciliation. God does not just fix us - He restores us to purpose, to beauty, to belonging.

Colossians 1:22 affirms this again: *"Yet He has now reconciled you in His body of flesh through death, in order to present you before Him holy and blameless and beyond reproach."*

This is the gospel's heartbeat. Jesus' death was not symbolic - it was necessary. His blood did not just stain the cross - it cleansed the world. And now, because of Him, we can stand before God not in fear, but in freedom.

The Bloody Book: Why Blood Matters

The Bible has often been called a "bloody book," and rightly so. From Eden's first sacrifice to the crimson-stained robes of Revelation, blood flows through Scripture not as a grotesque detail, but as a sacred thread - binding together justice and mercy, holiness and love. It is the language of life and the cost of reconciliation. In the biblical story, blood is never wasted. It is poured out with purpose.

The First Shedding: Grace in the Garden

The first glimpse of this truth appears quietly in Genesis 3:21: *"And the Lord God made garments of skin for Adam and his wife and clothed them."*

Adam and Eve, having disobeyed God, stand exposed - naked not just in body, but in soul. Their shame is palpable. And God responds not with immediate wrath, but with a gesture of grace. He clothes them - but not with fig leaves. He uses animal skins. Something innocent dies so that the guilty may be covered. This is the first recorded death in Scripture, and it is not accidental. It is theological. **Blood is shed so that shame can be hidden.** The altar of grace is built on the cost of life.

This moment foreshadows the entire redemptive arc of Scripture: sin brings death, and only through death can its consequences - shame, separation, guilt - be addressed.

Blood as Atonement: Life for Life

In the wilderness, surrounded by the rituals of the Tabernacle, Israel learns that blood is sacred. It is not just biological - it is theological. It carries life, and when poured out on the altar, it becomes the currency of atonement. The altar is not a place of sentiment - it is a place of exchange. Guilt meets grace. Death yields life.

Under the Mosaic Law, nearly everything had to be cleansed with blood - because sin defiles not just the sinner, but the space around them. Blood was God's appointed means of purification. But these sacrifices were shadows. They pointed forward to something greater. The blood of bulls and goats could cover sin, but they could not remove it. Only the blood of Christ could do that.

The Incarnate Sacrifice

And so, in Hebrews 2:14, we read: *"Therefore, since the children share in flesh and blood, He Himself likewise also partook of the same, so that through death He might destroy the one who has the power of death, that is, the devil."*

Jesus did not remain distant. He entered into our humanity - flesh and blood. He became vulnerable to death so that He could destroy its power. The devil, who wields death like a sword, is disarmed by the very thing he thought would be his triumph. Jesus' death is not just payment - it is victory. **His blood does not just cleanse - it conquers**.

This victory is celebrated in Revelation 1:5–6: *"To Him who loves us and released us from our sins by His blood - and He made us into a kingdom, priests to His God and Father - to Him be the glory and the dominion forever and ever. Amen."*

His love is not abstract - it is embodied in sacrifice. His blood is not merely spilled - it is poured out with purpose. Through it, we are not only forgiven - we are transformed. We become part of a kingdom, called to serve as priests - those who stand in the presence of God and minister His grace to the world. Imagine a prisoner not only pardoned but crowned. That is the power of the blood. It does not just erase - it elevates.

The Robe Dipped in Blood

And finally, in Revelation 19:13, we see the returning Christ: *"He is clothed with a robe dipped in blood, and His name is called The Word of God."*

It is a striking image - majestic and haunting. This is not the blood of defeat, but of triumph. It is the blood that speaks of justice satisfied, mercy extended, evil overcome. Even in glory, Christ bears the marks of His love. His robe is dipped in blood - not to remind us of suffering, but to declare victory.

Taken together, these passages reveal a profound truth: blood is not incidental to the gospel - it is essential. It is the language of covenant, the cost of reconciliation, and the seal of victory. In a world that often sanitizes or sentimentalizes faith, the Bible confronts us with the raw, red reality of redemption. It tells us that sin is serious, that forgiveness is costly, and that love is willing to bleed.

Blood matters because it is the price of peace. It is the ink with which God writes our names into His story. And it is the thread that ties Eden to Calvary, the Tabernacle to the empty tomb, the altar to the throne.

Atonement: The Path to Reconciliation

If reconciliation is the restored relationship between God and humanity, then atonement is the bridge that makes that restoration possible. It is not a soft word - it is a sacred transaction. Atonement is where justice meets mercy, where holiness embraces love, and where the cost of sin is not ignored but absorbed.

The English word *atonement* can be poetically broken down as "at-one-ment" - a reflection of its goal: to make us "at one" with God again. But this unity is not cheap. It comes at a cost so staggering that only God Himself could pay it.

In Hebrew, the word for atonement is *kippur* (כִּפֵּר), from the root *kaphar*, meaning "**to cover**," "**to purge**," or "**to reconcile**." It evokes the image of a protective covering - like a shield placed between judgment and the guilty. In the Old Testament, this covering was achieved through sacrifice. Blood was shed, not as a ritual of cruelty, but as a symbol of substitution. The innocent bore the penalty so the guilty could go free.

Leviticus 16 describes the Day of Atonement (*Yom Kippur*), when the high priest would enter the Holy of Holies and sprinkle blood on the mercy seat to make atonement for the people. It was a solemn day - a day of reckoning and release. But even this ritual pointed forward to something greater.

The Cost of Sin

Sin is not just a mistake - it is a debt. It is not just a flaw - it is a fracture. And the payment for that debt is death. Not metaphorical death, but real separation from the source of life. God, in His holiness, cannot overlook sin. But God, in His love, refuses to abandon the sinner. So, He provides a way - a costly, blood-stained way - through atonement. To repeat this important verse, Hebrews 9:22 makes it clear: *"Without the shedding of blood there is no forgiveness."*

This is not divine cruelty - it is divine consistency. Life must be given to restore life. In the Old Testament, animals were sacrificed as substitutes. Their blood covered sin temporarily. But these sacrifices had to be repeated year after year. They were shadows of a greater reality. That reality is Christ.

Atonement is Rescue

Jesus is not just the high priest - He is the sacrifice. He does not enter the earthly temple - He enters the heavenly one. And He does not offer the blood of animals - He offers His own.

Hebrews 10:10 declares: *"By this will, we have been sanctified through the offering of the body of Jesus Christ once for all."*

This is the heart of the gospel. Jesus, sinless and pure, takes our place. He becomes the Lamb of God, whose blood does not just cover sin - it removes it. His death is not symbolic - it is substitutionary. He dies so we can live. He is condemned so we can be accepted. He is forsaken so we can be embraced.

Imagine a burning building, and inside, a child trapped by flames. A firefighter rushes in, not because the child deserves rescue, but because love compels action. The rescuer absorbs the heat, the smoke, the danger - and carries the child to safety. That is atonement. It is not just rescue - it is sacrifice.

Romans 5:11 says: *"And not only this, but we also celebrate in God through our Lord Jesus Christ, through whom we have now received the reconciliation."*

Atonement leads to reconciliation. The debt is paid, the barrier removed, the relationship restored. We are no longer enemies - we are children. No longer condemned - we are called. No longer distant - we are home.

Atonement Is Love in Action

At its deepest level, atonement reveals the character of God. He is not indifferent to sin, nor is He indifferent to sinners. He is both just and merciful. And in Christ, these attributes meet - not in contradiction, but in harmony.

1 John 4:10 captures it beautifully: *"In this is love, not that we loved God, but that He loved us and sent His Son to be the propitiation for our sins."*

The word *propitiation* (Greek: *hilasmos*, ἱλασμός) means "a sacrifice that **satisfies wrath**." It is not about appeasing a temperamental deity - it is about restoring a broken relationship through a costly gift. **God does not demand blood - He provides it**. He does not wait for us to earn love - He demonstrates it.

5

The Tabernacle: A Blueprint for Redemption

In the wilderness, far from the permanence of cities or the grandeur of temples, God gave Israel a stunning command: *"Have them construct a sanctuary for Me, so that I may dwell among them"* (Exodus 25:8).

This was no ordinary tent. The Tabernacle was a mobile meeting place between heaven and earth - a sacred space where the infinite God chose to dwell among finite, flawed people. Every detail of its construction was divinely dictated, from the materials used to the layout of its courts, because it was meant to reflect heavenly realities in earthly form. It was not just architecture - it was theology in fabric and gold.

The Tabernacle was divided into three main areas:

<u>The Outer Court</u> – where sacrifices were made.

<u>The Holy Place</u> – where daily priestly duties occurred.

<u>The Holy of Holies</u> – the innermost chamber, where God's presence dwelled.

This progression - from outer to inner - symbolized the journey from sin to sanctity, from distance to intimacy with God. It was a visual and spiritual roadmap of redemption.

I. The Outer Court: Where Sacrifice Begins

The Outer Court was the first area one would enter upon approaching the Tabernacle. It was open to Israel and marked the beginning of their encounter with God. But it was not a place of comfort - it was a place of confrontation. Here, sin was dealt with through sacrifice.

The Bronze Altar

At the heart of the Outer Court stood the bronze altar, where animals were offered as sacrifices for sin.

"You shall make the altar of acacia wood, five cubits long and five cubits wide; the altar shall be square, and its height shall be three cubits" (Exodus 27:1).

The altar was a place of blood and fire - a place where the cost of sin was made visible. The Israelites would bring animals without blemish, lay their hands on them to symbolically transfer their guilt, and watch as the innocent died in their place. This was not a gruesome ritual - it was a grace-filled exchange. The altar taught that sin brings death, but that God provides a substitute. It pointed forward to the cross, where Jesus, the Lamb of God, would offer Himself as the final sacrifice.

The Bronze Basin

Next to the altar stood the bronze basin, filled with water for ceremonial washing.

"You shall also make a basin of bronze, with its stand of bronze, for washing; and you shall put it between the tent of meeting and the altar, and put water in it" (Exodus 30:18).

Before entering the Holy Place, priests had to wash their hands and feet. This symbolized purification - not just from physical dirt, but from spiritual defilement. It was a reminder that approaching God requires cleansing. It was also of utmost importance. If a priest forgot to wash at the basin or wash improperly, the moment he enters the Holy Place – he would die instantly. Not a minor detail – but a profound action.

The basin foreshadowed the cleansing we receive through Christ: *"If we confess our sins, He is faithful and righteous, so that He will forgive us our sins and cleanse us from all unrighteousness"* (1 John 1:9).

The Outer Court, then, was a place of preparation - a place where sin was confronted, forgiveness was offered, and hearts were made ready to draw closer to God.

II. The Holy Place: Where Service and Sanctification Meet

Beyond the Outer Court lay the Holy Place, accessible only to the priests. This chamber was filled with symbolic furnishings, each pointing to a deeper spiritual truth. It was a place of daily ministry, where sanctification - the process of being made holy - was lived out.

The Golden Lampstand

To the left stood the golden lampstand, or menorah.

"You shall also make a lampstand of pure gold. The lampstand shall be made of hammered work; its base and its shaft, its cups, its bulbs and its flowers shall be from it" (Exodus 25:31).

The lampstand held seven lamps, which kept burning continually. In a room with no windows, this was the only source of light. The lampstand symbolized God's guidance and presence.

"Your word is a lamp to my feet and a light to my path" (Psalm 119:105).

It also pointed to Christ, who declared: *"I am the Light of the world; the one who follows Me will not walk in the darkness, but will have the Light of life"* (John 8:12).

The light in the Holy Place reminded the priests - and us - that we are called to walk in the light, to live by truth, and to reflect God's glory.

The Table of Showbread

To the right stood the table of showbread, holding twelve loaves representing the twelve tribes of Israel.

"You shall also make a table of acacia wood... And you shall set the bread of the Presence on the table before Me continually" (Exodus 25:23, 30).

This bread was a symbol of God's provision and fellowship. It reminded Israel that they lived not by bread alone, but by every word that comes from God. *"Man shall not live on bread alone, but on every word that comes out of the mouth of God"* (Deuteronomy 8:3).

Jesus fulfilled this image when He said: *"I am the bread of life; the one who comes to Me will not be hungry, and the one who believes in Me will never be thirsty"* (John 6:35).

The table of showbread invited the priests into communion with God - a foretaste of the fellowship we now enjoy through Christ.

The Altar of Incense

Directly in front of the veil stood the altar of incense.

"You shall make an altar as a place for burning incense; you shall make it of acacia wood" (Exodus 30:1).

Incense was burned morning and evening, symbolizing the prayers of the people rising to God. *"May my prayer be counted as incense before You; the raising of my hands as the evening offering"* (Psalm 141:2). The sweet aroma filled the Holy Place, reminding the priests that God delights in the prayers of His people.

"The smoke of the incense, with the prayers of the saints, went up before God" (Revelation 8:4). The altar of incense teaches us that prayer is not peripheral - it is central. It is the fragrance of relationship, the breath of intimacy with God.

III. The Holy of Holies: Where Glory Dwells

At the very center of the Tabernacle - beyond the bronze altar, past the golden lampstand, behind the veil - stood the Holy of Holies, the most sacred space in all of Israel's worship. It was not a place of routine or ritual. It was a place of awe, mystery, and trembling reverence. Only one person - the High Priest - could enter, and only once a year, on the Day of Atonement.

"But into the second, only the high priest enters once a year, not without taking blood, which he offers for himself and for the sins of the people committed in ignorance" (Hebrews 9:7).

Inside this chamber rested the Ark of the Covenant, a golden chest overlaid with pure gold, constructed according to God's precise instructions.

"They shall construct an ark of acacia wood... You shall overlay it with pure gold, inside and out" (Exodus 25:10–11).

The Ark was more than a container - it was a throne. It represented the seat of God's rule and the center of His covenant with Israel. And within it were three deeply symbolic items:

1. The Jar of Manna

"Put an omerful of manna in a jar, and place it before the Lord to be kept throughout your generations" (Exodus 16:33).

This jar held a sample of the miraculous bread God provided in the wilderness. It was a reminder that God sustains His people - not just physically, but spiritually. Manna was daily provision, undeserved and unearned. It pointed forward to Christ, who said: *"I am the bread of life; the one who comes to Me will not be hungry"* (John 6:35).

The manna in the Ark whispered of grace that meets us in dry places, of nourishment that comes not from the ground, but from heaven.

2. Aaron's Staff That Budded

"The staff of Aaron... had sprouted and produced blossoms, and it yielded ripe almonds" (Numbers 17:8).

This was no ordinary staff. It was a dead piece of wood that miraculously came to life - sprouting, blooming, bearing fruit. It was God's way of affirming Aaron's priesthood and silencing rebellion. The staff symbolized divine authority and intercession. It pointed forward to Jesus, our eternal High Priest, whose resurrection was the ultimate sign of divine approval.

"Christ was faithful as a Son over His house - whose house we are" (Hebrews 3:6). The budding staff reminds us that God chooses His mediators, and that life can spring from what was once dead.

3. The Stone Tablets of the Law

"You shall put into the ark the testimony which I shall give you" (Exodus 25:16).

These tablets contained the Ten Commandments - the moral foundation of God's covenant. They represented His holiness, His justice, and His expectations for His people. But they also reminded Israel of their failure to keep the law, and their need for mercy.

Together, these three items told the story of Israel's relationship with God:

- Provision - through manna
- Leadership - through Aaron's staff
- Covenant - through the tablets of the Law

But above them sat something even more profound - the Mercy Seat.

The Mercy Seat: Where Justice Meets Grace

The Mercy Seat was a slab of pure gold, placed atop the Ark, flanked by two cherubim whose wings stretched upward and inward, overshadowing the space where God's presence would dwell.

"You shall make a mercy seat of pure gold... and the cherubim shall have their wings spread upward, covering the mercy seat with their wings" (Exodus 25:17, 20). This was the throne of God on earth. And it was here - between the cherubim, above the Law - that God said He would meet His people.

"There I will meet with you; and from above the mercy seat... I will speak to you" (Exodus 25:22).

But access to this throne was not casual. On the Day of Atonement, the High Priest would enter with blood - not his own, but that of a spotless animal. He would sprinkle it (seven times) on the Mercy Seat to make atonement for the sins of the people. *"He shall take some of the blood of the bull and sprinkle it with his finger on the mercy seat"* (Leviticus 16:14).

This act was the climax of Israel's worship. It was the moment when justice was satisfied, and mercy was extended. The blood covered the Law, symbolizing that the penalty for sin had been paid. The Mercy Seat pointed forward to Christ, who became both the sacrifice and the High Priest.

"Whom God displayed publicly as a propitiation in His blood through faith" (Romans 3:25). The word *propitiation* here is the Greek word *hilastērion* (ἱλαστήριον) - the same word used in the Septuagint for "Mercy Seat." In other words, Jesus is our Mercy Seat. He is the place where wrath is absorbed, and grace is poured out.

The Heart of Worship

The Holy of Holies teaches us that worship is not just about songs or rituals - it is about encounter. It is about stepping into the presence of a holy God, not with fear, but with faith. It is about recognizing that the God who dwelled between the cherubim now dwells within us.

"Do you not know that your body is a temple of the Holy Spirit within you, whom you have from God?" (1 Corinthians 6:19).

We are now 'living' sanctuaries. The journey from the Outer Court to the Holy of Holies is not just a physical path - it is a spiritual one. It is the journey of every believer, moving from guilt to grace, from distance to intimacy, from ritual to relationship. The Holy of Holies is the heart of divine encounter. And through Christ, that heart now beats within us.

What is a Cheribum? And Why Does It Matter

The cherubim on the Mercy Seat atop the Ark of the Covenant are deeply significant in biblical theology, reflecting God's presence, holiness, and covenant relationship with His people.

Exodus 25:22 states: *"There I will meet with you; and from above the mercy seat, from between the two cherubim which are upon the ark of* the testimony, I will speak to you about all that I will give you in commandment for the sons of Israel."

They are symbols of God's Presence and Holiness. Cherubim are angelic beings associated with God's glory and throne. In Ezekiel 10:1-22, they are depicted as part of God's heavenly throne, emphasizing His majesty and power. Their placement on the Mercy Seat signifies that the Ark was a earthly representation of God's heavenly throne, where His presence dwelt among His people.

The cherubim's wings spread over the Mercy Seat symbolize protection and reverence, guarding the sacred space where God's law (the Ten Commandments) was kept. This reflects God's holiness and the seriousness of His covenant.

They are the Guardians of God's Covenant. In Genesis 3:24, cherubim guard the way to the Tree of Life after Adam and Eve's sin, showing their role as protectors of divine boundaries. Similarly, the cherubim on the Ark guard the covenant, symbolizing that access to God's presence is restricted to those who approach Him on His terms - through obedience and atonement.

The Mercy Seat was sprinkled with blood during the Day of Atonement (Leviticus 16:14-15), symbolizing forgiveness of sins. The cherubim, positioned above, witness this act of reconciliation, highlighting God's justice (punishing sin) and mercy (offering forgiveness).

They are always in the presence of Divine Communication. The space between the cherubim was where God promised to meet and speak with Moses and the high priests (Exodus 25:22). This made the Mercy Seat a unique point of connection between God and humanity, emphasizing His desire for a relationship with His people, despite their sinfulness.

The cherubim and Mercy Seat teach that God is both holy (demanding justice) and merciful (offering forgiveness). This balance is crucial today, reminding us that while God is loving, He is also just. We are called to approach Him with reverence and faith in Christ's sacrifice.

Their presence underscores the importance of worshiping God in the way He prescribes. Today, this encourages believers to live in alignment with God's will, honoring Him through obedience and a life of faith. The promise of God meeting His people "between the cherubim" points to His desire for relationship. In a world of uncertainty, this assures us that God is accessible through Jesus, offering guidance, forgiveness, and hope.

The Day of Atonement

The Day of Atonement, called *Yom Kippur* in Hebrew, was an annual event where the high priest performed specific rituals to atone (make amends) for the sins of the Israelites, both individually and as a nation. It took place on the tenth day of the seventh month and was a solemn day of fasting, repentance, and seeking God's forgiveness.

Leviticus 16:29-30 summarizes its purpose: *"This shall be a permanent statute for you: in the seventh month, on the tenth day of the month, you shall humble your souls and not do any work, whether the native, or the alien who sojourns among you; for on this day atonement shall be made for you to cleanse you; you will be clean from all your sins before the Lord."*

The importance and meaning of the Day of Atonement is of enormous significance. It represented a cleansing from sin. It was unique because it addressed all sins - intentional and unintentional - of the entire nation, including the priests. Leviticus 16:16 says, *"He shall make atonement for the holy place, because of the impurities of the sons of Israel and because of their transgressions in regard to all their sins."* Sin separated the people from God's holiness, and this day was God's way of providing a path to forgiveness and reconciliation, ensuring they could remain in His presence.

The high priest, after purifying himself, entered the Holy of Holies only once a year - on this day. He offered sacrifices: a bull for his own sins and two goats for the people. One goat was sacrificed, and its blood was sprinkled on the Mercy Seat to atone for Israel's sins (Leviticus 16:15). The second, the "scapegoat," symbolically carried the people's sins into the wilderness (Leviticus 16:21-22). This showed that atonement required both payment for sin (the blood sacrifice) and removal of sin (the scapegoat), emphasizing God's justice and mercy.

The high priest's entry into the Holy of Holies was extraordinarily solemn, as God's holiness could not tolerate sin. The blood sprinkled on the Mercy Seat symbolized the covering of sin, allowing God's mercy to prevail over judgment. If the High Priest made even the smallest error – he would die instantly. That is why every time he entered the Holy of Holies, there was a cord (like a rope) tied to his ankle. In other words, if he were to make a mistake and die, the other priests would be able to 'drag' him out of the inner sanctuary and back into the Holy Place.

It was a day of humility and repentance. The Israelites were commanded to "humble their souls" (fast and repent) and refrain from work (Leviticus 16:29). This showed that atonement was not just about rituals but required a heart of humility and dependence on God's grace.

The Day of Atonement holds profound meaning for us today, especially in understanding Jesus Christ's work and our relationship with God. The New Testament presents Jesus as the fulfillment of the Day of Atonement. He is both the high priest and the sacrifice. Hebrews 9:11-12 says:

"But when Christ appeared as a high priest of the good things to come, He entered through the greater and more perfect tabernacle, not made with hands... and not through the blood of goats and calves, but through His own blood, He entered the holy place once for all, having obtained eternal redemption."

Think of the Day of Atonement like a divine "reset button" for Israel's relationship with God. Their sins created a barrier, but God provided a way to wipe the slate clean through sacrifices and repentance. Today, this points to Jesus, who is the ultimate reset button. Understanding this helps us see the seriousness of sin, the depth of God's love, and the incredible gift of forgiveness through Christ. It is a reminder that we can approach God confidently, not because we are perfect, but because Jesus' sacrifice makes us clean.

This also challenges us to live with gratitude and purpose, knowing our sins are forgiven, and to share this hope with others in a world that often feels broken and unforgiving. Most Christians today have no knowledge (or understanding) of *Yom Kippur*. But this is our 'heritage' as a foundation for the New Testament. It was the most solemn moment of the (Jewish) year - a dramatic picture of reconciliation. The blood covered the Law, symbolizing that mercy triumphs over judgment.

The Veil

When Jesus died, something extraordinary happened: *"And behold, the veil of the temple was torn in two from top to bottom; and the earth shook, and the rocks were split"* (Matthew 27:51).

This was no ordinary curtain and was fifteen feet high. The veil that separated the Holy of Holies was thick - woven with precision, designed to shield sinful humanity from the overwhelming holiness of God. (In Jesus' day in Herod's Temple, the Veil was sixty feet tall). Only the high priest could pass through it, and only once a year. It was a barrier, a boundary, a reminder that access to God was limited and costly. Three golden cherubim were woven into the curtain – guarding the presence of God within.

The Veil itself was made of fine linen and richly embroidered with blue, purple, and scarlet threads (along with the golden cherubim). It hung from golden hooks supported by four pillars of acacia wood overlaid with gold and anchored into silver sockets. As mentioned previously, every item, every covering, curtain, metal, color, piece of furniture, and measurement of the Tabernacle of Moses – had enormous meaning and significance.

We will study this one example – the four colors of the Veil:

Blue – represents divinity, heaven, and the spiritual realm. It was always associated with God's presence and divine commandments.

Purple – symbolizes royalty, majesty, and sovereignty. Because royal dye was rare and costly, it was reserved for kings, significant leaders and sacred places. This is why Jesus wore a purple robe (from the Roman guards) on the day of His crucifixion. It is interesting to note – Ceasar always wore a purple robe and his private Praetorian Guard all wore purple capes to distinguish themselves from other Roman soldiers.

Scarlet – stands for sacrifice, atonement, and redemption. Its deep red hue evoked the shedding of blood required for the forgiveness of sins. Some critics believe that there is an error in Scripture – i.e. – Mark (Mark 15:17) and John (John 19:2) describe Jesus as wearing a purple robe, whereas Matthew (Matthew 27:28) describes Jesus wearing a scarlet robe. When a purple robe as drenched in blood – it turns scarlet. Matthew was describing a purple robe full of the blood of Jesus.

Gold – embodies divine glory, purity, perfection and holiness. That is why the Mercy Seat, the Cherubim, even the Golden Lampstand (representing the Holy Spirit) was made of pure gold.

The Veil Torn: Access Restored

When Jesus breathed His last, that veil was torn - not from bottom to top, as if by human effort, but from top to bottom, as if by divine hands. The message was unmistakable: the way into God's presence was now open. The sacrifice had been made. The blood had been shed. The barrier was gone.

"Therefore, brothers and sisters, since we have confidence to enter the holy place by the blood of Jesus... Let us approach God with a sincere heart in full assurance of faith" (Hebrews 10:19, 22).

The torn veil is the symbol of a new covenant. No longer do we need a human priest to mediate for us. Christ Himself is our High Priest, and through Him, we have direct access to the Father. *"For there is one God, and one mediator also between God and mankind, the man Christ Jesus"* (1 Timothy 2:5).

This is the climax of the Tabernacle's message: the journey from the Outer Court to the Holy of Holies is no longer reserved for a select few. In Christ, all who believe are invited to draw near.

The Tabernacle Fulfilled: Christ in Every Detail

The Tabernacle was never meant to be permanent. It was a shadow, a symbol, a sacred blueprint pointing forward to something greater. Every piece of furniture, every ritual, every curtain and covering whispered of Christ.

The **bronze altar** pointed to the cross, where the final sacrifice was made.

The **bronze basin** foreshadowed the cleansing we receive through Christ's blood.

The **lampstand** revealed Jesus as the Light of the World.

The **table of showbread** declared Him as the Bread of Life.

The **altar of incense** reflected His intercession on our behalf.

The **Ark of the Covenant** symbolized His throne and His covenant.

The **mercy seat** revealed the place where justice and mercy meet - fulfilled in Jesus.

Even the structure itself - the progression from outer to inner - mirrors the spiritual journey of every believer. We begin in the Outer Court, confronted by our sin and drawn to the sacrifice. We move into the Holy Place, where we are nourished, enlightened, and invited into communion. And finally, through Christ, we enter the Holy of Holies - not with fear, but with confidence.

"Let us draw near with confidence to the throne of grace, so that we may receive mercy and find grace for help at the time of our need" (Hebrews 4:16).

Living as Tabernacle People

The Tabernacle is not just ancient history - it is a living invitation. Through Christ, we are now the dwelling place of God. *"Do you not know that you are a temple of God and that the Spirit of God dwells in you?"* (1 Corinthians 3:16).

This means that the journey of redemption is not just something we study - it is something we live. We are called to be people of the altar, people of the lampstand, people of the mercy seat. We carry the presence of God into the world, becoming mobile sanctuaries of grace.

"But you are a chosen people, a royal priesthood, a holy nation, a people for God's own possession, so that you may proclaim the excellencies of Him who has called you out of darkness into His marvelous light" (1 Peter 2:9).

Just as the Tabernacle moved with Israel through the wilderness, so God moves with us through the wilderness of life. He does not wait for us to reach perfection - He meets us in our imperfection. He does not dwell in distant temples - He dwells in hearts made holy by His grace.

Final Reflection: From Tent to Throne

The Tabernacle began as a tent in the desert. It was humble, temporary, and fragile. But it pointed to something eternal - the throne of God, surrounded by worship, filled with glory.

In Revelation, we see the fulfillment of this vision: *"Behold, the tabernacle of God is among the people, and He will dwell among them, and they shall be His people, and God Himself will be among them"* (Revelation 21:3).

This is the end of the journey - not just proximity to God, but perfect union. No more veils. No more altars. No more separation. Just God with His people, face to face.

Until that day, the Tabernacle reminds us of the path we walk from sacrifice to sanctification to glory. It teaches us that redemption is not a moment - it is a movement. And it invites us to draw near, to dwell, and to delight in the presence of the One who made a way.

The Cross: The Final Altar

The Tabernacle was a shadow, a rehearsal for the true and final sacrifice. The blood of animals could cover sin, but it could not remove it. Only the blood of Christ could do that.

"But now He has appeared by the sacrifice of Himself to put away sin" (Hebrews 9:26b).

At Calvary, Jesus became both priest and offering. He did not bring the blood of another - He brought His own. He did not sprinkle it on gold - He poured it out on wood. The cross became the final altar, and His blood the final payment.

"Knowing that you were not redeemed with perishable things... but with precious blood, as of a lamb unblemished and spotless, the blood of Christ" (1 Peter 1:18–19).

This was not a symbolic gesture - it was a cosmic transaction. Life for life. The innocent for the guilty. The Son for the sinner. And unlike the sacrifices of old, this one was sufficient.

"For by one offering He has perfected for all time those who are sanctified" (Hebrews 10:14). The blood of Christ does not just cover - it cleanses. It does not just **delay judgment - it defeats it.** It does not just echo the Tabernacle - it fulfills it.

6

The Blood That Speaks

In the Old Testament, blood cried out from the ground - like Abel's, demanding justice.

"The voice of your brother's blood is crying out to Me from the ground" (Genesis 4:10).

But in the New Testament, blood speaks a better word. *"You have come... to Jesus, the mediator of a new covenant, and to the sprinkled blood, which speaks better things than the blood of Abel"* (Hebrews 12:24).

The blood of Christ does not cry for vengeance - it declares forgiveness. It does not accuse - it acquits. It does not condemn - it cleanses. This is the heart of the gospel: that the life of One was poured out so that the lives of many could be restored.

The Sacred Logic of Redemption

The shedding of blood is not primitive - it is profound. It reveals the sacred logic of redemption: that sin is deadly, but grace is costly. That justice must be satisfied, but mercy can be extended. That life must be given, but love is willing to give it.

The Tabernacle taught this through repetition. The cross declared it through finality. Now, we live not under the shadow of bulls and goats, but under the light of the Lamb.

"Worthy is the Lamb that was slaughtered to receive power, wealth, wisdom, might, honor, glory, and blessing" (Revelation 5:12). The blood has been shed. The price has been paid. The way has been opened. And we are invited to draw near - not with fear, but with faith.

Christ: The Fulfillment of the Tabernacle

When Jesus died on the cross, He became both High Priest and sacrificial Lamb. He did not enter the earthly Tabernacle, stitched with human hands and shadowed by ritual. He entered the heavenly one - eternal, perfect, and real.

"But when Christ appeared as a high priest of the good things having come, He entered through the greater and more perfect tabernacle, not made by hands... not by the blood of goats and calves, but by His own blood, He entered the Holy Place once for all time, having obtained eternal redemption" (Hebrews 9:11–12).

This was not repetition - it was resolution. Jesus did not sprinkle animal blood on golden furniture. He poured out His own blood on the altar of the cross. And when He did, the veil of the Temple was torn in two.

The Mercy Seat Fulfilled

The Mercy Seat, once hidden behind the veil and sprinkled with animal blood, finds its ultimate fulfillment in Christ. He is the place where judgment meets mercy, where law meets love, where death meets resurrection.

"Whom God displayed publicly as a propitiation in His blood through faith" (Romans 3:25).

Jesus **is** our Mercy Seat. He is the meeting place between God and humanity. His blood does not merely cover sin - it removes it. It cleanses the conscience. It restores the soul.

"How much more will the blood of Christ... cleanse your conscience from dead works to serve the living God?" (Hebrews 9:14).

A Living Invitation

The Tabernacle of Moses was more than a tent - it was a living prophecy, a divine blueprint of redemption. Every curtain, every vessel, every ritual pointed forward to Christ. The bronze altar whispered of the cross. The lampstand glowed with the light of the world. The bread of the Presence foretold the Bread of Life. The incense rose like the prayers of the saints. And the Holy of Holies, once shrouded in mystery, now shines with invitation.

"Behold, the tabernacle of God is among the people, and He will dwell among them, and they shall be His people, and God Himself will be among them" (Revelation 21:3).

The Tabernacle was a shadow. Christ is the substance. The rituals were rehearsals. The cross was the performance. The veil was a barrier. His body was the breakthrough.

To meditate on the Tabernacle is to see the gospel in architecture, in ritual, in symbol. It is to witness the lengths to which God will go to dwell with His people - not in spite of their sin, but through the shedding of blood that removes it.

Dwelling with God: From Tent to Temple

Now, through Christ, we are not just visitors to the Tabernacle - we are its fulfillment. We are living temples, indwelt by the Spirit of God.

The journey from the Outer Court to the Holy of Holies is no longer a physical path - it is a spiritual reality. We begin at the altar, where sin is confessed and grace is received. We move through the Holy Place, where light, nourishment, and prayer shape our daily walk. And we enter the Holy of Holies - not with fear, but with faith - because the blood has been shed, the veil has been torn, and the invitation has been extended.

"Let us draw near with confidence to the throne of grace, so that we may receive mercy and find grace for help at the time of our need" (Hebrews 4:16).

Reflection: The Tabernacle in Us

The Tabernacle is not just history - it is identity. It teaches us that God desires to dwell with His people. That holiness is not distant - it is accessible. That redemption is not abstract - it is architectural, woven into the very fabric of worship. And now, through Christ, we carry the presence of God into the world. We are mobile sanctuaries, living testimonies, walking tabernacles of grace.

"But you are a chosen people, a royal priesthood, a holy nation, a people for God's own possession..." (1 Peter 2:9).

The Tabernacle began as a tent in the wilderness. It ends as a people in the world - redeemed, restored, and radiant with the glory of God.

Calvary and the Blood

The old system was a shadow, a rehearsal for the true sacrifice to come. Every drop of animal blood spilled on the altar was a whisper of something greater - a longing for cleansing that could reach not just the surface, but the soul.

"For it is impossible for the blood of bulls and goats to take away sins" (Hebrews 10:4). The blood of animals could cover sin like a blanket over a stain. But it could not erase the guilt, silence the shame, or restore the broken heart. It was mercy on credit - awaiting the day when the debt would be paid in full. That day came on a hill called Calvary.

When Jesus hung on the cross, His blood was not spilled - it was **poured out**. Not by accident, but by intention. Not as a ritual, but as a ransom. His blood was not the blood of a creature - it was the blood of the Creator. Pure. Powerful. Permanent.

The Blood of Abel

Abel's blood cried out from the ground for justice (Genesis 4:10). But Christ's blood speaks a better word.

As Hebrews 12:24 revealed, Abel's blood cried, "Injustice!" Jesus' blood cries, "It is finished." Abel's blood demanded vengeance. Jesus' blood delivers forgiveness. Abel's blood marked the earth with sorrow. Jesus' blood marks the believer with salvation.

The blood of Christ does not merely cleanse the altar - it cleanses the conscience. It does not just remove guilt - it restores intimacy. It does not just satisfy the law - it satisfies the heart of God.

To repeat Hebrews 9:14, *"How much more will the blood of Christ... cleanse your conscience from dead works to serve the living God?"*

This is not surface-level forgiveness. It is soul-deep restoration. The blood of Jesus reaches into the hidden places - the regrets, the secrets, the wounds - and washes them clean. It is not a temporary fix. It is a permanent transformation.

The Altar Within

In the Tabernacle, the altar was made of bronze and stood outside the Holy Place. It was the first stop on the journey to God. But now, through Christ, the altar is not a piece of furniture - it is a posture of the heart.

We come not with animals, but with repentance. Not with ritual, but with faith. And the blood is already there - waiting, speaking, cleansing.

"Therefore, brothers and sisters, since we have confidence to enter the holy place by the blood of Jesus... let us approach God with a sincere heart in full assurance of faith" (Hebrews 10:19, 22).

The blood of Jesus is not just the end of the old system - it is the beginning of new life. It is the river that flows from the cross to the heart, washing away sin and watering the seeds of grace.

To trust in His blood is to trade death for life, guilt for peace, distance for closeness. It is to stand at the altar - not in fear, but in freedom. Not condemned but cleansed.

"In Him we have redemption through His blood, the forgiveness of our wrongdoings, according to the riches of His grace" (Ephesians 1:7).

Jesus: The Final Atonement

The cross was not a tragic accident - it was a divine appointment. From eternity past, God had prepared a way for justice and mercy to meet, for holiness and love to embrace. That way was Jesus.

"He was foreknown before the foundation of the world, but has appeared in these last times for the sake of you" (1 Peter 1:20).

When Jesus cried out, "It is finished," He was not just announcing the end of His suffering - He was declaring the completion of atonement. The debt was paid. The veil was torn. The wrath was absorbed. The way was opened.

"For by one offering He has perfected for all time those who are sanctified" (Hebrews 10:14). No more sacrifices. No more bloodshed. No more waiting. The final Lamb had been slain, and His blood speaks louder than any ritual ever could.

Though the sacrifice was once for all, the power of the blood is ongoing. It still cleanses. It still speaks. It still invites. *"If we walk in the Light as He Himself is in the Light... the blood of Jesus His Son cleanses us from all sin"* (1 John 1:7).

The blood of Jesus is not a relic - it is a river. It flows from Calvary to every heart that dares to believe. It washes away guilt. It quenches spiritual thirst. It marks us as His own.

The Cross as a Compass

The cross is not just a moment in history - it is the compass of eternity. It points us to the heart of God. It anchors our identity. It defines our hope.

To gaze upon the cross is to see the cost of grace and the depth of love. It is to realize that we are not just saved - we are wanted. **Not just forgiven - we are invited**.

The Old Testament rituals were sacred shadows, preparing the way for the reality of Christ. The Tabernacle, the Mercy Seat, the Day of Atonement - all of it was a divine drama pointing to the cross. And now, because of Jesus, the curtain has been torn, the blood has been shed, and the way to God is open.

"For the Law, since it has only a shadow of the good things to come and not the form of those things itself, can never... make the worshipers perfect" (Hebrews 10:1).

These rituals were not empty - they were anticipatory. They taught Israel that sin was serious, that holiness was costly, and that access to God required sacrifice. But they also taught that God was near, that He desired relationship, and that He was preparing something greater.

But the wilderness was not the final destination. The Tabernacle was not the final temple. And the High Priest was not the final mediator. Enter Christ. *"But now He has obtained a more excellent ministry... He is the mediator of a better covenant"* (Hebrews 8:6).

Satan and the Blood: The Transfer of Authority

When Adam and Eve sinned in the Garden of Eden, it was not simply a moment of disobedience - it was a spiritual transaction with eternal consequences. By trusting the serpent's voice over God's command, they surrendered their divine authority and unknowingly invited spiritual occupation. In essence, they handed over the stewardship of humanity's soul to Satan, exchanging truth for deception. Sin entered not just their actions, but their very bloodline - like a virus that corrupts the spiritual DNA of all who follow.

Paul reveals this haunting reality in 2 Corinthians 4:4, writing that *"the god of this world has blinded the minds of the unbelieving so that they will not see the light of the gospel of the glory of Christ."* Satan is not divine, but he has jurisdiction - temporary influence over a world now bent away from the light. His power lies not in force but in falsehood. He weaves lies so fine that they resemble truth, cloaking humanity in confusion and rebellion.

Imagine a beautiful tapestry torn from its frame and replaced with counterfeits: philosophies that sparkle, pleasures that promise, but all stitched with spiritual decay. Satan's mission is not just to tempt, but to enslave - and his dominion operates through deception, leading souls deeper into darkness.

The Dominion of Darkness: A Hidden Captivity

Paul intensifies this picture in Ephesians 2:2, describing Satan as *"the prince of the power of the air."* It is a poetic way of saying his influence saturates the unseen - like pollution in the atmosphere, invisible but toxic. Before Christ illuminates the soul, each person walks in this fog: living by the world's rhythms, chasing hollow values, and unknowingly aligning with the rebellion of darkness.

John echoes this in 1 John 5:19: *"We know that we are of God, and that the whole world lies in the power of the evil one."* The language here is not metaphor - it is a spiritual diagnosis. Humanity is not wandering in neutral territory; we are born onto a battleground, inheriting an internal tilt away from God.

Satan's dominion is parasitic. He cannot create beauty, only corrupt it. He cannot redeem life, only resist it. His grip is not made of chains - it is sewn into the inherited sin nature that pulses within us. David lays this bare in *Psalm 51:5*: *"Behold, I was brought forth in guilt, and in sin my mother conceived me."* Sin is more than behavior - it is a spiritual inheritance, a bent posture toward rebellion.

The Gospel as Rescue

This is the soul's condition before redemption - a spiritual bloodstream infected with rebellion, a blindness that keeps truth out of reach. But the gospel does not just forgive - it heals, restores, and reclaims authority. Through Christ's blood, not ours, the curse is reversed.

Think of it like a transfusion. Our corrupted blood is replaced by the pure blood of Christ, a transaction described in *Colossians 1:13–14*: *"For He rescued us from the domain of darkness and transferred us to the kingdom of His beloved Son, in whom we have redemption, the forgiveness of sins."* It is not behavior modification - it is rebirth, a re-alignment with divine authority.

The Blood: Heaven's Counterattack

Into this bleak battlefield steps Jesus - not as a distant deity cloaked in majesty, but as a baby wrapped in mortality. Born of a virgin and conceived by the Holy Spirit, He entered the human story untouched by Adam's fallen inheritance. Matthew 1:18–25 underscores this miraculous entrance: before Mary and Joseph came together, she was found to be with child - by divine overshadowing, not by human seed. This was not poetic flourish or religious symbol - it was a tactical maneuver in the spiritual war. Jesus came through a back door Satan could not guard, bypassing the corrupted bloodline and emerging beyond the reach of sin's jurisdiction.

The virgin birth was Heaven's declaration: "This One is different." No inherited rebellion. No internal decay. He alone could become the substitute - the Lamb without blemish, whose blood held no trace of guilt, and whose death would carry explosive spiritual consequence.

Hebrews 2:14 gives language to the mystery: *"Since the children share in flesh and blood, He Himself likewise also partook of the same..."* Jesus put on our skin, entered our fragility, and walked into the very realm where death reigned. But He did not come to survive it - He came to dismantle it. By dying, He detonated the enemy's most feared weapon. The cross was not a tragic misstep - it was a trap set in divine brilliance. Satan, blinded by pride, took the bait. And when Christ's innocent blood hit the dust, it wrote a new story - one where death lost its sting and the grave its victory.

Jesus' crucifixion was Heaven's thunderclap in the underworld. It was God's counterattack wrapped in suffering. With arms outstretched and blood poured out, He stormed the gates of hell - not to negotiate, but to conquer. The cross became a cosmic reversal: what looked like weakness was the triumph of divine strength; what seemed like defeat was the doorway to redemption.

Redemption: Bought Back by Blood

Imagine being held captive in a shadowed fortress - not just physically chained, but spiritually imprisoned. No windows. No exit. No light. This was our condition under sin - a soul-level captivity beneath Satan's dominion. But then came the sound of footsteps... not from within, but from above. Colossians 1:13–14 declares it: *"He rescued us from the domain of darkness and transferred us to the kingdom of His beloved Son..."* This is not religious jargon - it is a jailbreak. A divine extraction. We did not wander out - we were rescued. Pulled from darkness, relocated into light.

And the price? Blood. Not just any blood, but innocent, royal, divine blood. Redemption is not a sentiment - it is a transaction. To redeem is to buy back what was lost, stolen, or enslaved. Jesus did not negotiate with evil - He paid in full. His blood is our receipt of purchase, stamped with Heaven's seal. It says to every demonic claim: *"Paid. Nullified. Canceled."*

But redemption goes even deeper. It is not just being freed from - it is being freed for. Freedom to belong. Freedom to inherit. Freedom to call God *Abba*. Acts 26:18 captures this epic reversal: *"...that they may turn from darkness to light, and from the power of Satan to God..."* Redemption opens our eyes to a reality that was always near but never accessible. Through Christ's sacrifice, we do not just get forgiven - we get family.

We are no longer spiritual orphans wandering through theological fog. We have been given a last name: Son. Daughter. Heir. And with that identity comes inheritance - not just in some distant afterlife, but now. Redemption means we walk with spiritual authority, clothed in righteousness, carrying passports stamped with the seal of the King.

So, when you hear the word *redemption,* do not think abstract theology. Think adoption papers signed in blood. Think - shackles snapped by grace. Think a prison cell swung wide open - and a child stepping into the light of a forever home.

The Great Reversal: From Condemnation to Victory

Condemnation is not just a feeling - it is a verdict. Humanity, apart from Christ, stands guilty beneath the weight of sin's decree. But into this courtroom enters a Savior with pierced hands and a sinless record. In *John 3:18,* Jesus renders the life-altering judgment: *"The one who believes in Him is not judged; the one who does not believe has been judged already..."* The gavel has fallen, but faith rewrites the case. This is not a loophole - it is the law of grace enacted through blood.

Apart from Christ, our condition is not neutral - it is occupied. We live under spiritual jurisdiction, and sin aligns us with the dominion of darkness. As *1 John 3:8* declares with piercing clarity: *"The one who practices sin is of the devil...The Son of God appeared for this purpose, to destroy the works of the devil."* This is not poetry - it is warfare. Jesus came not merely to inspire, but to crush evil's infrastructure. Every miracle He performed was not just compassionate - **it was confrontational.** Every healing and exorcism tore holes in hell's agenda.

The cross was Heaven's invasion point. It did not just absorb wrath - it deployed victory. The resurrection was not a recovery - it was a roar. As *1 Corinthians 15:57* proclaims: *"But thanks be to God, who gives us the victory through our Lord Jesus Christ."* This is not distant theology - it is current position. We do not fight <u>for</u> victory; we fight - <u>from</u> it. The blood is our defense against accusation, our song in suffering, our emblem in spiritual conflict.

Picture a reversal so complete that slaves become sons, convicts become co-heirs, enemies become ambassadors. That is the gospel: condemnation swallowed by mercy, judgment overturned by justice, defeat swallowed up in triumph. The cross stands forever as the pivot point of history - where wrath met grace, and grace prevailed.

So, lift your eyes, saint and soldier. You carry the name of Victor. The blood is not just a past event - it is a present power. It is your shield in temptation, your banner in warfare, and your anthem in every hour of darkness.

Satan's Defeat and Our Defense

Revelation 12:11 is more than a footnote in apocalyptic drama - it is a battle cry for every believer: *"And they overcame him because of the blood of the Lamb and because of the word of their testimony…"* This is the strategy of Heaven against hell's schemes. The blood of Jesus is not only our rescue - it is our resistance. It dismantles accusation, severs chains, and secures our citizenship in the kingdom of God. The cross did not merely redeem us - it armed us.

Satan is more than a tempter; he is an accuser. His native tongue is deception. He whispers guilt into the ears of the redeemed, trying to reopen wounds that Christ has already healed. But the blood speaks louder. As Hebrews 12:24 reminded us - it is not vengeance, but mercy; not condemnation but covering. **Where Satan points, the blood defends**. Where sin shouts, the blood silences.

The blood of Jesus is Heaven's legal answer to hell's indictment. It is not mystical sentiment - it is divine evidence. The courtroom of eternity has already issued its verdict: *Justified. Adopted. Free.* The devil may accuse, but he holds no authority over those sealed in Christ.

Some ask - *Was Jesus born under Satan's rule, like us?* Scripture answers with clarity. Matthew 1:18–25 reveals His origin: conceived by the Holy Spirit, born of a virgin. No tainted lineage. No inherited rebellion. Jesus was not subject to Adam's curse. He entered humanity, but not its corruption. This is why His blood matters - it was unstained. Innocent. Powerful enough to substitute for the guilty and crush the serpent's head.

Paul punctuates the story with a victory cry – and once again it comes from 1 Corinthians 15:57: *"But thanks be to God, who gives us the victory through our Lord Jesus Christ."* This victory is not theoretical - it is experiential. It belongs to us. Through Christ, we do not just escape sin - we overcome it. We do not just survive spiritual war - we dominate it. We walk forward not as survivors, but as sons armed with the blood.

Tetelestia – It Is Finished

The word *Tetelestai* comes from the Greek verb *teleo*, meaning "**to complete**," "**to fulfill**," or "**to pay**." In the ancient world, it was used in various contexts, such as a servant reporting to a master that a task was done or a merchant declaring a debt fully paid. When Jesus said *"Tetelestai"*, He was proclaiming that His work on the cross - His sacrificial death - was complete, fulfilling God's plan for salvation. This moment marked the climax of His mission to redeem humanity from sin and defeat the powers of evil, including Satan.

Think of *Tetelestai* as Jesus saying, "Mission accomplished!" He was not just saying He was done suffering; He was declaring that He had fully paid the price for humanity's sins, won the victory over evil, and opened the way for people to be reconciled with God.

John 19:30 states: *"Therefore when Jesus had received the sour wine, He said, 'It is finished!' And He bowed His head and gave up His spirit."* This verse shows that *Tetelestai* was Jesus' final declaration before His death, signaling the completion of His atoning work.

To understand its deeper meaning, especially regarding Satan, let us explore what this moment accomplished:

Fulfillment of God's Plan for Salvation. Jesus' death on the cross was the ultimate sacrifice for humanity's sins, fulfilling Old Testament prophecies and the requirements of God's justice. Isaiah 53:5 foreshadows this: *"But He was pierced through for our transgressions, He was crushed for our iniquities; the chastisement for our well-being fell upon Him, and by His scourging we are healed."*

By saying *Tetelestai,* Jesus confirmed that He had completed the work of atonement, paying the full price for sin so that humanity could be forgiven and restored to God. This was a devastating blow to Satan, whose power relied on humanity's separation from God due to sin.

Victory Over Satan and the Powers of Evil. Satan, as the adversary, sought to keep humanity enslaved to sin and death. Jesus' death and resurrection broke this power. Colossians 2:15 explains: *"When He had disarmed the rulers and authorities, He made a public display of them, having triumphed over them through Him [the cross]."*

Here, *"rulers and authorities"* refer to spiritual forces, including Satan and his demonic powers. On the cross, Jesus stripped Satan of his authority to hold humanity captive. *Tetelestai* was a declaration that Satan's claim over humanity - through sin and death - was nullified.

Breaking the Power of Sin and Death. Satan's primary weapon is sin, which leads to death and separation from God. Jesus' sacrifice destroyed this power. Hebrews 2:14-15 states: *"Therefore, since the children share in flesh and blood, He Himself likewise also partook of the same, that through death He might render powerless him who had the power of death, that is, the devil, and might free those who through fear of death were subject to slavery all their lives."*

Tetelestai marked the moment when Jesus rendered Satan "powerless" by breaking the chains of death. Satan could no longer hold the fear of death over humanity, as Jesus' sacrifice provided eternal life for those who believe.

Establishing a New Covenant. Jesus' death inaugurated a new covenant, making forgiveness and direct access to God available to all who trust in Him. Hebrews 9:15 says: *"For this reason He is the mediator of a new covenant, so that, since a death has taken place for the redemption of the transgressions that were committed under the first covenant, those who have been called may receive the promise of the eternal inheritance."*

This new covenant undermined Satan's ability to accuse or condemn believers, as their sins were now forgiven through Christ's finished work.

What "Tetelestai" Meant for Satan

For Satan, Tetelestai was a declaration of defeat. Here is what it meant specifically for him:

Loss of Authority: Satan's power depended on humanity's sinfulness and separation from God. Jesus' perfect sacrifice paid the debt of sin, stripping Satan of his legal claim over humanity. As 1 John 3:8 says: *"The Son of God appeared for this purpose, to destroy the works of the devil."*

Public Defeat: The cross was a public humiliation for Satan. Colossians 2:15 (quoted above) describes Jesus making a *"public display"* of Satan's defeat. Picture Satan as a villain who thought he had won when Jesus was crucified, only to realize that the cross was his downfall.

Foreshadowing Ultimate Judgment: While Satan was defeated at the cross, his final judgment is still to come (Revelation 20:10). *Tetelestai* was a decisive blow, ensuring his ultimate fate. It was like Jesus landing a knockout punch in a boxing match, even if the final bell has not rung yet.

When Jesus said Tetelestai - "It is finished"- This was a game-changer for Satan. Jesus' death on the cross paid the price for our sins, broke Satan's power over death, and made it possible for people to be right with God. For Satan, it meant he lost his grip on humanity, his accusations were silenced, and his defeat was guaranteed.

7

The Permanent Sacrifice and Our Living High Priest

The ancient Hebrews followed God's instructions carefully, offering animal sacrifices year after year to atone for their sins. As they settled in the Promised Land and grew as a nation, their temporary Tabernacle was replaced by the magnificent Temple in Jerusalem. This permanent building became the center of their worship, housing the Holy of Holies where God's presence descended and dwelt once a year. However, one thing remained temporary: the sacrificial system itself.

Every year, on the Day of Atonement, the High Priest entered the Holy of Holies to offer blood for the people's sins, knowing he would have to repeat the process the next year. But God had a greater plan - a permanent sacrifice that would change everything. When Jesus died on the cross, His perfect sacrifice replaced the temporary system, offering eternal redemption. No matter how many animals were offered, the High Priest would return the next year, repeating the ritual. It was a constant reminder that something greater was needed - a permanent solution to sin. That solution came through Jesus Christ, whose death on the cross and resurrection changed everything forever. He became the ultimate sacrifice, proved His victory by rising from the dead, and now stands as our High Priest, always interceding for us.

One Offering for All Time

Imagine trying to paint a masterpiece using only charcoal outlines. The shapes are there, the intention is clear - but the color, the depth, the life of the image is missing.

The old system of sacrifices was like this sketch, a faint outline of something far greater. It could not erase sin - it could only cover it temporarily. Picture the High Priest, year after year, carrying the blood of goats and bulls into the Holy of Holies, knowing it was not enough. God was never improvising, He had a plan from before time began, a perfect sacrifice, not drawn from the herd in the field but born of heaven. A sacrifice that would not just cover sin but conquer it.

The book of Hebrews opens a window into this dilemma. *"For the Law, since it has only a shadow of the good things to come and not the very form of things, can never, by the same sacrifices which they offer continually year by year, make perfect those who draw near"* (Hebrews 10:1). They were not wrong - but they were preparatory. Every sacrifice was a whisper of longing, a cry for something more.

Hebrews continues: *"For it is impossible for the blood of bulls and goats to take away sins"* (Hebrews 10:4). **The repetition of sacrifice was not a sign of strength - it was a sign of insufficiency**. Year after year, the Day of Atonement came and went, and with it, the reminder: "You are still sinful. You are still waiting."

But then, a voice breaks through the shadows. Quoting Psalm 40, the writer of Hebrews imagines Jesus speaking to the Father: *"SACRIFICE AND OFFERING YOU HAVE NOT DESIRED, BUT A BODY YOU HAVE PREPARED FOR ME; IN WHOLE BURNT OFFERINGS AND sacrifices FOR SIN YOU HAVE TAKEN NO PLEASURE. THEN I SAID, 'BEHOLD, I HAVE COME (IN THE SCROLL OF THE BOOK IT IS WRITTEN OF ME) TO DO YOUR WILL, O GOD'"* (Hebrews 10:5–7). This is the turning point of history. God did not ultimately desire the blood of animals - He desired obedience, holiness, and a heart fully surrendered. And so, He prepared a body - not a symbolic offering, but a living, breathing vessel of divine love.

Jesus came not to perpetuate the old system, but to fulfill it. *"Then He said, 'BEHOLD, I HAVE COME TO DO YOUR WILL.' He takes away the first in order to establish the second"* (Hebrews 10:9).

The cross was not an accident - it was the culmination of God's eternal plan. And by that will - by Jesus' perfect obedience - we have been *"sanctified through the offering of the body of Jesus Christ once for all"* (Hebrews 10:10). Not temporarily. Not conditionally. But permanently.

Then comes one of the most breathtaking declarations in all of Scripture: *"For by one offering He has perfected for all time those who are sanctified"* (Hebrews 10:14).

This is the paradox of grace. In Christ, we are already perfect - declared righteous, fully accepted - even as we are still being transformed. It is like being adopted into a royal family: the moment you are chosen, your identity changes, even if you are still learning how to live like royalty. **The blood of Jesus does not just forgive - it redefines.** It speaks a new name over us: *Beloved. Redeemed. Holy.*

Paul echoes this truth in Romans: *"Therefore there is now no condemnation at all for those who are in Christ Jesus"* (Romans 8:1).

So, we walk forward - not in fear, but in faith. Not trying to earn what has already been given but learning to live in the light of it. The offering has been made. The door is open. The sketch has become a masterpiece.

A Greater Priest, A Greater Offering

Hebrews 9 takes us deeper still. *"But when Christ appeared as a high priest of the good things to come, He entered through the greater and more perfect tabernacle, not made with hands, that is to say, not of this creation"* (Hebrews 9:11). Jesus did not enter the earthly tent, stitched by human hands - He entered the heavenly sanctuary, the true dwelling place of God. And He did not carry the blood of animals - He carried His own blood, shed on a Roman cross, poured out in love.

"And not through the blood of goats and calves, but through His own blood, He entered the holy place once for all, having obtained eternal redemption" (Hebrews 9:12). Eternal. Not annual. Not provisional. The old sacrifices could cleanse the body, but they could not touch the soul. They could purify the flesh, but they could not silence the conscience.

The writer of Hebrews draws a vivid contrast: *"For if the blood of goats and bulls and the ashes of a heifer sprinkling those who have been defiled sanctify for the cleansing of the flesh, how much more will the blood of Christ, who through the eternal Spirit offered Himself without blemish to God, cleanse your conscience from dead works to serve the living God?"* (Hebrews 9:13–14). The reference to the ashes of a heifer comes from Numbers 19, where a red heifer was burned and its ashes used to purify those who had touched death. It was a ritual of cleansing, a way to restore worshipers to community and holiness.

Jesus' blood goes deeper. It does not just cleanse the hands - it cleanses the heart. It does not just restore ritual purity - it liberates the soul. Imagine a river cutting through a desert, turning dry ground into a garden. That is what His sacrifice does to the human spirit. It reaches into the hidden places - guilt, shame, regret - and washes them clean. It silences the voice that says, *"You are not worthy."* It breaks the chain that whispers, *"You'll never change."* It opens the door to a life of purpose, joy, and communion with the living God.

Paul echoes this in Romans: *"Much more then, having now been justified by His blood, we shall be saved from the wrath of God through Him"* (Romans 5:9). And again, in Ephesians: *"In Him we have redemption through His blood, the forgiveness of our wrongdoings, according to the riches of His grace"* (Ephesians 1:7).

A Word to the Weary and the Wandering

If you have ever felt like you are not enough - like you have failed too many times, wandered too far, or sinned too deeply - this is your invitation. You do not need to earn God's approval. You do not need to offer your own sacrifices. The offering has already been made. The blood has already been shed. The veil has already been torn. Jesus' sacrifice is once for all - for all people, for all sin, for all time. It is the final word in the story of redemption. And it speaks over you: Forgiven. Redeemed. Made holy.

So, come. Not with fear, but with faith. Not with shame, but with confidence. The way is open. The blood has been sprinkled - not on a golden lid in a tent, but on the mercy of God's heart. And it is enough.

As Hebrews reminds us: *"Therefore, brothers and sisters, since we have confidence to enter the holy place by the blood of Jesus... let's approach God with a sincere heart in full assurance of faith"* (Hebrews 10:19, 22a).

The Eternal Priest

In the ancient world of Israel, the priesthood was a lineage - a sacred office passed from father to son, generation after generation. Each priest served for a time, then died, and another took his place. The system was holy, but it was fragile. Human priests were mortal. They sinned. They aged. They failed. And so, the sacrifices continued, day after day, year after year - atonement layered upon atonement, like patchwork over a broken soul.

Hebrews 7 lifts our eyes to a new kind of priesthood - one not bound by time or death. *"but because He continues forever, He has an unchangeable priesthood"* (Hebrews 7:24). The Greek word here for *"unchangeable"* is *aparabatos* (ἀπαράβατος) – and has a meaning of **unchangeable, inviolable, indestructible**. His priesthood cannot be interrupted, revoked, or replaced. Why? Because He lives forever. The resurrection was not just a miracle - it was a coronation. Jesus rose not only as Savior, but as High Priest eternal, seated at the right hand of God, never to be dethroned.

And because He lives forever, *"Therefore He is able also to save <u>forever</u> those who draw near to God through Him, since He always lives to make intercession for them"* (Hebrews 7:25). The word *"forever"* here is *pantelēs* (παντελὲς) - meaning **fully, entirely, to the uttermost**. Not partially. Not temporarily. Not conditionally. Jesus saves to the depths and to the edges. There is no corner of your heart too dark, no failure too frequent, no wound too deep. He saves forever.

Why? "Because He always lives to intercede for them." This is one of the most tender truths in all of Scripture. Jesus is not just your past Savior - He is your **present Intercessor**. Right now, in this moment, He is praying for you. Not generically. Not abstractly. But personally. He knows your name. He knows your story. And He is speaking it before the throne of God with love and authority.

No More Layers of Blood

The contrast with earthly priests is stark. *"For it was fitting for us to have such a high priest, holy, innocent, undefiled, separated from sinners and exalted above the heavens; who does not need daily, like those high priests, to offer up sacrifices, first for His own sins and then for the sins of the people, because this He did once for all when He offered up Himself"* (Hebrews 7:26–27). Human priests had to purify themselves before they could help others. But Jesus is sinless - holy, undefiled, and pure. He did not need to offer sacrifices for Himself. He was the sacrifice.

"He offered up Himself." This is the heart of the gospel. The phrase *"once for all"* is *ephapax* (ἐφάπαξ) – means a **decisive, unrepeatable act**. Jesus did not die to begin a new cycle of offerings. He died to end the cycle. His blood was not a placeholder - it was the final payment. His life was not taken - it was freely given.

Hebrews 9:22 reminds us why blood was necessary: *"And according to the Law, one may almost say, all things are cleansed with blood, and without shedding of blood there is no forgiveness"*. Sin demands a life. It is not a minor offense - it is a rupture in the fabric of holiness. Animal blood was symbolic, a temporary covering. But it could not erase guilt. It could not cleanse the conscience. It could not restore the soul.

Only perfect blood could do that. Blood that was innocent. Blood that was willing. Blood that came from a heart that loved the sinner more than it feared the cross.

A Word to the Wounded and the Wondering

So, what does this mean for you?

It means your salvation is not fragile. It is not hanging by a thread. It is anchored in the eternal priesthood of Jesus, who never dies, never sleeps, and never stops praying for you. It means your past does not define you. Your failures do not disqualify you. Your doubts do not displace you.

Jesus has already offered Himself. The altar is empty. The veil is torn. The blood has been poured out - not in a temple made by hands, but in the presence of God Himself. And it is enough. You are forgiven. You are free. You are held by a Savior who saves forever and intercedes constantly.

So, come. Not with fear, but with faith. Not with shame, but with boldness. The High Priest is waiting - not to judge, but to welcome. And His arms are open forever.

Unbreakable Love

If Jesus is the eternal High Priest - if His sacrifice was once for all, and His intercession never ceases - then what could possibly threaten your place in God's heart?

Paul answers this not with a whisper, but with a thunderclap. In Romans 8, he does not offer vague comfort - he declares unshakable truth: *"Who will separate us from the love of Christ? Will tribulation, or distress, or persecution, or famine, or nakedness, or peril, or sword?"* (Romans 8:35).

This is not a poetic list - It is a battlefield inventory. Trouble. Hardship. Hunger. Danger. These are the jagged edges of life in a broken world. Paul was not theorizing- he had lived them. Beaten, imprisoned, starved, hunted. And yet, his answer is unwavering: *None of it can separate us.*

Then he builds to a crescendo: *"For I am <u>convinced</u> that neither death, nor life, nor angels, nor principalities, nor things present, nor things to come, nor powers, nor height, nor depth, nor any other created thing, will be able to separate us from the love of God, which is in Christ Jesus our Lord"* (Romans 8:38–39).

The Greek word for *"convinced"* is *pepeismai* (πέπεισμαι) - a **settled, immovable certainty**. Paul is not speaking from a safe distance. He is speaking from the trenches. His conviction has been tested, and it holds.

And what is he convinced of? That death cannot sever it. Life cannot dilute it. Angels cannot override it. Demons cannot destroy it. Today's failures cannot undo it. Tomorrow's fears cannot outrun it. No power - spiritual, political, emotional - can touch it. No height of joy, no depth of despair, no created thing in all existence can break it.

This is the crescendo of grace. The love of God is not fragile. It is not conditional. It is not distant. It is in Christ Jesus - anchored in His death, sealed by His resurrection, and carried by His eternal priesthood. You are not just loved - you are securely loved. Held. Known. Protected.

A Word to the Anxious and the Afraid

Maybe you have wondered: What if I mess up too badly? What if I drift too far? What if I lose my faith?

Paul's answer is clear: Nothing can separate you. Not your worst day. Not your deepest doubt. Not your darkest secret. **The love of Christ is not a feeling - it is a fact**. **It is not a mood - it is a mission**. Jesus did not die for you on a whim. He chose the cross with you in mind. And now, risen and reigning, He holds you with hands that still bear the scars.

Jesus did not stumble into the cross. He chose it - with you in mind. When you feel unworthy, remember: He is interceding for you. *"Christ Jesus is He who died, but rather, was raised, who is at the right hand of God, who also intercedes for us"* (Romans 8:34).

When you feel unloved, remember: He has already proven His love and this verse should be memorized: *"But God demonstrates His own love toward us, in that while we were still sinners, Christ died for us"* (Romans 5:8).

When you feel unsafe, remember: Nothing can separate you. This is the security of salvation. Not built on your strength, but on His. Not held by your grip, but by His embrace. **You are not dangling - you are anchored.**

Picture this: You are facing a tough day. Maybe you are stressed about exams, arguing with a friend, or feeling invisible in a crowded room. Paul says nothing - not failure, not fear, not even supernatural forces - can cut you off from God's love. Jesus' sacrifice has locked in your place in God's family. When life feels like a storm, this promise is your anchor - holding you steady in the deep waters of God's unbreakable love.

He's Alive: The Proof of Victory

The cross was not the end - it was the turning point. Jesus' death was not a tragic finale, but a divine transaction. On that hill outside Jerusalem, sin was judged, wrath was absorbed, and mercy was unleashed. But the world did not know it yet. The sky darkened, the earth shook, and the tomb was sealed. For three days, silence reigned. And then - He rose.

The resurrection is not a footnote to the gospel - it is the proof that the gospel is true. Without it, Jesus' death would be noble but incomplete. Like the 300 Spartans at Thermopylae, who stood against impossible odds. Like the defenders of the Alamo, who died for freedom. Their courage was real. Their sacrifice was inspiring. But they stayed dead. Their stories stir the heart, but they cannot save the soul.

If Jesus had stayed in the grave, He would be remembered - but not worshiped. Admired - but not trusted. His teachings might live on, but His power would not. That is why Paul writes with such urgency in 1 Corinthians 15: "*and if Christ has not been raised, then our preaching is vain, your faith also is <u>vain</u>*" (1 Corinthians 15:14).

The Greek word for "vain" is kenos (κενός) – meaning **empty, hollow, without substance**. Without resurrection, Christianity collapses. The cross becomes a tragedy, not a triumph. Faith becomes fantasy. Hope becomes delusion.

Paul continues: "*and if Christ has not been raised, your faith is worthless; you are still in your sins. Then those also who have fallen asleep in Christ have perished. If we have hoped in Christ in this life only, we are of all men most to be pitied*" (1 Corinthians 15:17–19). If

Jesus did not rise, then we are clinging to a lie. We are building our lives on a myth. We are trusting a Savior who could not even save Himself. And those who died believing in Him? Lost. Forgotten. Deceived.

But Paul does not stop there. He declares with fire and certainty. His words in 1 Corinthians 15:20–22 are not just doctrinal - they are cosmic in scope and intimate in impact. He writes, *"But now Christ has been raised from the dead, the <u>first fruits</u> of those who are asleep. For since by a man came death, by a man also came the resurrection of the dead. For as in Adam all die, so also in Christ all will be made alive"* . The resurrection is not a private miracle - it is the beginning of a harvest, the first sprouting of life in a field long scorched by death.

The Greek word for *'first fruits'* - *aparche*, refers to the **first portion** of a harvest offered to God, symbolizing the beginning and guarantee of the full harvest to come. Jesus' resurrection is the first of its kind: a glorified, eternal resurrection - meaning that it guarantees believers will also be raised to eternal life. Just as the first fruits in the Old Testament were a pledge to the full harvest, Jesus is the pledge of the resurrection of all who belong to Him.

At the start of harvest, the first sheaf of grain was offered to God - not just in gratitude, but in expectation. It was a pledge that more was coming. The first fruits were holy, set apart, and representative of the full harvest yet to come. So, when Paul calls Jesus the *"first fruits,"* he is saying: His resurrection is not the end of the story - it is the beginning of yours.

Jesus did not rise alone. He rose as the prototype, the forerunner, the new Adam. Through Adam, the first man, death entered the world like a virus - infecting every soul, every body, every generation. Adam's sin fractured creation, severed communion, and unleashed mortality. *"For as in Adam all die..."* - not just physically, but spiritually. We inherit his brokenness, his exile, his dust-bound destiny.

But then comes Christ - the second Adam, the true Man, the sinless Son. *"...so also in Christ all will be made alive."* This is not poetic - it is prophetic. Jesus did not just undo Adam's curse - **He rewrote humanity's future**. Where Adam brought death, Christ brings life. Where Adam fell, Christ stood. Where Adam hid, Christ revealed. And where Adam returned to dust, Christ burst from the grave.

Paul reinforces this in Romans: *"But if the Spirit of Him who raised Jesus from the dead dwells in you, He who raised Christ Jesus from the dead will also give life to your mortal bodies through His Spirit who dwells in you"* (Romans 8:11).

A Word to the Doubting and the Dreaming

Maybe you have wondered: Is this all real? Is my faith just a story I have inherited or indoctrinated?

Paul would say: Look at the resurrection. It is not a metaphor. It is a historical event. Eyewitnesses saw Him. Touched Him. Ate with Him. *"Then He appeared to more than five hundred brethren at one time, most of whom remain until now, but some have fallen asleep"* (1 Corinthians 15:6). These were not hallucinations - they were encounters. And many of those witnesses died for their testimony, refusing to recant. People do not die for what they know is a lie. It means your faith is not blind - it is anchored. Your hope is not wishful - it is historical. Your future is not uncertain - it is resurrected.

Jesus did not rise to impress the world. He rose to defeat death, to vindicate the cross, and to open the grave for all who believe. His resurrection is the Father's "Amen" to the Son's *"It is finished."* It is the dawn after the darkness. The roar after the silence. The victory after the battle. And because He lives, you will live too.

Adam's sin fractured creation, severed communion, and unleashed mortality. Paul echoes this in Romans: *"So then as through one transgression there resulted condemnation to all men, even so through one act of righteousness there resulted justification of life to all men"* (Romans 5:18).

Jesus did not just survive death - He conquered it. **He did not just escape the grave - He emptied it.**

A Word to the Mortal and the Hopeful

You live in a world that fears death. It hides it behind hospital curtains, masks it with euphemisms, distracts from it with entertainment. But Scripture does not flinch. It names death as the enemy - and then declares that the enemy has been defeated.

"The last enemy that will be abolished is death" (1 Corinthians 15:26).

Because Jesus rose, you too will rise. Not metaphorically. Not symbolically. But bodily, eternally, gloriously. Death is no longer a wall - it is a doorway. A passage from the broken to the whole, from the temporary to the eternal, from the ache of exile to the joy of home.

This is your hope: not that you will escape death, but that you will pass through it into life. Jesus went first. He walked into the grave and came out holding the keys.

"I was dead, and behold, I am alive forevermore, and I have the keys of death and of Hades" (Revelation 1:18).

Remember - He is the first fruits - and you are part of the harvest. When you face loss, remember: Christ has been raised. When you fear the future, remember: You will be made alive. When you wonder if it is all worth it, remember: This is not the end.

The resurrection is not just a doctrine - it is a promise, a person, and a power that reaches into your present and pulls you toward eternity. It is the sunrise after the longest night. The seed that breaks open to become a tree. The heartbeat of a new creation.

"He Is Not Here"

The angel's declaration - *"He is not here, for He has risen, just as He said. Come, see the place where He was lying"* (Matthew 28:6) - is not merely a statement of fact. It is a cosmic disruption, a divine interruption in the story of death. These words echo through the corridors of history, shaking the foundations of despair and rewriting the narrative of humanity.

The tomb was supposed to be the end. It was sealed, guarded, final. But on that first Easter morning, the stone was rolled away - **not to let Jesus out, but to let the witnesses in**. *"Come and see the place where He lay."* The invitation is gentle, almost tender. It is as if heaven itself stoops down to our level, knowing our doubts, our grief, our need to see for ourselves.

This was not a demand - it was a gracious summons. The angel did not rebuke the women for their fear or confusion. He invited them to look, to witness, to believe. The empty tomb was not just evidence - it was an open door to faith. It was the moment when silence gave way to proclamation, when mourning turned to marvel.

"Just as He Said"

Jesus had foretold His resurrection. *"From that time Jesus began to show His disciples that He <u>must</u> go to Jerusalem and suffer many things from the elders and chief priests and scribes, and be killed, and be raised up on the third day"* (Matthew 16:21). He spoke plainly, repeatedly, and with purpose. And now, in the quiet of the garden, His words are vindicated. He keeps His promises - even the ones that seemed impossible.

This verse marks a pivotal moment in Jesus' ministry, often referred to as the "turning point" in the Gospel of Matthew. Up until this point, Jesus had focused on teaching, healing, and proclaiming the kingdom of God. Now, He explicitly reveals His mission to His disciples: He must go to Jerusalem, the religious and political center of Judaism, to face suffering, death, and resurrection.

The use of *"must"* (Greek: *dei*, meaning **divine necessity**) emphasizes that this was not a random event but part of God's redemptive plan, foretold in Scripture (e.g., Isaiah 53). The opposition from the *"elders, chief priests, and scribes"* represents the religious establishment, which would reject Jesus as the Messiah, fulfilling prophecies of a suffering servant.

The mention of the resurrection *"on the third day"* is significant. In Jewish tradition, the "third day" carried symbolic weight, often associated with divine deliverance or vindication (e.g., Hosea 6:2). Jesus' prediction was not vague; it was specific and tied to His identity as the Son of God. Yet, the disciples struggled to grasp this (as seen in Peter's rebuke in Matthew 16:22), reflecting their expectation of a political Messiah rather than a suffering one.

Matthew 16:21 establishes Jesus as a prophet who not only foretells the future but fulfills it through His actions. His willingness to face suffering and death demonstrates His obedience to the Father's will and His love for humanity. The resurrection, promised here, is the linchpin of Christian faith (1 Corinthians 15:14), validating Jesus' authority over sin and death. For believers, this verse is a reminder that God's plans often defy human expectations but are always purposeful. Jesus' clear foretelling of His death and resurrection invites trust in His foresight and sovereignty, even when His path seems incomprehensible.

The certainty of Jesus' prediction encourages believers to trust God's plan in their own lives, even in seasons of suffering or uncertainty. Just as Jesus faced the cross with purpose, Christians can face trials knowing that God's promises hold true, and resurrection power is at work in their lives.

<u>This matters deeply.</u> Because if Jesus kept His word about death and resurrection, then He will keep His word about everything else:

"and lo, I am with you always, even to the end of the age." Matthew 28:20

This verse concludes the Great Commission (Matthew 28:18–20), where the resurrected Jesus commands His disciples to make disciples of all nations. Spoken after His resurrection, these words carry the weight of His victory over death. The phrase *"I am with you always"* echoes God's covenantal promises to Israel (e.g., Genesis 28:15, Joshua 1:5) and underscores Jesus' divine presence.

The Greek phrase for '*I am with you*', *ego meth* (*hymon eimi*) emphasizes **continuity** and **permanence,** assuring the disciples that Jesus' presence is not limited by His physical absence. "*Even to the end of the age*" points to the eschatological scope of His promise - His presence endures until the consummation of history at His return.

The resurrection validates this promise. If Jesus could conquer death, as He predicted, then His assurance of ongoing presence is equally trustworthy. In the first-century context, the disciples faced persecution, cultural opposition, and the daunting task of spreading the gospel to a hostile world. Jesus' promise was not abstract; it was a lifeline, empowering them through the Holy Spirit (Acts 1:8) to fulfill their mission. This verse also reflects the doctrine of the Immanuel ("*God with us,*" Matthew 1:23), fulfilled in Jesus' incarnation and now extended through His abiding presence.

For believers, this promise is a source of comfort and courage. Whether facing personal struggles, societal pressures, or spiritual battles, Christians can rely on Jesus' constant presence. This assurance transforms mission and ministry, reminding believers that they are never alone in their calling to share the gospel or live out their faith.

"Come to Me, all who are weary and heavy-laden, and I will give you rest." Matthew 11:28

This invitation comes during a time of growing opposition to Jesus' ministry, particularly from the religious leaders who burdened people with legalistic interpretations of the Law (Matthew 23:4). The *"weary and heavy-laden"* likely refers to those exhausted by religious demands and the weight of sin. Jesus positions Himself as the source of true rest, contrasting the yoke of the Pharisees with His "easy yoke" (Matthew 11:29–30). In Jewish culture, a "yoke" symbolized teaching or obligation; Jesus' yoke represents His grace-filled teachings and the rest found in a relationship with Him.

The resurrection undergirds this promise. If Jesus can defeat death, He has the authority to offer spiritual rest - freedom from the guilt of sin and the striving for self-righteousness. This rest is not merely physical but existential, addressing the soul's deepest needs. In the context of first-century Judaism, this was revolutionary: Jesus offered direct access to God without the oppressive requirements of religious performance. Theologically, this rest points to the Sabbath rest fulfilled in Christ (Hebrews 4:9–10), where believers find peace through His finished work on the cross.

This verse speaks to anyone burdened by life's pressures - whether guilt, anxiety, or societal expectations. Jesus' invitation is universal (*"all"*) and personal (*"come to Me"*). Believers can find rest by trusting in His completed work, surrendering their burdens through prayer, and embracing His grace. This promise also challenges Christians to extend compassion to others, reflecting Jesus' heart for the weary.

"In My Father's house are many dwelling places; if it were not so, I would have told you; for I go to prepare a place for you." John 14:2

Spoken during the Last Supper, this verse is part of Jesus' farewell discourse to His disciples, who were troubled by His impending departure (John 13:36–14:1). *"My Father's house"* refers to heaven, the eternal dwelling place of God. The phrase *"many dwelling places" monai pollai,* means **rooms** or **abodes** and suggests **abundant space in God's presence** for all believers. Jesus' assurance that He is preparing a place conveys His active role in securing their eternal future. The phrase *"if it were not so, I would have told you,"* underscores His honesty and reliability, reinforcing the theme of trustworthiness.

The resurrection is the guarantee of this promise. By rising from the dead, Jesus demonstrated His authority to grant eternal life (John 10:17–18). In the cultural context, a bridegroom would prepare a home for his bride; Jesus, as the Bridegroom (John 3:29), prepares an eternal home for His church. This promise counters the disciples' immediate fears and points to the hope of eternal communion with God.

Theologically, it affirms the doctrine of eternal security - believers have a reserved place in heaven: "to *obtain* an inheritance *which is* imperishable, undefiled, and will not fade away, reserved in heaven for you, (1 Peter 1:4).

This verse offers hope in the face of death and uncertainty. Believers can live with confidence, knowing their eternal destiny is secure in Christ. It also motivates a forward-looking faith, encouraging Christians to prioritize eternal values over temporal concerns. The promise of a prepared place invites believers to trust Jesus' ongoing work in their lives, even when His plans are unseen.

Each of these promises - His presence, rest, and eternal home - rests on the reality of the resurrection. In a first-century world of competing philosophies and religions, the resurrection set Jesus apart as the trustworthy Son of God. Today, in a world of broken promises and uncertainty, the resurrection remains an anchor for faith. Jesus' fulfillment of His prediction in Matthew 16:21 validates every other promise, assuring believers that He is both mighty and faithful.

The resurrection is not just proof of power - **it is proof of character**. Jesus is not only mighty - He is trustworthy. Again, in a world of broken promises and fragile hopes, this is your anchor: He said He would rise - and He did.

For the Doubting, the Fearful, the Weary

If you are facing uncertainty, if your faith feels thin, if fear whispers louder than hope - remember the angel's words. *"He is not here."* Death could not hold Him. The grave could not silence Him. And your darkest night is not beyond His reach.

The risen Christ is not a distant figure in stained glass - He is alive, present, and active. He meets you in your questions, walks with you in your pain, and speaks peace into your chaos. The empty tomb is not just a past event - it is a present reality. It means Jesus is available, attentive, and able.

So come and see. Not just the place where He lay - but the life He now offers. The tomb is empty so your heart can be full. The risen Christ is not a distant figure in stained glass - He is alive, present, and active. He meets you in your questions, walks with you in your pain, and speaks peace into your chaos.

"Peace be to you" (Luke 24:36), He said to His disciples after rising - and He says it still. The empty tomb is not just a past event - it is a present reality. It means Jesus is available, attentive, and able. He is not confined to history - He is alive in your story.

So come and see. Not just the place where He lay - but the life He now offers. The tomb is empty so your heart can be full. The silence of the grave has been replaced by the voice of heaven. And that voice still speaks: *"Do not be afraid... He has risen"* (Matthew 28:5–6).

8

"Behold the Lamb"

When John the Baptist cried out, *"Behold, the Lamb of God who takes away the sin of the world!"* (John 1:29), he was not offering a metaphor - he was announcing a revolution. In one sentence, he connected the ancient rhythms of Israel's worship to the unfolding drama of salvation. The Lamb was not just symbolic - it was sacrificial, substitutionary, and sacred.

In Exodus 12, the Passover lamb was chosen, spotless, and slain. Its blood marked the doorposts of Israelite homes, shielding them from judgment as death passed through Egypt. That lamb did not just represent protection - it purchased freedom. It was the price of deliverance.

Now John points to Jesus and says: This is the Lamb. Not a lamb for one family. Not a lamb for one nation. But a Lamb for the world. A Lamb whose blood does not just cover sin - it removes it. A Lamb whose death does not just delay judgment - it defeats it.

"You were not redeemed with perishable things... but with precious blood, as of a lamb unblemished and spotless, the blood of Christ" (1 Peter 1:18–19).

This Lamb is not passive. He walks willingly toward the altar. He does not resist the nails or recoil from the cross. He embraces it - because He knows what it will accomplish.

The Weight of Sin and the Wonder of Grace

Sin is heavy. It clings to memory like smoke to clothing. It distorts identity, whispering lies about who we are and what we are worth. It convinces us we are too far gone, too broken, too stained to be loved. But John's declaration cuts through that fog:

"Behold! The Lamb of God who takes away the sin of the world!" John 1:29

Not just the sins you confess. Not just the ones you regret. But the ones you carry in silence. The ones that haunt your dreams and shadow your joy. The ones that shame you into hiding. Jesus does not flinch. He takes them all. Not reluctantly, but willingly. Not abstractly, but personally.

"Surely our griefs He Himself bore, and our sorrows He carried... But He was pierced for our offenses, He was crushed for our wrongdoings" (Isaiah 53:4–5).

He became the Lamb so you could become free.

This is not a limited offer. It is not reserved for the righteous or the religious. It is for the world. For the addict and the skeptic. For the weary and the proud. For the one who's never heard and the one who's heard a thousand times but never believed it could be true.

"The one who comes to Me I certainly will not cast out" (John 6:37).

If you have ever longed for a reset - for the slate wiped clean, the guilt lifted, the story rewritten - this is it. The Lamb of God does not just forgive; He renews. He does not just erase the past; **He reclaims it**. His sacrifice opens a door no one can shut.

You do not have to earn this. You do not have to prove yourself. You simply behold the Lamb - see Him, trust Him, follow Him. And in that gaze, you find grace.

Resurrection Boldness

Before the resurrection, the disciples were shattered. Their 'Teacher' was dead. Their hopes were buried. Their future was uncertain. John 20:19 captures the mood: *"So when it was evening on that day, the first day of the week, and when the doors were shut where the disciples were, for fear of the Jews..."*. They were not planning a movement - they were trying to survive.

But then Jesus came. Not as a memory. But bodily, gloriously, unmistakably alive. He stood among them and said, *"Peace be with you"* (John 20:19). And in that moment, everything changed. Fear gave way to faith. Silence gave way to proclamation. Hiding gave way to heralding. The resurrection did not just prove Jesus was divine - it ignited a revolution in the hearts of ordinary men. They had seen death undone. They had touched eternity. And now, they could not be silent.

"When He had said this, He showed them both His hands and His side. The disciples then rejoiced when they saw the Lord" (John 20:20). The scars were not just proof - they were power. Proof that pain had been transformed. Power that suffering had been redeemed.

"We Cannot Help Speaking"

In Acts 4, Peter and John are dragged before the authorities. The same system that crucified Jesus now threatens them. But they do not flinch. They do not negotiate. They speak with a clarity that cuts through intimidation:

"Whether it is right in the sight of God to give heed to you rather than to God, you be the judge; for we cannot stop speaking about what we have seen and heard" (Acts 4:19–20).

This is not arrogance - it is conviction. They are not defending a theory. They are testifying to an encounter. They saw the scars. They heard His voice. They ate with Him. And now, the truth burns in their bones.

"But Peter and John answered and said to them, 'As for us, we cannot help but speak...'" It is like a fire shut up in their hearts, too fierce to contain.

This kind of boldness does not come from personality - it comes from presence. The presence of the risen Christ. The indwelling of the Holy Spirit. The certainty that death is not the end, and that love has conquered fear.

"For God has not given us a spirit of timidity, but of power and love and discipline" (2 Timothy 1:7).

Your Story, Your Voice, Your Witness

You may not have seen Jesus with your eyes, but if He has changed your life, you have seen Him with your soul. And that story matters. It is not about having perfect words - It is about bearing witness. To grace. To healing. To hope.

You do not have to be eloquent. You just have to be honest. You do not have to be fearless. You just have to be faithful. You do not have to convince the world. You just have to share what you have seen and heard.

"Let the redeemed of the Lord say so" (Psalm 107:2). Your voice is part of the resurrection echo. Every testimony is a tremor from the empty tomb.

The resurrection did not just happen - it is still happening. In you. Through you. Around you. Every time you speak life into someone's despair, every time you forgive, every time you love radically - you echo the empty tomb.

You are not just a believer - you are a witness. And the world needs your voice.

Eyewitness to Eternity

John's words in 1 John 1:1–2 are not abstract theology - they are personal memory, sacred testimony, and spiritual invitation. He writes with the voice of someone who has lived through the unthinkable: the death of hope and the resurrection of glory.

"What was from the beginning, what we have heard, what we have seen with our eyes, what we have looked at and touched with our hands, concerning the Word of Life - and the life was manifested, and we have seen and testify and proclaim to you the eternal life, which was with the Father and was manifested to us" (1 John 1:1–2).

This is not secondhand faith. It is not folklore passed down through whispers. It is firsthand encounter. The apostles did not build their message on dreams or legends - they built it on contact. On presence. On truth they could feel in their bones.

Imagine standing in the aftermath of a storm, touching the soaked earth, breathing the charged air, knowing something powerful just passed through. That is how John writes. He heard Jesus speak. He saw Him heal. He touched the scars. And now, he invites us into that experience.

The Word of Life: More Than a Message

John calls Jesus the *"Word of Life."* Not just a word *about* life. Not a philosophy or moral code. But the living Word - the embodiment of divine truth and eternal vitality. In Greek, the phrase is *logos tēs zōēs (λόγος τῆς ζωῆς)* - the logic, the meaning, the heartbeat of life itself.

This Word was not distant. He came close. He became flesh. He entered the dust and ache of human existence. *"And the Word became flesh, and dwelt among us"* (John 1:14). And after dying, He rose - not as a ghost, but as flesh renewed, life unstoppable, hope incarnate.

John continues: *"and the life was manifested, and we have seen and testify and proclaim to you the eternal life, which was with the Father and was manifested to us"* (1 John 1:2). This is the foundation of Christian confidence: God has made Himself known - not just in words, but in a Person. And that Person has been seen, touched, and proclaimed.

For you, this means the Bible is not a collection of myths – it is a record of revelation. The apostles did not invent Jesus – they encountered Him. Their testimony was not wishful thinking – it is eyewitness truth, preserved by the Spirit, passed down through generations, and offered to you as a foundation of faith.

You can trust the Scriptures - not because they are comforting, but because they are true. You can trust Jesus - not because He is a good idea, but because He is alive. And you can share your story - not because you have all the answers, but because you have met the Answer.

The Gospel's Revolutionary Power

When the people of Thessalonica cried out, "These men who have upset the world have come here also" (Acts 17:6), they were not exaggerating - they were witnessing a seismic shift that defied containment. The apostles, unarmed with swords or political influence, wielded a force far more disruptive: the proclamation of a risen King, Jesus Christ. This message was not a mere religious idea but a divine declaration that upended empires, traditions, and hearts. As Paul wrote, "For I am not ashamed of the gospel, for it is the power of God for salvation to everyone who believes" (Romans 1:16). The Gospel's power lay in its ability to transform lives and challenge the very structures of the world.

The resurrection of Jesus was not a private miracle confined to a small circle of disciples; it was a public upheaval that redefined reality itself. Paul declared, *"If Christ has not been raised, your faith is worthless; you are still in your sins"* (1 Corinthians 15:17). The empty tomb was God's decisive act, shattering the chains of death and inaugurating a new kingdom. This truth unleashed a cascade of revolutionary implications, each challenging the core assumptions of the Greco-Roman world and offering timeless hope for humanity:

<u>Death no longer has the final word.</u>

The resurrection of Jesus is the ultimate triumph over humanity's greatest enemy: death. As Scripture proclaims, *"O death, where is your victory? O death, where is your sting?"* (1 Corinthians 15:55). Jesus Himself declared, *"I am the resurrection and the life; he who believes in Me will live even if he dies"* (John 11:25).

In the Greco-Roman world, where philosophies like Stoicism accepted death's finality and mystery religions offered vague hopes of an afterlife, the Gospel's promise of bodily resurrection was radical. It gave believers unshakable hope, transforming how they faced persecution, suffering, and mortality. Today, this truth continues to offer assurance that death is not the end but a doorway to eternal life in God's presence, empowering Christians to live fearlessly in a world shadowed by mortality."

<u>Caesar is not the ultimate authority.</u>

In the Roman Empire, Caesar was often deified, hailed as "lord" and "savior," demanding absolute allegiance. The Gospel's proclamation of Jesus as *"Lord of lords and King of kings"* (Revelation 17:14) was a direct challenge to this imperial cult. When Peter and John declared, *"We must obey God rather than men"* (Acts 5:29), they asserted that Jesus' authority superseded all earthly powers. This was revolutionary in a society where defying Caesar could mean death. The Gospel stripped away the illusion of human sovereignty, revealing that true power belongs to the risen Christ, who *"disarmed the rulers and authorities"* through His cross (Colossians 2:15).

For believers today, this truth calls us to prioritize God's kingdom over worldly systems, trusting in Christ's ultimate reign even amidst political and cultural pressures.

<u>The poor, the outcast, and the broken are invited into divine fellowship.</u>

The Gospel shattered social barriers, declaring that God's kingdom is open to all, regardless of status. Jesus Himself said, *"Blessed are the poor in spirit, for theirs is the kingdom of heaven"* (Matthew 5:3), and Paul affirmed, *"There is neither Jew nor Greek, there is neither slave nor free man, there is neither male nor female; for you are all one in Christ Jesus"* (Galatians 3:28).

In a Roman society rigidly divided by class, ethnicity, and gender, this message was scandalous. The early church welcomed tax collectors, sinners, and Samaritans, reflecting Jesus' ministry to the marginalized (Luke 5:30-32).

This invitation to divine fellowship redefined human worth, offering dignity to those in society deemed worthless. Today, this truth challenges us to embrace the marginalized and to see every person as bearing the image of God, worthy of love and inclusion in His kingdom.

<u>Love - not fear - is the new currency of the kingdom.</u>

The Roman world operated on fear - fear of gods, emperors, and death. Yet the Gospel introduced a new paradigm: *"There is no fear in love; but perfect love casts out fear"* (1 John 4:18). Jesus' command to "love one another, just as I have loved you" (John 13:34) redefined relationships, calling believers to sacrificial love modeled on Christ's cross. This love transformed communities, as seen in the early church's care for widows and orphans (Acts 6:1-3) and Paul's call to *"do good to all people"* (Galatians 6:10).

In a culture driven by power and self-interest, this ethic of love was revolutionary, turning enemies into family and strangers into brothers. For modern believers, this principle compels us to live out Christ's love in a world often marked by division and fear, building communities that reflect the kingdom's values.

This message shook the foundations of Roman society, religious hierarchies, and personal identities. It turned slaves into brothers, as seen in Paul's appeal for Onesimus, a runaway slave, to be received as "*a beloved brother*" (Philemon 1:16). It transformed enemies into family, as Jews and Gentiles were reconciled in Christ (Ephesians 2:14-16). And it turned skeptics like Thomas, who doubted until he saw the risen Lord (John 20:27-28), into saints who proclaimed, "*My Lord and my God!*" The Gospel's power continues to disrupt and transform, calling us to live as citizens of a kingdom that turns the world upside down.

From Upside Down to Right Side Up

When the people of Thessalonica accused the apostles of turning the world upside down, they were not wrong - but they were not entirely right either.

To reiterate Acts 17:6 again, "*These men who have upset the world have come here also*". The irony is that the apostles were not disrupting order - they were restoring it. The world had already been turned upside down by sin, injustice, and death. The gospel came not to destabilize, but to realign. To redeem. To reorder everything according to God's original design.

Creation had been fractured. Humanity had lost its way. But the resurrection of Jesus was the beginning of a cosmic reset - a divine restoration project. And that restoration did not come through violence or political power. **It came through witness**. Through ordinary people who had encountered the extraordinary love of Jesus and could not keep it to themselves.

You Are Part of the Upside-Down Revolution

You do not need a pulpit or a passport to shake the world. You just need the presence of Jesus and the courage to share Him. When you speak truth in love, when you forgive radically, when you serve sacrificially, when you proclaim hope in a hopeless place - you are continuing the apostolic legacy.

You are part of the same movement that began in Jerusalem, spread to Thessalonica, and now reaches into classrooms, coffee shops, and digital spaces. The resurrection did not end with the empty tomb - it continues in you.

"You are the light of the world. A city set on a hill cannot be hidden" (Matthew 5:14). Your life is a beacon. Your story is a spark. Your faith is a flame that can light up the shadows around you.

This revolution is not loud - It is lasting. It is not built on force - It is built on faith. And every time you choose grace over revenge, truth over silence, love over fear - you turn the world a little more 'right side up'.

The Ripple of Resurrection

Imagine tossing a stone into a still lake. The impact is small, but the ripples spread far beyond the point of contact. That is what happens when you share Jesus. Your words, your love, your story - they create ripples of redemption that move through hearts, homes, and histories.

"So will My word be which goes out of My mouth; it will not return to Me empty, Without accomplishing what I desire, and without succeeding in the purpose for which I sent it" (Isaiah 55:11).

You may never see the full effect. You may never know how far the ripples reach. But heaven does. And the Spirit moves through every act of obedience, every moment of courage, every whisper of hope.

The resurrection is not just a past event - It is a present force. And you are part of its movement.

Living for Christ, Longing for Glory

Paul's declaration in Philippians 1:21 is breathtaking in its simplicity and depth:

"For to me, to live is Christ and to die is gain". It is as if he's saying, "Every breath I take is for Jesus. And when I stop breathing, I will be with Him face to face."

This is not escapism - It is anchored hope. Paul is not weary of life; he's consumed by purpose. Whether preaching in freedom or chained in prison, his heartbeat remains the same: Christ is everything. To live is not comfort, success, or safety. To live is Christ - His mission, His presence, His glory. To die is not loss, fear, or finality. To die is gain - because it means union with the One he loves most.

"But I am hard-pressed from both directions, having the desire to depart and be with Christ, for that is very much better" (Philippians 1:23). Paul does not romanticize death - he redefines it. Not as an end, but as a beginning.

A Life Reoriented by Resurrection

The resurrection of Jesus Christ is the cornerstone of Christian hope, the radiant truth that reorients every aspect of existence. As mentioned before and another key memory verse, Philippians 1:21, is not a fleeting sentiment but a declaration forged in the crucible of suffering and sustained by the reality of Christ's triumph over the grave.

The resurrection transforms death from an ominous threat into a doorway - a passage into unfiltered communion with God. Because Jesus rose, death is no longer the end; it is the beginning of an eternal embrace with the Creator.

This resurrection should reshape how we navigate the contours of life:

Consider Suffering. Pain, though searing, is imbued with divine purpose when Christ is your life. Picture a refiner's fire purifying gold: the heat is intense, but it yields something precious. Similarly, suffering refines the believer, aligning them with God's redemptive plan. Paul assures us in Romans 8:18, *"For I consider that the sufferings of this present time are not worthy to be compared with the glory that is to be revealed to us."* When Christ is your center, every trial becomes a brushstroke in God's masterpiece, sculpting you for eternity.

Consider Success. Earthly achievements, like flowers that bloom and wither, pale in the light of eternal impact. Imagine a merchant chasing coins that tarnish, only to discover a treasure of infinite worth. Success is redefined when Christ is your pursuit, as Paul testifies in Philippians 3:7-8, *"But whatever things were gain to me, those things I have counted as loss for the sake of Christ. More than that, I count all things to be loss in view of the surpassing value of knowing Christ Jesus my Lord."* Achievements become steppingstones, not ultimate goals, when your life is anchored in eternity.

Consider Fear. The resurrection disarms fear, even the fear of death. Picture a sailor navigating a stormy sea, confident because the harbor is in sight. Death, for the believer, is not a plunge into darkness but a passage to joy, a step into God's presence. Hebrews 2:14-15 declares that Christ, *"through death… render[ed] powerless him who had the power of death, that is, the devil, and… free[d] those who through fear of death were subject to slavery all their lives."* With Christ as your anchor, fear loses its hold, and even the grave becomes a gateway to glory.

Paul's words pierce the heart with a question: What am I living for? What fills the blank in *"To live is ____"*? If it is wealth, it will rust; if fame, it will fade; if comfort, it will falter. Anything less than Christ will ultimately disappoint, for only He is eternal. But if Christ fills that blank, then even death becomes a promotion - a joyful transition into the fullness of His presence, as promised in John 14:2-3: *"In My Father's house are many dwelling places… I go to prepare a place for you… that where I am, there you may be also."*

Imagine your heart as a compass, its needle swaying in a world of competing winds - comfort, ambition, approval. For most, the needle spins aimlessly, chasing fleeting desires. But Paul's compass is steadfast, its true north fixed on Christ. Whether in the storm of persecution, the confinement of a prison cell, or the shadow of execution, his direction never wavers.

You are invited to recalibrate your compass, to let Christ be your orientation, destination, and motivation. This is not a call to asceticism but to alignment - to live with eternity as your lens, as Paul urges in Colossians 3:2, *"Set your mind on the things above, not on the things that are on earth."*

This reorientation does not mean abandoning the present; it means embracing it with eternal purpose. You love more deeply, as Christ loved, reflecting John 13:34: *"A new commandment I give to you, that you love one another, even as I have loved you."* You serve more boldly, knowing your labor is not in vain (1 Corinthians 15:58). You speak more freely, proclaiming the hope within you (1 Peter 3:15). Your life becomes a vessel of grace, a testimony of hope, a light piercing the darkness - because it is not your own. It belongs to Christ, who bought it with His blood.

When your time comes, you do not lose; you gain. Death is not a defeat but a homecoming, a step into the fullness of the relationship you have been living for all along. As 2 Corinthians 5:8 assures, to be "*absent from the body*" is to be "*at home with the Lord.*" This is the resurrection hope: a life so anchored in Christ that it shines through every shadow, transforms every trial, and triumphs over every fear, until you stand face-to-face with the One who is your life.

The Altar of Witness

In Revelation 6:9, John shares an incredible vision:

"When the Lamb broke the fifth seal, I saw underneath the altar the souls of those who had been slain because of the word of God, and because of the testimony which they had maintained."

This is not just a random image - it is like looking into God's heavenly courtroom, a holy place where those who stayed faithful to Him are remembered and honored. These souls are martyrs, people who died not by accident or for some random cause, but because they stood up for God's truth and their belief in Jesus, no matter what it cost them.

The "*souls*" under the altar are people killed for believing in God's Word - the Bible and the message of Jesus - and for boldly sharing their faith. The word "*testimony*" means they spoke up about Jesus, even when it was dangerous. In Greek, "*testimony*" is tied to "martyr," showing they were witnesses who gave everything.

Think of early Christians who died under Roman emperors for refusing to worship fake gods. But this vision also includes anyone, from any time, who dies for their faith.

They are not just victims - they are heroes, as Revelation 12:11 describes: *"And they overcame him because of the blood of the Lamb and because of the word of their testimony, and they did not love their life even when faced with death."* Their courage shows what it means to stay true to Jesus.

The altar in this vision is more than a place - it is a symbol of God's love and care. The martyrs being "*under*" it means they are near God, protected and remembered. Their lives were like a sacrifice, like Romans 12:1: *"Therefore I urge you, brothers and sisters, by the mercies of God, to present your bodies as a living and holy sacrifice, acceptable to God, which is your spiritual service of worship."* Their deaths show their total devotion to Jesus, just like His sacrifice on the cross.

What is going on in this vision?

Revelation is full of intense visions, and in chapter 6, Jesus (the Lamb) is opening seals on a scroll that reveal God's plan for the world. The first four seals show things like war and hunger on earth, but the fifth seal takes us straight to heaven. John sees an altar, a special place that represents God's presence and worship. This altar reminds us of the Old Testament, where priests poured out blood at the base of the altar as a sacrifice (Leviticus 4:7) - *"The priest shall then put some of the blood on the horns of the altar of fragrant incense which is before the Lord in the tent of meeting; and all the rest of the blood of the bull he shall pour out at the base of the altar of burnt offering".*

In heaven, this altar is where the martyrs' lives are honored, like a monument to their faithfulness. Being *"underneath the altar"* means They are close to God, safe in His care, just like Psalm 91:1 says: *"One who dwells in the shelter of the Most High will lodge in the shadow of the Almighty."*

Who Are the Martyrs?

In Revelation 6:10, the martyrs cry out: *"How long, O Lord, holy and true, will You refrain from judging and avenging our blood on those who live on the earth?"* They are not asking for revenge; they want God to fix the world's wrongs.

This is like Abel's blood crying out in Genesis 4:10, *"The Lord said, 'What have you done? The voice of your brother's blood is crying out to Me from the ground.'"*

God tells them to *"rest a little while longer"* (Revelation 6:11), meaning He has a plan, and His timing is perfect, as 2 Peter 3:9 explains: *"The Lord is not slow about His promise, as some count slowness, but is patient toward you, not wishing for any to perish but for all to come to repentance."*

The martyrs did not stay quiet - they shared their faith, even when it meant death. Jesus said in Matthew 10:32, *"Therefore, everyone who confesses Me before people, I will also confess him before My Father who is in heaven."* Their courage pushes us to speak up for Jesus, too.

They are part of a *"cloud of witnesses"* cheering us on, like Hebrews 12:1: *"Therefore, since we have so great a cloud of witnesses surrounding us... let us run with endurance the race that is set before us."*

The martyrs get white robes (Revelation 6:11), showing They are pure and victorious because of Jesus' sacrifice, as Revelation 7:14 says: *"These are the ones who come out of the great tribulation, and they have washed their robes and made them white in the blood of the Lamb."* They are waiting for God's final victory, when He will make everything right, as Revelation 21:4 promises: *"He will wipe away every tear from their eyes; and there will no longer be any death; there will no longer be any mourning, or crying, or pain."* This gives hope to anyone facing hard times for their faith - God sees you, and He will make it right.

What This Means for Us

Be Bold in Faith: The martyrs show us how to stand up for Jesus, even when it is tough. You might not face death, but you might feel pressure to hide your beliefs. Their story encourages us to be brave, like 1 Peter 3:15: *"Always be ready to make a defense to everyone who asks you to give an account for the hope that is in you."*

Whether it is speaking up or making hard choices, your faith matters. When life feels unfair, the martyrs show us God hears our cries. He is working out His plan, and He'll make things right in His time. And live your faith: You do not have to die to be a witness. Every choice to follow Jesus - being kind, honest, or bold - makes your faith shine, as Ephesians 5:8 says: *"For you were once darkness, but now you are light in the Lord; walk as children of light."*

Trust God's Timing: The martyrs' cry for justice reminds us that God hears us when life feels unfair. He is working out a bigger plan, and He will bring justice when the time is right.

Live as a Witness: You do not have to die to be a witness. Every day, you can show your faith by how you live and what you say, as Jesus said in Luke 9:23: *"If anyone wishes to come after Me, he must deny himself, and take up his cross daily and follow Me."*

Their courage, as shown in Revelation 12:11 - inspires us to live boldly, and as Matthew 10:32 says: *"Everyone who confesses Me before people, I will also confess him before My Father who is in heaven."*

The Greek word *martyrs* means "**witness**," and these believers did not die because they were careless - they died because they stayed true to God. Their lives shouted a truth so strong that even death could not stop it. They stood firm, never giving up their belief in the gospel, no matter the cost.

These martyrs - they were committed. They held tightly to their faith in Jesus, even when it meant facing death. The passage says they *"maintained"* their testimony, which means they stayed strong and loyal, refusing to back down. This is what Jesus calls us to in Revelation 2:10, *"Be faithful until death, and I will give you the crown of life."*

Their deaths were not failures - they were bold messages, speaking louder than words ever could. They showed the world that God's truth is worth everything. They are resting in God's presence, honored for their sacrifice, as Psalm 116:15 says: *"Precious in the sight of the Lord is the death of His godly ones."*

Their deaths cry out for God's justice, trusting He'll make things right, like Psalm 9:12, *"For He who requires blood remembers them; He does not forget the cry of the afflicted."* Their bravery shows us what it looks like to live for Jesus, even when it is hard.

You might not face death, but you might deal with people making fun of your faith, losing friends for doing what's right, or feeling out of place for following God. The martyrs' lives tell us to keep going, to hold onto our faith no matter what. They are like runners passing a torch of faith to us, urging us to keep it burning bright.

The Empty Tomb and the Unstoppable Truth

The resurrection of Jesus is not just a theological claim - It is a historical disruption. If Jesus had not risen, silencing the movement would have been simple: produce the body. But no one could. Not the Roman authorities. Not the Jewish leaders. Not the guards who had every reason to protect their reputation and their lives.

Instead, Matthew records a cover-up:

"And they said, 'You are to say, "His disciples came by night and stole Him away while we were asleep." And if this should come to the

governor's ears, we will win him over and keep you out of trouble.' And they took the money and did as they had been instructed; and this story was widely spread among the Jews and is to this day" (Matthew 28:13–15).

But this story is riddled with contradictions. If the guards were asleep, how could they know who took the body? Roman soldiers faced severe punishment for failing their duty - why would they risk their lives unless they were coerced? And if the disciples had stolen the body, why were they not arrested? Why did they instead become bold, public witnesses?

The answer is simple: they could not stop the truth. Because Jesus was alive.

The resurrection was not a private miracle - it was a public shockwave. Consider the evidence:

- The tomb was guarded, sealed, and watched - yet it was found open and empty.

- The disciples, once fearful and scattered, became bold and unstoppable, willing to die for what they saw.

- The early church exploded in growth - not because of clever marketing, but because of eyewitness testimony and transformed lives.

Even nonbeliever sources - Roman historians like Tacitus and Jewish writings like the Talmud - acknowledge Jesus' existence, His crucifixion, and the claims of resurrection. The silence of His enemies speaks volumes. If they could have disproved it, they would have. But they could not. So, they lied.

"God raised Him up again, putting an end to the agony of death, since it was impossible for Him to be held in its power" (Acts 2:24).

The resurrection is not just a claim - It is a collision between heaven and history.

9

Your Life: Living Evidence of Resurrection

The most compelling proof of Jesus' resurrection today is not found in ancient artifacts or scholarly debates - it is found in the transformed life you live. Your life, reshaped by the risen Christ, is a testament to His victory over death.

<u>When anxiety surrenders to peace</u>, that is resurrection power. Jesus promises, *"Peace I leave with you; My peace I give to you; not as the world gives do I give to you. Let not your heart be troubled, nor let it be fearful"* (John 14:27). His peace in you is a living echo of the empty tomb.

<u>When bitterness gives way to forgiveness</u>, that is resurrection power. As Christ forgave us, so we forgive others: *"Be kind to one another, tender-hearted, forgiving each other, just as God in Christ also has forgiven you"* (Ephesians 4:32). Your forgiveness reflects His triumph over sin.

<u>When despair transforms into joy</u>, when weakness becomes strength, when shame is overwhelmed by grace - that is resurrection power. The Psalmist proclaims, *"Weeping may last for the night, but a shout of joy comes in the morning"* (Psalm 30:5). Your renewed life displays the strength of Christ*: "My grace is sufficient for you, for power is perfected in weakness"* (2 Corinthians 12:9)

Your story declares: "Jesus is alive, and He is transforming me." You may not have every theological answer, but you possess something far greater: a life touched and changed by the risen Christ. Your changed life is evidence of His resurrection power at work.

Picture your life as both a mirror and a window. As a mirror, it reflects the radiant light of Christ - His peace, His love, His truth - shining for all to see. As a window, it invites others to peer through and glimpse the reality of Jesus for themselves. *"Let your light shine before men in such a way that they may see your good works, and glorify your Father who is in heaven"* (Matthew 5:16)

When you share your story, you are not merely recounting events - you are bearing witness to the living Christ. You are proclaiming, "I have seen the empty tomb - not with my physical eyes, but with the eyes of my soul. I know He lives because He lives in me." As John testifies, *"And the life was manifested, and we have seen and testify and proclaim to you the eternal life, which was with the Father and was manifested to us"* (1 John 1:2). Your life, transformed by resurrection power, is a living invitation to others to encounter the risen Savior.

Jesus the only Mediator

Paul writes: *"For there is one God, and one mediator also between God and men, the man Christ Jesus"* (1 Timothy 2:5).

This verse is a theological diamond - compact, brilliant, and unshakably true. Access to God is not earned through rituals, saints, or spiritual performance. It is granted through a Person - Jesus Christ, who stands in the gap between a holy God and a hurting world. He is the only mediator - not one among many, but the one and only. Why? Because He alone is both fully divine and fully human.

As God, Jesus carries the authority, purity, and power of heaven. He knows the heart of the Father because He shares it. He does not just speak on your behalf - He speaks as One who is God, who knows the justice and mercy of heaven, and who perfectly fulfills its demands.

He does not beg for your forgiveness - He secures it. He does not hope you will be accepted - He guarantees it. As man, Jesus knows what It is like to be tired, tempted, rejected, and misunderstood. He walked dusty roads, felt hunger, wept at gravesides, and endured betrayal. He does not just sympathize - He empathizes.

Hebrews 4:15 says: *"For we do not have a high priest who cannot sympathize with our weaknesses, but One who has been tempted in all things as we are, yet without sin"*. That means He understands your anxiety, He knows your grief, and He feels your weakness. Yet He remained sinless - which makes Him not just relatable but qualified to stand in your place.

Because Jesus is your mediator, you do not need to go through a priest, a prophet, or a spiritual hierarchy. You can go straight to Him. Right now. With your doubts, your pain, your praise, your questions.

He welcomes you - not reluctantly, but joyfully. His throne is not a place of judgment - it is a throne of grace.

Imagine a vast chasm between humanity and God - caused by sin, fear, and separation. Religion tries to build ladders. Morality tries to build ropes. But they all fall short.

Then Jesus comes - not to build a bridge, but to *be* the bridge. His cross spans the gap. His resurrection secures the path. And now, anyone who walks across in faith finds life, peace, and communion with God.

As your mediator, He invites you to pray with confidence knowing He hears you; live with assurance knowing He intercedes for you; and rest in grace knowing He understands you and the situations of your life. You do not have to clean yourself up first. You do not have to pretend. You just have to come. *"Come to Me, all who are weary and heavy-laden, and I will give you rest"* (Matthew 11:28).

No Condemnation, No Separation

Romans 8:1–2 opens like a sunrise breaking through storm clouds: *"Therefore there is now no condemnation for those who are in Christ Jesus. For the law of the Spirit of life in Christ Jesus has set you free from the law of sin and of death"*.

This is not wishful thinking - It is a legal declaration from the highest court in heaven. The verdict has been rendered: Not guilty. Free. Redeemed. Why? Because Jesus did not just forgive your sin - He fulfilled the law, shattered the chains, and replaced condemnation with life.

Imagine two laws at work: one pulls downward like gravity - the law of sin and death. The other lifts upward like wings - the law of the Spirit of life. In Christ, you are no longer bound to the gravitational pull of guilt and shame. You've been given wings. You are not defined by your past - you are **redefined by His presence.**

Jesus the Advocate

John writes with pastoral tenderness: *"My little children, I am writing these things to you so that you may not sin. And if anyone sins, we have an Advocate with the Father, Jesus Christ the righteous; and He Himself is the propitiation for our sins; and not for ours only, but also for those of the whole world"* (1 John 2:1–2).

Notice the realism in John's words. He does not say "if" as if sin were rare - he knows it is inevitable. But instead of shame, he offers hope. Jesus is your Advocate - not a passive observer, but an active defender. He stands before the Father and says:

"I paid for that." "They belong to Me." "My righteousness covers their failure."

And this is not just for a select few - It is for the whole world. That means your story matters. Your testimony is part of a global invitation to grace.

Picture a courtroom again. You stand accused. But Jesus does not just argue your case - He presents Himself as the evidence. His righteousness becomes your defense. His sacrifice becomes your freedom.

The Throne of Grace

Hebrews 4:14–16 lifts your eyes to a throne - not of judgment, but of grace: *"Therefore, since we have a great high priest who has passed through the heavens, Jesus the Son of God, let us hold fast our confession. For we do not have a high priest who cannot sympathize with our weaknesses, but One who has been tempted in all things as we are, yet without sin. Therefore, let us draw near with confidence to the throne of grace, so that we may receive mercy and find grace to help in time of need"*.

Jesus has ascended, but He has not abandoned. He has been tempted in every way - rejection, loneliness, pressure, betrayal - and yet He never sinned. That makes Him uniquely qualified to help you. You do not have to tiptoe into God's presence. You can run boldly. Mercy is waiting - not punishment. Grace is available - not judgment.

Hebrews 2:18 adds a tender layer: *"For since He Himself was tempted in that which He has suffered, He is able to come to the aid of those who are tempted"*. Jesus does not help from a distance - He helps from experience. He knows what It is like to be hungry, tired, misunderstood, and tempted. He does not just sympathize - He strengthens.

Think of Him like a friend who's walked the same dark valley. He does not shout encouragement from the edge - He climbs down, wraps His arm around you, and says: "I've been here. I know the way out. Hold on to Me."

Imagine falling into a deep pit - cold, dark, hopeless. Religion might shout advice from above. Philosophy might offer theories. But Jesus descends into the pit, lifts you up, and walks with you toward light.

Trust Over Tension and Turmoil

Jesus offers a radical reordering of priorities in Matthew 6:33–34, *"But seek first His kingdom and His righteousness, and all these things will be added to you. So do not worry about tomorrow; for tomorrow will care for itself. Each day has enough trouble of its own"*.

Instead of chasing security, success, or control, Jesus invites you to chase Him. To make His kingdom - His reign, His values, His mission - your first pursuit.

But what does it mean to *"Seek first?"* This verse, part of Jesus' Sermon on the Mount, calls believers to prioritize God's kingdom and righteousness above all else, with the promise that their needs will be met. To go deeper, let's explore the meaning of "seek" in its Greek and Latin linguistic contexts, its theological implications, and its application to life today.

The Greek word for "seek" in Matthew 6:33 is *zēteō* (ζητέω). This verb carries a rich range of meanings. According to Strong's Concordance (G2212), *zēteō* can mean to **seek after**, **inquire into**, or **desire to obtain** something. It often conveys a **diligent**, **focused effort**, as in **searching for something valuable** or **essential**. In some contexts, it can also mean to demand or require, suggesting urgency or priority.

In Matthew 6:33, *zēteō* is a present imperative active verb, indicating a continuous, ongoing command. Jesus is instructing His followers to continually seek God's kingdom and righteousness as a way of life, not a onetime act. The adverb *"first"* (Greek: *prōton*, πρῶτον) emphasizes **priority** - God's kingdom must take precedence over all other pursuits.

I think it appropriate to also consider the Latin meaning of 'to seek'. In the Latin Vulgate, the translation uses the verb *quaerite*, from *quaero*. *Quaero* means to seek, search for, inquire, or strive after. Like *zēteō*, it implies an active effort to find or attain something. It can also mean to ask, question, or investigate, suggesting a thoughtful and intentional process.

According to Lewis and Short's Latin Dictionary, *quaero* can denote seeking something lost, striving for a goal, or earnestly desiring something. In a legal context, it could mean 'to investigate' or 'demand justice'. In Matthew 6:33, *quaerite* carries a spiritual weight, urging believers to pursue God's kingdom with **diligence and devotion**. The imperative form *quaerite* mirrors the Greek present imperative, emphasizing a continuous action. The Latin reinforces the idea that seeking God's kingdom is an **ongoing, active commitment**.

The use of *zēteō* and *quaerite* in Matthew 6:33 reveals that seeking God's kingdom and righteousness is not a casual or secondary activity but a deliberate, lifelong priority requiring effort, focus, and intentionality.

This should challenge us to:

Pursue God Intentionally: Seeking God's kingdom requires active engagement - through prayer, studying Scripture, and aligning decisions with God's will. For example, in a fast-paced world driven by productivity and success, this might mean carving out daily time for spiritual reflection or making ethical choices that reflect God's righteousness, even at personal cost.

Prioritize God Above All: The emphasis on *"first"* (*prōton/primum*) calls for reordering priorities. In today's context, this could mean evaluating whether social media, work, or entertainment overshadows devotion to God. For instance, choosing to serve in a community outreach program over personal leisure time reflects seeking God's kingdom first.

Trust God's Provision: The promise of provision addresses modern anxieties about financial stability, health, or future uncertainties. *Zēteō's* sense of diligent pursuit encourages believers to trust that God will meet their needs as they focus on His priorities, reducing reliance on self-driven solutions.

Live Counterculturally: In a secular age, seeking God's righteousness means embracing values that may clash with societal norms - such as humility, generosity, or forgiveness. The investigative nuance of *quaero* suggests discerning God's will in complex issues, like navigating ethical dilemmas in the workplace or advocating for justice in a polarized world.

Sustain a Lifelong Pursuit: The present imperative of *zēteō* and *quaerite* calls for consistency. In present day, this might look like maintaining spiritual disciplines amid distractions, such as regular worship or small group accountability, to keep God's kingdom central over time.

Entomology is fine – But what does that look like? Here are a few examples:

- Choosing integrity over popularity.
- Serving others instead of self.
- Trusting God's timing instead of forcing your own.
- Living with eternal purpose, not temporary pressure.

When you seek His kingdom first, you are not ignoring your needs - you are entrusting them. Jesus promises: *"All these things will be added to you."* That includes food, clothing, direction, and peace. He's not indifferent to your needs - He is committed to meeting them.

Jesus continues: *"So do not worry about tomorrow; for tomorrow will care for itself. Each day has enough trouble of its own."*

This is not a call to irresponsibility - It is a call to faithful presence. Worry pulls you into a future you cannot control. Trust anchors you in a present where God is already working. Think back to the wilderness in Exodus. God gave Israel manna - daily bread. But they couldn't store it up. If they tried, it spoiled. Why? Because God wanted them to trust Him daily.

Jesus echoes that rhythm here. He is saying: "I'll give you what you need - today." "Don't hoard anxiety about tomorrow." "Come back tomorrow - I'll be here, and so will My grace."

Maybe you need to 'refocus' – what are you seeking first? It is God's kingdom or your own plans and comfort? Maybe you need to 'release' something – what worries are you carrying that belongs to tomorrow? Maybe you need to 'rest' – are you able to trust Jesus with your situations, concerns, your future?

You do not have to have it all figured out. You just have to walk with Jesus today. And when tomorrow comes, He will be there too.

Living Proof of Redemption

You are not just a spectator in God's plan - you are a participant. A character in the unfolding drama of grace. Jesus' sacrifice did not just change history - it changed your history. His resurrection did not just defeat death - it breathed life into your identity. His priesthood is not just cosmic - It is intimately personal. He knows your name. He knows your battles. And He's writing your story with purpose, beauty, and redemption.

When you trust Jesus, your life becomes a living letter. Paul writes: *"You are our letter, written in our hearts, known and read by all men; being manifested that you are a letter of Christ, cared for by us, written not with ink but with the Spirit of the living God, not on tablets of stone but on tablets of human hearts"* (2 Corinthians 3:2–3).

This means your life is not just a message - it is a manifestation. A visible, tangible reflection of Christ's work in you. Your peace in chaos whispers of His presence. Your joy in hardship echoes His resurrection. Your forgiveness in conflict reveals His grace. Your endurance in temptation displays His strength.

You do not have to be perfect - you just have to be real. Your story, with all its ups and downs, becomes a mirror of mercy and a window of hope for others. Imagine your life as a stained-glass window. Each piece - joy, pain, failure, growth - is part of the design. On its own, a shard may seem broken. But when the light of Christ shines through, the whole picture glows with beauty.

That is what happens when you let Jesus use your story. He does not erase your past - He redeems it. He does not hide your scars - He heals through them. Your brokenness becomes a canvas for His grace.

Jesus said: *"You are the light of the world. A city set on a hill cannot be hidden; nor does anyone light a lamp and put it under a basket, but on the lampstand, and it gives light to all who are in the house. Let your light shine before men in such a way that they may see your good works and glorify your Father who is in heaven"* (Matthew 5:14–16).

Your story shines brightest when you choose kindness in a culture of gossip. When you speak truth even when it costs you. When you show compassion to someone hurting. When you share your faith - even if your voice shakes.

You do not need a stage. **You just need authenticity**. Your story is your strongest witness because it is undeniably yours - and it points to the One who changed everything. Think of your life as a lampstand - not flashy, but faithful. It holds the light. It lifts it high. It gives light to everyone in the room. You do not have to generate the flame - Jesus is the light. You just have to hold it up.

Philippians 2:15–16 echoes this: *"...so that you will prove yourselves to be blameless and innocent, children of God...among whom you appear as lights in the world, holding firmly the word of life..."*. Your life becomes a lighthouse in the fog. A signal of safety. A beacon of belonging. Not because you are flawless, but because you are faithful.

Navigating the Maze of Beliefs

Step into the world today, and it feels like walking through a vast spiritual marketplace. Imagine a stadium the size of a city, filled with booths and banners, each one claiming to offer the ultimate path to God.

Some shout with confidence, "Follow our rituals!" Others whisper seductively, "Discover the divine within." A few offer sleek presentations, promising peace through philosophy, mindfulness, or moral living. It is dazzling, overwhelming, and deeply confusing.

This spiritual stadium mirrors the culture around us. From TikTok theologians to bestselling spiritual authors, the marketplace of beliefs is crowded. But beneath all the noise, a critical question echoes: Can all paths lead to God?

The Bible answers with **clarity** - not with cruelty, but with **conviction**. It does not offer a spiritual buffet. It offers a singular feast, prepared by one Host: Jesus Christ.

The Apostle John, writing to early Christians surrounded by spiritual confusion, does not soften the truth. In 1 John 2:22–23, he writes, *"Who is the liar but the one who denies that Jesus is the Christ? This is the antichrist, the one who denies the Father and the Son. Whoever denies the Son does not have the Father; the one who confesses the Son has the Father also."*

These words are not just theological – they are relational. To deny Jesus is to sever the connection to God Himself. It is like trying to power a lamp without plugging it into the outlet. No matter how beautifully the lamp is designed, without the source, it remains dark.

John's warning introduces the concept of the "antichrist" - not just a future villain, but any spirit or mindset that opposes Christ's identity and mission. In his time, this included Gnostic teachers who claimed secret knowledge but denied Jesus' incarnation. Today, it might be influencers who reduce Jesus to a metaphor or a moral teacher. John's logic is clear: if you deny the Son, you cannot access the Father. But if you confess the Son, you are welcomed into full relationship with God.

Picture salvation as a grand mosaic - thousands of tiles forming a breathtaking image of God's love. Without Jesus, the centerpiece is missing. The image blurs. The story breaks. Colossians 1:15–20 paints this picture vividly: *"He is the image of the invisible God, the firstborn of all creation... For it was the Father's good pleasure for all the fullness to dwell in Him, and through Him to reconcile all things to Himself."*

Jesus is not just part of the picture - He is the image of God. He is the lens through which we see the Father clearly. Without Him, we are left guessing, grasping, and ultimately lost.

Jesus Himself makes this truth unmistakable in John 14:6, *"I am the way, and the truth, and the life; no one comes to the Father but through Me."* He does not say He knows the way. He says He is the way. It is not a map He hands us - it is Himself.

Think of a mountain trail carved by the Creator. Jesus does not just point to it; He walks it with us and *is* the trail. In a world of half-truths and spiritual spin, He is the unchanging reality. He does not just speak truth - He embodies it. And when it comes to life, He offers more than existence. He offers eternal, vibrant, resurrected life. He is the breath in our lungs and the hope beyond the grave.

Other belief systems may offer glimpses of morality, beauty, or wisdom. But only Jesus offers reconciliation with God. Only He bridges the chasm of sin. He expands this teaching in Matthew 7:13–14: *"Enter through the narrow gate; for the gate is wide and the way is broad that leads to destruction, and there are many who enter through it. For the gate is narrow and the way is constricted that leads to life, and there are few who find it."* This is not about elitism – it is about clarity. The narrow gate is not hidden; it is simply unpopular. It requires humility, surrender, and faith in Jesus alone.

Visualize a crowded carnival with dozens of entrances. Most lead to temporary thrills. But one quiet gate, tucked away, leads to a kingdom. Few notice it. Fewer choose it. But it is the only one that leads home.

John's Gospel opens with a radiant metaphor. In John 1:4–5, we read, *"In Him was life, and the life was the Light of mankind. And the Light shines in the darkness, and the darkness did not grasp it."* Jesus is the light that exposes false paths and illuminates the true one. In a world of spiritual shadows, He shines with divine clarity. Imagine being in a pitch-black cave. You hear voices, feel walls, stumble over stones. Then someone turns on a flashlight - not just any light, but one that reveals the exit. That is Jesus. Not just illumination, but direction.

In the wilderness of beliefs, Jesus is the compass that always points true north. Other compasses may be magnetized by emotion, culture, or charisma - but only His needle is calibrated by eternity. To follow Jesus is not to reject others with arrogance, but to walk with conviction. It is to say, "I've found the way - and I want you to find it too."

Discerning Truth from Falsehood

In a world overflowing with spiritual voices, John offers a lifeline - a kind of spiritual GPS for those trying to navigate the maze of beliefs. He begins with a tender word: "Beloved." It is not just a greeting; it is the voice of a mentor, a coach, a spiritual father urging his children to stay alert. In 1 John 4:1, 3, he writes, *"Beloved, do not believe every spirit, but test the spirits to see whether they are from God, because many false prophets have gone out into the world... and every spirit that does not confess Jesus is not from God; this is the spirit of the antichrist, of which you have heard that it is coming, and now it is already in the world."*

John's concern is not paranoia - it is pastoral. He knows that not every spiritual message comes from the Holy Spirit. Some teachings are powered by deception, cloaked in charisma, and designed to lead hearts away from Christ. The *"spirits"* he refers to are the unseen influences behind people's words - whether divine or deceptive. In his day, false prophets were spreading confusion among believers. Today, the same dynamic plays out through podcasts, influencers, spiritual movements, and even well-meaning friends who offer advice that sounds wise but subtly sidesteps Jesus.

To *"test the spirits"* is to become a spiritual detective. It is like examining a diamond under a magnifying glass - not just admiring its sparkle but checking for authenticity. John's test is simple yet profound: Does this teaching confess Jesus as the Son of God, come in the flesh to save us? If not, it is not from God. It may sound inspiring, even compassionate, but if it leaves out Jesus, it is missing the heart of truth.

Imagine scrolling through social media and stumbling upon a post promising inner peace through meditation or self-love. It is beautifully written, maybe even backed by science. But if it never mentions Jesus - if it offers peace without the Prince of Peace – it is incomplete. Or picture being invited to a group that talks about "spirituality" and "energy" but avoids the cross, the resurrection, and the name of Jesus. John's warning urges you to ask the deeper question: Does this message point to Jesus as the Christ? If not, it may be dressed in light, but it is not from (or of) the Light.

Paul echoes this concern in 2 Corinthians 11:13–15, writing, *"For such men are false apostles, deceitful workers, disguising themselves as apostles of Christ. No wonder, for even Satan disguises himself as an angel of light. Therefore, it is not surprising if his servants also disguise themselves as servants of righteousness, whose end will be according to their deeds."* These words are sobering. False teachings do not always come with flashing red warnings. Sometimes they wear halos. They speak in gentle tones. They quote Scripture out of context. They offer a version of righteousness that feels good but lacks the power to save.

It is like biting into a beautifully decorated cake only to find it is made of cardboard. The appearance is convincing, but the substance is hollow. For those seeking truth, this means learning to think critically - not cynically, but wisely. It means holding every teaching up to the light of Scripture and asking, "Does this align with the gospel of Jesus?"

At the center of all this discernment is one question: Who is Jesus? That is the heartbeat of salvation. In both 1 John 2 and 1 John 4, the issue is not just morality or spirituality – it is identity. Jesus is not one spiritual leader among many. **He does not merely point to the path - He is the path**. He does not just teach about God - He is God, wrapped in human flesh, sent to rescue us from sin.

The Bible teaches that sin is not just a mistake – it is a barrier. Isaiah 59:2 says, *"But your wrongdoings have caused a separation between you and your God, and your sins have hidden His face from you so that He does not hear."* Sin creates a chasm between us and God, and no amount of good deeds, rituals, or positive thinking can bridge that gap. It is like standing on one side of a canyon, shouting across, hoping your voice will reach the other side. But the distance is too great. The echo fades. The silence remains.

That is where Jesus steps in - not as a motivational speaker, but as a Savior. Think of sin like a massive debt you could never repay. Jesus did not negotiate the terms - He paid it in full. Romans 5:8 declares, *"But*

God demonstrates His own love toward us, in that while we were yet sinners, Christ died for us." This love is not conditional. God did not wait for us to clean up our act. He moved toward us while we were still lost, still broken, still running.

Again, Ephesians 2:8–9 drives the point home: *"For by grace you have been saved through faith; and that not of yourselves, it is the gift of God; not as a result of works, so that no one may boast."* **Salvation is not a trophy we earn – it is a gift we receive**. You do not have to perform for God's approval. You do not have to join the right group or follow a checklist. You simply trust in Jesus, and the door to grace swings open.

But this also means we must reject teachings that add requirements to salvation - those that say you must follow certain rules, adopt specific rituals, or belong to a particular organization to be saved. These teachings, however well-intentioned, undermine the sufficiency of Jesus' sacrifice. It is like trying to add paint to a masterpiece. The moment you do, you distort the original beauty.

Jesus is enough. His cross is enough. His resurrection is enough.

So how do you live out John's warnings in a world overflowing with spiritual noise? It begins with a posture of curiosity - but not blind trust. When you encounter a spiritual claim - whether it is from a friend, a teacher, a TikTok video, or a religious group - pause and ask yourself: *Does this point to Jesus as the Son of God and the only way to salvation?* If the message centers on human effort, vague spirituality, or alternative paths to God, it may sound comforting, but it does not align with the truth of Scripture.

Think of it like navigating a city with dozens of signs pointing in different directions. Some are flashy, some are ancient, and some are handwritten. But only one leads to the destination. The Bible is your guide in this spiritual landscape. It does not just offer information - it offers illumination. Psalm 119:105 says, *"Your word is a lamp to my feet and a light to my path."* In a world full of shadows and spiritual shortcuts, God's Word shines like a lantern in the fog, helping you see where to step and what to avoid.

Reading Scripture regularly - especially the Gospels, which reveal Jesus' life, teachings, and heart - trains your spiritual instincts. It is like learning to recognize a familiar voice in a crowded room. The more you know Jesus through His Word, the easier it becomes to spot when something does not sound like Him.

But even with a map, you still need guidance. That is where prayer comes in. Ask the Holy Spirit to help you discern truth from error. James 1:5 offers this promise: *"But if any of you lacks wisdom, let him ask of God, who gives to all generously and without reproach, and it will be given to him."* God is not stingy with wisdom. He is eager to guide you - like a loving parent helping a child learn to walk through a busy street.

Imagine you are invited to a group that seems spiritual. They talk about peace, love, and purpose. But something feels off. They never mention Jesus. They avoid the cross. They speak of "energy" and "awakening," but not of sin or salvation. In that moment, pray.

Open your Bible. Ask the hard question: *Does this teaching confess Jesus as the Christ?* If not, it is time to walk away - not with anger, but with clarity. Your relationship with Jesus is too precious to compromise.

The world is full of voices claiming to have the answers. Some are loud, some are persuasive, and some are wrapped in kindness. But only one voice leads to life. Only one voice says, "I am the way." Jesus does not just point to salvation - He *is* salvation.

If by chance you still have not given your life over to Jesus, nor prayed the pray to receive Jesus in chapter three of this book, here is another opportunity to do so.

You just need an open heart. Revelation 3:20 gives us this beautiful image: *"Behold, I stand at the door and knock; if anyone hears My voice and opens the door, I will come in to him and will dine with him, and he with Me."* Picture Jesus standing at the door of your heart - not with judgment, but with love. He is not holding a checklist. He is holding a seat at His table.

He wants to share life with you. To forgive you. To walk with you. To never let you go. If you did not pray 'the prayer of salvation' in chapter three of this book, why not do it now? Here is a simple prayer to invite Him in:

Lord Jesus, I need You. I believe You are the Christ, the Son of God, who died for my sins and rose again. I open my heart and invite You into my life. Thank You for Your love and grace. Guide me to follow You every day. Amen.

If you pray this with sincerity, you can trust God's promise. Jesus has entered your life. He has forgiven your sins. He has given you eternal life. John 10:28 assures us, *"And I give eternal life to them, and they will never perish; and no one will snatch them out of My hand."*

It is like being held in the strongest arms imaginable - arms that never grow tired, never let go, and never forget you. In a world of shifting beliefs and uncertain truths, Jesus is your anchor. Your compass. Your light. Your life.

10
The 'I AM' - Said So (1)

Of all the claims that people make about salvation, there is one distinct difference in what Christ has claimed. Jesus did not say that He would lead us towards the way, nor did He give us a list of requirements to follow in order to gain the way. Jesus never said that He would lead us into a spiritual light for 'enlightenment.' Jesus never said that He would give us a list of rituals to satisfy a spiritual hunger. Jesus never said that He would show us a religious door to walk through in order to gain 'heavenly bliss.'

What Jesus did say was that He is 'The Light'; The Bread'; The Door.' The Apostle John recorded seven times Jesus personally identifying Himself using the phrase 'I am' metaphorically to distinguish Himself above all others. If you include His reference to the 'I AM' statement from God speaking to Moses (during the captivity in Egypt), and two times in the Book of Revelation, Jesus referred to Himself as 'I am' on ten different occasions. Each instance (briefly mentioned here) show us the depth of who Jesus is and helps us understand more about Him as 'The Son of God' and the 'Savior of the world.'

Why the "I AM" Matters

The "I AM" statements of Jesus are not just bold declarations - they are the heartbeat of the Gospel. They reveal not only who Jesus is, but why He alone can offer salvation. In a world filled with spiritual voices, philosophies, and religious systems, Jesus does not offer a method to reach God - He offers Himself as the way to God. That distinction is not just important; it is eternal.

Many belief systems present guides - teachers who claim to know the way to spiritual fulfillment. They might say, "Meditate this way," or "Perform these good deeds," or "Follow our sacred rules." These approaches offer a path, but they leave you walking alone, hoping you are headed in the right direction. Jesus, however, does not hand you a map and wish you luck. He says, "I am the way" (John 14:6). He is the road beneath your feet, the compass in your hand, and the destination at the end. He is not merely a guide - He is the source.

This is why Jesus never taught that salvation comes through rituals. He did not say, "Attend these services," or "Give this amount," or "Recite these words." Instead, He offered a relationship. He invited people to know Him, to walk with Him, to trust Him. In John 17:3, Jesus defines eternal life not as a reward for religious performance, but as the joy of knowing God: *"This is eternal life, that they may know You, the only true God, and Jesus Christ whom You have sent."* Salvation is not earned - it is received through intimacy with the living Christ.

And while today's culture often speaks of "enlightenment" or "finding your inner truth," Jesus offers something far more powerful. He does not promise a vague spiritual glow or a temporary emotional high. He promises transformation. He forgives sin, heals wounds, and gives new purpose. As Paul writes in 2 Corinthians 5:17, *"Therefore if anyone is in Christ, he is a new creature; the old things passed away; behold, new things have come."* Jesus does not just improve your life - He remakes it. He does not just inspire you - He adopts you into God's family.

The "I AM" of the Burning Bush

The "I AM" phrase first appears in the Old Testament, in a dramatic encounter between God and Moses. In Exodus 3:13-41 the Scripture says, *"... Moses said to God, "Behold, I am going to the sons of Israel, and I will say to them, 'The God of your fathers has sent me to you.' 'Now they may ask me, "What is His name?" What shall I say to them?" God said to moses, "I AM WHO I AM"; and He said, "Thus you shall say to the sons of Israel, 'I AM has sent me to you.'"*

Around 1446 B.C., the Israelites had been enslaved in Egypt for four hundred years, suffering under harsh conditions. God chose Moses, a former Egyptian prince turned fugitive, to lead His people to freedom. While tending sheep in the desert, Moses saw a bush on fire but not burning up – a miracle that caught his attention. When God spoke from the bush, commissioning Moses to confront Pharaoh, Moses asked for God's name to prove His authority. In Egypt, where people worshipped many gods like Ra or Qsiris, names carried power. God's response, *"I AM WHO I AM,"* was both simple and cataclysmic.

The name *"I AM"* (in Hebrew, Yahweh or Ehyeh) means God is **eternal**, **self-existent**, and **unchanging**. He does not depend on anything or anyone else to exist – He simply is. It is like saying, "I am the source of all reality, forever and always." This name set God apart from Egypt's false gods, showing He alone had the power to deliver His people. By telling Moses to say, "*I AM has sent me,*" God was declaring His supreme authority and personal presence with the Israelites.

Fast forward 1,500 years to Jesus' time – in John 8:56-58, Jesus makes this stunning claim: "*Your father Abraham rejoiced to see My day, and he saw it and was glad.*" *So, the Jews said to Him, "You are not yet fifty years old, and have you seen Abraham?" Jesus said unto them, "Truly, truly, I say to you, before Abraham was born, I am."*

When Jesus used this name, He was not being poetic – He was being precise. It was not a riddle – **but a revelation**. This conversation happened with the Jewish religious leaders in Jerusalem. They were questioning Jesus' authority, and He mentioned Abraham, the father of the Jewish nation who lived two thousand years earlier. When the religious leaders challenged Jesus, He did not just say He existed before Abraham – He said, "*I am*". The religious leaders immediately recognized this as a claim to be God, the same "*I AM*" who spoke to Moses.

Thus, as John 8:59 states, "*Therefore they picked up stones to throw at Him, but Jesus hid Himself and went out of the temple.*" Jesus left because His time for suffering (and dying) had not yet come, but His words left no doubt: He was declaring Himself to be God.

Think of this like a bold announcer on a global stage. Imagine someone walking on the stage and saying, "I'm the creator of the universe." That is the kind of claim Jesus made. It was not just about being a new rabbi or prophet – He was saying He is the eternal God who spoke to moses, now standing before them in human form. This sets Jesus apart from every other religious figure. No one else in history claimed to be God Himself in this way.

John's Gospel (John 1:1-3,14) opens with a thunderous affirmation of this truth: "*In the beginning was the Word, and the Word was with God, and the Word was God. He was in the beginning with God. All things came into being through Him, and apart from Him nothing came into being that has come into being .... And the Word became flesh, and dwelt among us."*

Jesus, the Word, was present at creation. He did not come into existence - He always was. He is eternal, uncreated, divine. Hebrews 1:3 adds that Jesus is *"the radiance of His glory and the exact representation of His nature,"* and that He *"upholds all things by the word of His power."* Jesus does not just reflect God - He is God in full. He sustains the universe with His voice.

Colossians 1:15-17 takes this even further: *"He is the image of the invisible God, the firstborn of all creation. For by Him all things were created... and in Him all things hold together."* Jesus is not a distant deity - He is the Creator and Sustainer of all things. He is before all things, and in Him everything finds its purpose and coherence. These verses do not just support Jesus' "I AM" claim - they explode it with cosmic significance.

This means Jesus is not just a historical figure or a wise teacher. He is the eternal God who knows you personally, who formed you in your mother's womb, who holds your life together even when everything feels like it is falling apart. He is not distant - He is near. He is not optional - He is essential.

Living the "I AM" Today

So, what does this mean for your everyday life? It means that in a world full of competing voices - social media influencers, spiritual trends, and cultural pressures - you have a foundation that does not shift. Jesus' *"I AM"* statements are your anchor in the storm.

When someone suggests another way to God - whether through good deeds, meditation, or self-improvement - remember Jesus' words in John 10:9: *"I am the door; if anyone enters through Me, he will be saved."* He is not one option among many - He is the only way. He is the door to salvation, and every other path leads to a dead end.

When doubts creep in, when friends question your faith, or when life feels overwhelming, you can find confidence in who Jesus is. Philippians 2:9-11 reminds us that *"at the name of Jesus every knee will bow... and every tongue will confess that Jesus Christ is Lord."* You are not following a trend – you are following the King of kings. His authority is unmatched, and His love is unshakable.

Even more, Jesus offers you a life of purpose. He did not come just to save you from sin - He came to give you abundant life. As He says in John 10:10, *"I came that they may have life, and have it abundantly."* Whether you are facing stress about grades, relationships, or your future, Jesus offers peace, direction, and joy. He is not just your Savior - **He is your purpose.**

Jesus, the Bread of Life

Picture the feeling of deep hunger after a long, exhausting day - your stomach growling, your energy fading, and your mind distracted by the need to eat. Then imagine the relief of biting into a warm, fresh slice of bread. It satisfies you for the moment, restores your strength, and gives you a sense of comfort. But as we all know that satisfaction does not last. A few hours later, the hunger returns. Physical food can only sustain us temporarily.

Now shift the scene inward. Imagine a hunger not of the body, but of the soul - a craving for meaning, peace, identity, and hope. It is the kind of hunger that no sandwich, no snack, no feast can satisfy. This is the hunger Jesus speaks to when He declares, *"I am the bread of life."* He is not offering a temporary fix or a spiritual snack. He is offering Himself as the eternal nourishment that fills the deepest emptiness in our hearts.

In John 6:35, Jesus says, *"I am the bread of life; he who comes to Me will not hunger, and he who believes in Me will never thirst."*

To grasp the full meaning of this statement, we need to step into its historical context. Around 30 A.D. Jesus had just performed one of His most famous miracles: feeding over five thousand people with only five loaves of bread and two fish. This event, recorded in John 6:1–14, took place near the Sea of Galilee and left the crowd amazed. Many followed Him afterward, hoping for more miracles - or more free food. They even brought up the story of manna, the miraculous bread God provided to the Israelites during their 40 years in the wilderness (Exodus 16:4–15).

That manna was a daily provision, a temporary fix for physical hunger. But it did not satisfy the deeper spiritual hunger of the people.

Jesus saw that the crowd was focused on physical bread, missing the deeper truth. He wanted them to seek something far greater - eternal nourishment for their souls. When He said, "*I am the bread of life,*" He was claiming to be the true and lasting source of spiritual sustenance, far surpassing the manna of old. His promise was clear: those who come to Him and believe in Him will never hunger or thirst again - not because life will be easy, but because their deepest needs will be met in Him. Forgiveness, purpose, peace, and connection with God are found in Jesus alone.

Think of it like this: the world offers vending machine snacks - quick fixes like popularity, success, or even spiritual practices that feel good for a moment but leave you empty again. Jesus offers a home-cooked meal that never runs out. He is not a temporary boost – He is the source of eternal sustenance.

From Manna to Messiah

The crowd's excitement after the miracle was understandable. They saw Jesus as a potential political leader, someone who could meet their physical needs and maybe even overthrow Roman rule. In John 6:14–15, we read, "*Therefore when the people saw the sign which He had performed, they said, 'This is truly the Prophet who is to come into the world.' So, Jesus, perceiving that they were intending to come and take Him by force to make Him king, withdrew again to the mountain by Himself alone.*"

They wanted a king who could feed them and fight for them. But Jesus had a greater mission. The next day, when they found Him in Capernaum, they asked for another sign, comparing Him to Moses and the manna. Jesus corrected their thinking. He explained that the manna was not from Moses - it was from God. And now, God was offering something far greater: the true bread from heaven.

In John 6:32–33, Jesus says, "*Truly, truly, I say to you, it is not Moses who has given you the bread out of heaven, but it is My Father who gives you the true bread out of heaven. For the bread of God is that which comes down out of heaven and gives life to the world."*

The manna sustained physical life for a day. Jesus gives eternal life to the whole world. The Israelites ate manna and still died. This ties directly to the *"I AM"* theme, connecting Jesus to the eternal name of God in Exodus 3:14. Just as God provided for His people in the desert, Jesus provides for all humanity as the divine Bread of Life.

What It Means to "Come" and "Believe"

The phrases *"he who comes to Me"* and *"he who believes in Me"* in John 6:35 are the keys to eternal satisfaction. To *"come"* to Jesus means to turn toward Him in faith, to approach Him as the source of life. It is like walking toward a friend who is holding out everything you need. To *"believe"* in Jesus means to trust that His death and resurrection are enough to forgive your sins and give you eternal life. It is not just agreeing with facts - it is entrusting your whole self to Him.

Jesus expands on this in John 6:47–51: *"Truly, truly, I say to you, he who believes has eternal life. I am the bread of life. Your fathers ate the manna in the wilderness, and they died. This is the bread which comes down out of heaven, so that one may eat of it and not die. I am the living bread that came down out of heaven; if anyone eats of this bread, he will live forever; and the bread also which I will give for the life of the world is My flesh."*

Here, Jesus connects the Bread of Life to His sacrifice on the cross. By giving His flesh - His body in death - He provides the means for eternal life. This points to the Lord's Supper, where bread symbolizes Jesus' body given for us (Luke 22:19). This means that faith in Jesus is not just a one-time decision - it is a daily choice to "feed" on Him through prayer, Scripture, and trust.

Galatians 2:20 deepens this truth: *"I have been crucified with Christ; and it is no longer I who live, but Christ lives in me; and the life which I now live in the flesh I live by faith in the Son of God, who loved me and gave Himself up for me."* When you trust in Jesus, your old self dies with Him. Christ lives in you, transforming your life. It is like trading a life of chasing temporary things for a life powered by Jesus' love. This might mean letting go of the pressure to fit in and instead living for the One who knows you completely and loves you unconditionally.

Additional Scriptures That Illuminate the Bread of Life

Jesus' promise in John 6 is echoed throughout Scripture. In John 4:13-14, Jesus tells the Samaritan woman, *"Everyone who drinks of this water will thirst again; but whoever drinks of the water that I will give him shall never thirst."* Just as He offers living water to quench spiritual thirst, He offers Himself as the Bread that satisfies spiritual hunger. Both images show that Jesus fulfills our deepest needs.

In 1 Corinthians 11:23–25, Paul recounts the Lord's Supper: *"The Lord Jesus in the night in which He was betrayed took bread... and said, 'This is My body, which is for you; do this in remembrance of Me.'"* This links the Bread of Life to Jesus' sacrifice, reminding us that His death is the nourishment of our salvation.

And in Isaiah 55:1–2, the prophet invites all to receive God's free gift: *"Why do you spend money for what is not bread, and your wages for what does not satisfy?"* This ancient call points forward to Jesus, who offers true satisfaction - without cost, without striving, without performance.

So, what does it actually look like to live with Jesus as your Bread of Life? How do you take this powerful truth and make it part of your everyday rhythm - between classes, work, family, friendships, sports, and the swirl of social media? It starts with daily dependence.

Just as your body needs food every day to stay strong, your soul needs Jesus daily to stay spiritually alive. Seeking Him is not a once-a-week activity – it is a daily invitation to be nourished by His presence. That might mean starting your morning with a short prayer, reading a chapter from the Gospel of John, or simply pausing during a stressful moment to remember His love. When exams or work pile up or friendships feel shaky, turning to Jesus in prayer can bring peace and strength that no grade or compliment can offer. Psalm 34:8 invites us into this experience: *"O taste and see that the Lord is good; how blessed is the man who takes refuge in Him!"* Jesus is not just good in theory – He is good in practice, and you will discover that as you lean on Him day by day.

At the same time, it is important to recognize the difference between lasting nourishment and temporary "fulfillment." The world is full of quick fixes for your soul's hunger - likes on a post, compliments from friends, new clothes, or even spiritual trends that promise peace without Jesus. These things might feel good for a moment, but they are like junk food: they leave you empty and craving more. When you find yourself chasing approval or comparing yourself to others, pause and ask, "Is this really filling my heart, or do I need to turn to Jesus?" Only He can satisfy the hunger for identity, belonging, and purpose.

And when life gets hard - when you feel lonely, anxious, or uncertain - remember Jesus' promise. He said that those who come to Him will never hunger or thirst. That does not mean life will be perfect, but it does mean He will meet your deepest needs. You can trust Him to be enough. In John 6:37, Jesus assures us, *"All that the Father gives Me will come to Me, and the one who comes to Me I will certainly not cast out."* That means you are never too broken, too confused, or too far gone for Jesus. He will never turn you away.

Finally, if Jesus is the Bread of Life, then it is worth sharing Him with others. You do not have to be a preacher or theologian to do this. Just tell a friend what Jesus means to you. Invite someone to church, youth group, or a Bible study. Share a verse that has helped you through a tough time. Your story matters, and you can help someone else find their way. Jesus said in Matthew 5:16, *"Let your light shine before men in such a way that they may see your good works, and glorify your Father who is in heaven."* When you live out your faith with love and authenticity, people will notice - and God will be glorified.

Jesus, the Light of the World

Imagine stumbling through a pitch-black room, unsure of where to step, tripping over furniture, and feeling the weight of uncertainty pressing in. Now picture lighting a single candle. Instantly, the darkness begins to retreat, and the room becomes visible. You can see the obstacles, the path forward, and the safety around you. That is the kind of power Jesus claims when He calls Himself the "Light of the World."

In a world filled with confusion, fear, and sin, Jesus does not just offer a flicker of hope - He offers a light that transforms everything. His light does not just brighten your path; it reveals truth, exposes lies, and leads you into life.

While other spiritual leaders may offer advice, rituals, or temporary fixes, Jesus declares that He is the light that overcomes all darkness. His claim sets Him apart as the source of truth, the presence of God, and the guide for every soul seeking clarity and peace.

In John 8:12, Jesus says, *"I am the Light of the world; he who follows Me will not walk in the darkness, but will have the Light of life."* To understand the weight of this statement, we need to step into its historical and spiritual context. It was around 30 A.D., during the Feast of Tabernacles in Jerusalem - a major Jewish festival celebrating God's provision for the Israelites during their wilderness journey (Leviticus 23:33–43). During this feast, the temple was illuminated with massive golden lampstands, symbolizing God's presence and guidance, much like the pillar of fire that led the Israelites by night (Exodus 13:21–22).

Against this backdrop of glowing light and sacred memory, Jesus stood in the temple courts and declared, *"I am the Light of the World."* This was not just a clever sermon illustration - it was a jaw-dropping moment. Jesus was claiming to be the fulfillment of the festival's symbolism, the divine presence that had guided Israel, now standing among them in human form. He was not just pointing to God's light - He was revealing Himself as that light.

The promise embedded in John 8:12 is profound. Jesus says that those who follow Him will not walk in darkness but will have the Light of life. In Scripture, darkness represents sin, confusion, and separation from God. In Jesus' time, people were burdened by religious legalism, spiritual blindness, and the weight of guilt. Today, darkness might look like anxiety, peer pressure, depression, or the chaos of conflicting messages on social media. Jesus promises that if you follow Him - if you trust His teachings, walk in His ways, and lean on His presence - you will not stumble in the dark. Instead, you will live in the light of His truth, love, and eternal hope.

Think of Jesus as the ultimate flashlight in a power outage. No matter how dark or uncertain life becomes - whether you are stressed about college applications, work deadlines, struggling with identity, or tempted to follow the wrong crowd - Jesus' light is stronger. He does not just show you the way out; He walks with you, illuminating every step.

Light in a Dark World: The Context of John 8

To understand John 8:12 more deeply, we need to look at the broader conversation. This verse comes during a tense exchange between Jesus and the Pharisees, the religious leaders who often opposed Him. In John 8:13–20, they challenged His claim, arguing that He could not testify about Himself without witnesses. Jesus responded by pointing to His Father – God - as His witness and reminded them that His miracles and teachings confirmed His divine authority.

The setting of the Feast of Tabernacles is crucial. The lampstands in the temple reminded the people of God's guidance in the wilderness. By saying, "I am the Light," Jesus was claiming to be the fulfillment of that guidance - the divine presence leading people not just through deserts, but through the spiritual wilderness of life.

This claim echoes powerful Old Testament imagery. Psalm 27:1 declares, *"The Lord is my light and my salvation; whom shall I fear? The Lord is the defense of my life; whom shall I dread?"* For the Jewish people, light symbolized God's truth, holiness, and protection. Jesus' statement would have stunned His audience. He was equating Himself with the God who had led their ancestors, the same "I AM" who spoke to Moses in Exodus 3:14. The Pharisees' resistance was not just theological - it was personal. Jesus' light exposed their pride, their legalism, and their spiritual blindness.

Light That Exposes and Transforms

Light does not just reveal - **it transforms**. The Bible teaches that humanity is naturally in darkness because of sin. Before knowing Jesus, we are trapped in spiritual blindness. We make choices based on fear, confusion, or selfishness. But Jesus, as the Light of the World, exposes that darkness - not to shame us, but to save us.

Ephesians 5:8 says, *"For you were formerly darkness, but now you are Light in the Lord; walk as children of Light."* This verse does not say we were merely in darkness - it says we were darkness. Sin is not just around us; it is within us. But when Jesus enters our lives, He changes our identity. We become light in Him.

John 1:4–5, deepens this truth: *"In Him was life, and the life was the Light of men. The Light shines in the darkness, and the darkness did not comprehend it."* The word *"comprehend"* can also mean **"overcome."** This means that no matter how deep the darkness, it cannot extinguish Jesus' light. His truth is stronger than any lie. His grace is deeper than any guilt. His presence is brighter than any fear.

Isaiah 9:2 prophesies this light: *"The people who walk in darkness will see a great light; those who live in a dark land, the light will shine on them."* This was fulfilled in Jesus, as Matthew 4:16 confirms. He is the sunrise after the longest night.

In John 12:46, Jesus says, *"I have come as Light into the world, so that everyone who believes in Me will not remain in darkness."* Faith in Jesus is not just a belief – it is a rescue. It is stepping out of confusion, out of guilt and into grace.

And in 1 John 1:5–7, we read, *"God is Light, and in Him there is no darkness at all... if we walk in the Light as He Himself is in the Light, we have fellowship with one another, and the blood of Jesus His Son cleanses us from all sin."* Jesus' light does not just guide us - it cleanses us. It brings us into community, into truth, and into freedom.

Living in the Light

So how can you live with Jesus as the Light of the World? It begins with following His guidance. That means trusting His teachings in the Bible and seeking His direction through prayer. When you are faced with tough choices - like whether to cheat on a test, gossip about a friend, or join in something you know is wrong - ask yourself, "What would Jesus want me to do?" Again, Psalm 119:105 says, *"Your word is a lamp to my feet and a light to my path."* Let Scripture illuminate your decisions.

Life can feel dark sometimes. Maybe you are dealing with anxiety, family struggles, or bullying. Jesus promises that His light is stronger than any darkness. When you feel overwhelmed, turn to Him. Pray. Read His Word. Trust that He is with you. 2 Corinthians 4:6 reminds us, *"For God, who said, 'Light shall shine out of darkness,' is the One who has shone in our hearts to give the Light of the knowledge of the glory of God in the face of Christ."* His light brings hope even in the hardest moments.

As a follower of Jesus, you are also called to reflect His light. That means letting His love shine through your actions. Small acts of kindness, standing up for what is right, or sharing your faith can make a big impact. If a friend is struggling, listen to them. Share how Jesus has helped you. Matthew 5:14–16 says, *"You are the light of the world... Let your light shine before men in such a way that they may see your good works and glorify your Father who is in heaven."* Your life can be a beacon that points others to God.

But be alert - because not every light is true. The world offers "lights" that seem bright but lead to darkness. Popularity, materialism, and misleading spiritual ideas can look appealing but leave you lost. Test everything against Jesus' truth. 1 John 4:1 warns, *"Beloved, do not believe every spirit, but test the spirits to see whether they are from God."* If a trend, teaching, or philosophy does not point to Jesus, it is not the true light.

A Call to Walk in the Light

Jesus' declaration, *"I am the Light of the World,"* is a call to step out of the shadows of confusion, guilt, and spiritual emptiness, and into the brilliance of His truth, grace, and eternal life. He does not ask you to earn salvation through flawless behavior or religious rituals. He does not demand perfection or performance. He simply asks you to follow Him.

To walk in the light means to trust Jesus - to believe that He is who He says He is: the Son of God, the Savior of the world, the Light that overcomes all darkness.

Jesus also gives a powerful promise to those who choose to follow Him. In John 8:31–32, He says, *"If you continue in My word, then you are truly disciples of Mine; and you will know the truth, and the truth will make you free."* Walking in the light is not just a one-time decision - **it is a daily journey**. It means continuing in His word, learning from His teachings, and allowing His truth to shape your thoughts, choices, and relationships. And as you walk in that light, you will discover freedom - not just from sin, but from fear, shame, and the pressure to be someone you are not.

Let Jesus' light shine in your life. Let it guide you through the ups and downs of friendships, family, and future plans. Let it illuminate your identity, showing you that you are loved, chosen, and called. Let it expose the lies that say you are not enough and replace them with the truth that you are deeply known and eternally valued.

To walk in the light is to walk with Jesus. It is to live in the glow of His grace, the warmth of His presence, and the clarity of His truth. And it is to know, with confidence, that no matter how dark the world may seem, the Light of the World is with you - and He will never let you walk alone.

Jesus – The Door

Imagine life as a long hallway filled with countless doors. Some lead to joy, growth, and purpose - like choosing good friends, working hard in school, or pursuing your passions. Others open into confusion, regret, or emptiness - like giving in to peer pressure, chasing popularity, or making reckless decisions. But among all these doors, one stands apart. It is not just another option - it is the entrance to forgiveness, peace, and eternal life. That door is Jesus. When He says, *"I am the door,"* He is not offering advice or pointing to a spiritual path. He is declaring that He *is* the way into God's presence. Jesus is not just a teacher or prophet; He is the gateway to salvation itself.

Provision and Sustenance

John 10:9 says: *"I am the door; if anyone enters through Me, he will be saved, and will go in and out and find pasture."*

To grasp the depth of this promise, picture the ancient shepherding practices of Jesus' time. Shepherds would guide their sheep into stone (walled) enclosures at night - safe spaces with only one entrance.

Sometimes, the shepherd himself would lie across the opening, becoming the literal "door" to guard the sheep from predators. In this context, Jesus is saying: I am your protection, your access, your safety, and your guide.

This verse offers a threefold promise:

> **Salvation**: *"If anyone enters through Me, he will be saved."* Entering through Jesus means trusting Him as your Savior - believing that His death and resurrection paid for your sins. This is not about earning God's love; it is about receiving it through faith.
>
> **Freedom**: *"He will go in and out."* This phrase suggests a life of security and confidence. Just as sheep trust their shepherd to lead them safely, you can live with boldness, knowing Jesus is always with you.
>
> **Provision**: *"And will find pasture."* Pasture symbolizes nourishment, rest, and abundance. Jesus does not just offer survival - He offers a life filled with meaning, peace, and spiritual richness.

Think of Jesus as the entrance to the most important event of your life - not a concert or college acceptance, but eternal life with God. Other doors might promise excitement or success, but only Jesus leads to lasting fulfillment.

The Context: Jesus as the True Shepherd's Door

To understand this metaphor more fully, let us explore the surrounding verses. In John 10:1–6, Jesus describes a shepherd who enters the sheepfold through the door, unlike thieves who sneak in another way. The Pharisees did not grasp His meaning, so He clarified in John 10:7–8: *"So Jesus said to them again, 'Truly, truly, I say to you, I am the door of the sheep. All who came before Me are thieves and robbers, but the sheep did not hear them.'"*

Here, Jesus contrasts Himself with false leaders - those who claimed to speak for God but led people astray. The Pharisees, with their rigid rules and burdensome traditions, created barriers between people and God. Jesus tears those barriers down. He is the Door that opens directly into God's grace.

This shepherd imagery echoes the Old Testament, where God is portrayed as Israel's shepherd. Psalm 23:1–3 says: *"The Lord is my shepherd, I shall not want. He makes me lie down in green pastures; He leads me beside quiet waters. He restores my soul; He guides me in the paths of righteousness for His name's sake."*

Jesus fulfills this ancient promise. He is both the Shepherd and the Door - the one who leads and the one who grants access.

The Door to a Relationship with God

The metaphor of "doors" reminds us that life is full of choices. But choosing Jesus is not just one good option - it is the only way to enter into a relationship with God. Other doors - like religion, self-help, or moral effort - might seem promising, but they do not lead to God. Only Jesus does.

Revelation 3:20 adds a personal dimension to this truth: *"Behold, I stand at the door and knock; if anyone hears My voice and opens the door, I will come in to him and will dine with him, and he with Me."*

This is not just about theology - it is about relationship. Jesus is knocking on the door of your heart, inviting you into friendship, forgiveness, and transformation. "Dining" with Jesus suggests **closeness**, **trust**, and **joy**. He does not want to be a distant figure - He wants to be your daily companion.

Additional Scriptures to Deepen the Truth

These verses highlight that entering through Jesus leads to a restored relationship with God, something no other door can offer.

Acts 4:12 - *"And there is salvation in no one else; for there is no other name under heaven that has been given among men by which we must be saved."* This confirms Jesus as the only 'Door' to salvation, emphasizing His exclusivity.

John 10:10 - *"The thief comes only to steal and kill and destroy; I came that they may have life and have it abundantly."* The 'thief' represents no only Satan, but false paths that rob you of true life: Jesus, the Door, offers abundant life – full of purpose, joy, and eternal security.

Ephesians 2:18 - *"For through Him we both have our access in one Spirit to the Father."* Jesus, the Door, provides direct access to God, uniting all believers in His family.

So how do you walk through the Door that is Jesus - not just once, but every day? Life constantly presents you with choices, like standing in that uncertain hallway filled with doors.

One way to do this is by choosing Jesus intentionally each day. Every morning, you face doors of temptation - whether it is the pressure to cheat on a test, lie to a friend, or follow the crowd into choices that do not reflect your values. Choosing Jesus means praying for strength, seeking His wisdom, and following His teachings in Scripture. Colossians 2:6–7 encourages this daily walk: *"Therefore as you have received Christ Jesus the Lord, so walk in Him, having been firmly rooted and now being built up in Him."* Staying rooted in Jesus means letting His truth shape your decisions, your relationships, and your sense of identity.

Another way to walk through the Door is by learning to recognize and avoid false doors. The world offers many alternatives that seem appealing - doors labeled with social media fame, material success, or spiritual trends that promise peace without Jesus. These doors may glitter, but they do not lead to God. When you are faced with a choice, pause and ask: Does this align with Jesus' truth? **Does this door lead me closer to Him or farther away?**

Walking through the Door also means finding rest in His pasture. Jesus does not just offer salvation - He offers peace, provision, and renewal. When you are overwhelmed by school, sports, relationships, or anxiety, remember that Jesus invites you to rest in Him. Jesus' pasture is not just a place - it is a way of life. It is where your soul finds quiet, your heart finds healing, and your mind finds clarity.

And finally, walking through the Door means inviting others in. If Jesus has changed your life, do not keep that to yourself. Share His love with friends, family, or classmates. You do not need to preach - just tell your story. A simple conversation about how Jesus helped you through a tough time can open someone else's heart. 1 Peter 3:15 encourages this kind of witness: *"Always being ready to make a defense to everyone who asks you to give an account for the hope that is in you."* Your hope matters. And your story might be the key that helps someone else find the Door.

11

The 'I AM' - Said So (2)

In this chapter, we continue our exploration of the profound "I Am" statements of Jesus, turning our attention to the final five declarations that reveal His divine identity and redemptive mission. Each statement offers a window into the heart of Christ - His care, His power over death, His guidance, His sustaining presence, and His eternal nature. As the Good Shepherd, He tenderly leads and protects His flock. As the Resurrection and the Life, He conquers death and offers eternal hope. In declaring Himself the Way, the Truth, and the Life, Jesus becomes our path to the Father. As the Vine, He invites us into abiding relationship and spiritual fruitfulness. And as the Alpha and the Omega, He stands as the beginning and the end of all things. These declarations are not mere metaphors -they are invitations into deeper intimacy with the One who holds all things together. They are not 'well defined slogans' for a marketing campaign. They reveal the essence and being of the Savior of the world.

Jesus, the Good Shepherd

Imagine being lost in a vast, unfamiliar wilderness. Around you are steep cliffs, wild animals, and poisonous plants. You feel vulnerable, unsure of where to go or whom to trust. Then, out of the shadows, a skilled and compassionate guide appears - someone who knows every path, shields you from danger, and leads you to safety and nourishment. This is the role Jesus claims when He says, *"I am the good shepherd."* He is not just a spiritual advisor or distant deity - He is the one who walks with you, fights for you, and laid down His life to save you.

When Jesus says, *"I am the good shepherd,"* He is declaring that He is not a hired hand who might flee when danger comes. He is the one who knows His sheep, loves them deeply, and sacrifices everything for their safety. Let us explore John 10:11 and its surrounding context to discover how Jesus, as the Good Shepherd, can guide you through the challenges of life.

In John 10:11, Jesus says, *"I am the good shepherd; the good shepherd lays down His life for the sheep."* This statement was made around 30 A.D. in Jerusalem, possibly during or just after the Feast of Tabernacles. Jesus was speaking to a crowd familiar with shepherding. Sheep were valuable but defenseless, prone to wandering and vulnerable to predators. A good shepherd did not just point the way; he led the sheep and protected them to keep danger out.

When Jesus calls Himself the Good Shepherd, He is claiming to be the ultimate protector and provider - not just for a flock of animals, but for all humanity. The phrase *"lays down His life"* foreshadows His death on the cross, where He would sacrifice Himself to save us from sin and eternal separation from God. Unlike a hired hand who might abandon the sheep when wolves approach (John 10:12–13), Jesus willingly gives His life to ensure our safety. This sets Him apart from every other spiritual leader - He does not just offer wisdom; **He offers Himself.**

Think of Jesus as the ultimate coach - not one who shouts from the sidelines, but one who steps into the game, takes the hits, and carries you to victory. In a world filled with peer pressure, anxiety, and tempting but harmful choices, Jesus is the Good Shepherd who knows you personally, leads you to safety, and sacrifices everything to keep you secure.

The Context: Jesus vs. False Shepherds

To understand the depth of Jesus' claim, we need to look at the verses surrounding John 10:11. Just before this, in John 10:9, Jesus says, "I am the door," declaring that He is the only way into God's kingdom. In John 10:1–10, He contrasts Himself with "thieves and robbers" - likely referring to the religious leaders of His day, the Pharisees. These leaders burdened people with strict rules and rituals, claiming to guide them to God but often leading them astray through legalism and pride.

Jesus' audience would have connected this to Ezekiel 34:2–4, where God condemns false shepherds: *"Woe, shepherds of Israel who have been feeding themselves! Should not the shepherds feed the flock? ... Those who are sickly you have not strengthened, the diseased you have not healed, the broken you have not bound up, the scattered you have not brought back, nor have you sought for the lost."*

In contrast, Jesus fulfills God's promise to send a true shepherd - one who strengthens the weak, heals the broken, and seeks the lost. His listeners would have recognized Him as the Messiah, the Shepherd who leads with love and sacrifice.

John 10:27–28 expands this promise: *"My sheep hear My voice, and I know them, and they follow Me; and I give eternal life to them, and they will never perish; and no one will snatch them out of My hand."*

This is a stunning assurance. Jesus knows His followers personally, like a shepherd who recognizes each sheep by name. When you listen to His voice - through Scripture and the Holy Spirit - He gives you eternal life, a gift that cannot be taken away. The phrase *"no one will snatch them out of My hand"* means that once you belong to Jesus, you are forever secure. This means you are never to be totally alone, no matter what challenges you face.

The Shepherd's Love and Sacrifice

The image of the Good Shepherd reveals profound truths about Jesus' character and mission. His willingness to *"lay down His life"* points directly to the cross. As 1 John 3:16 says: *"We know love by this, that He laid down His life for us; and we ought to lay down our lives for the brethren."*

Jesus' sacrifice was not just for a select few - it was for all humanity. He offers forgiveness, healing, and reconciliation with God. His love is personal and unconditional. Romans 5:8 affirms this: *"But God demonstrates His own love toward us, in that while we were still sinners, Christ died for us."*

The Good Shepherd also reflects God's heart throughout the Old Testament. Psalm 23:1–3 paints a picture of a shepherd who provides, guides, and restores. Jesus fulfills this perfectly, as seen in John 10:14–15: *"I am the good shepherd, and I know My own and My own know Me, even as the Father knows Me and I know the Father; and I lay down My life for the sheep."*

This mutual knowing is intimate and deep - like a close friendship built on trust and love. Jesus knows your fears, dreams, and struggles, and He invites you to know Him in return.

Other scriptures deepen this truth:

Isaiah 40:11 - *"Like a shepherd He will tend His flock, in His arm He will gather the lambs and carry them in His bosom; He will gently lead the nursing ewes."* This prophecy points to Jesus, the gentle yet powerful Shepherd who cares for the vulnerable.

Hebrews 13:20-21 - *"Now the God of peace, who brought up from the dead the great Shepherd of the sheep through the blood of the eternal covenant, even Jesus our Lord, equip you in every good thing to do His will, working in us that which is pleasing in His sight, through Jesus Christ, to whom be the glory forever and ever. Amen."* Jesus' resurrection confirms His role as the eternal Shepherd, equipping us to live for God.

1 Peter 2:24-25 - *"and He Himself bore our sins in His body on the cross, so that we might die to sin and live to righteousness; for by His wounds, you were healed. For you were continually straying like sheep, but now you have returned to the Shepherd and Guardian of your souls."* This connects Jesus' sacrifice to His role as Shepherd, healing and guiding us back to God.

Following the Good Shepherd

So how can you follow Jesus as the Good Shepherd in your everyday life? It starts with listening to His voice. Jesus says His sheep *"hear My voice."* You hear Him by reading the Bible, praying, and seeking the Holy Spirit is guidance. When you are faced with tough choices - like whether to join friends in something you know is wrong - ask yourself, "What is Jesus' voice telling me?"

Following the Good Shepherd means trusting His protection. Life can feel like a wilderness, full of stress, temptation, and uncertainty. But Jesus is with you. Romans 8:38–39 assures us: *"Neither death, nor life, nor angels, nor principalities… will be able to separate us from the love of God, which is in Christ Jesus our Lord."* Lean on Jesus when you feel vulnerable - He is guarding you even when you cannot see it.

Another way to follow is by trusting His lead. Instead of chasing popularity or success, seek to live with integrity and kindness. Proverbs

3:5–6 offers this wisdom: *"Trust in the Lord with all your heart and do not lean on your own understanding. In all your ways acknowledge Him, and He will make your paths straight."* Let Jesus guide your steps, even when the path feels uncertain.

Finally, **share His care**. As Jesus loves and protects you, reflect that love to others. Help a struggling classmate, stand up for someone at work, or share your faith with a friend. Matthew 5:16 encourages: *"Let your light shine before men in such a way that they may see your good works, and glorify your Father who is in heaven."* Your kindness can be a glimpse of the Good Shepherd's heart.

Jesus, the Resurrection and the Life

Picture yourself standing at a funeral, surrounded by grief, weighed down by the finality of death. It feels like the end - like death has the last word. Now imagine someone stepping forward, speaking with authority, and calling the deceased back to life. That is the astonishing power Jesus claims when He says, *"I am the resurrection and the life."* In a world where death seems like the ultimate enemy, Jesus declares that He is the source of life - both now and forever. This is not just comfort in sorrow; it is a bold proclamation that Jesus holds authority over death itself and offers eternal life to all who believe in Him. Jesus proves His power by raising His friend Lazarus from the dead.

Jesus' Power Over Death

In John 11:25–26, Jesus says to Martha: *"I am the resurrection and the life; he who believes in Me will live even if he dies, and everyone who lives and believes in Me will never die. Do you believe this?"*

To grasp the weight of this statement, we need to step into the scene. It is in Bethany, a village near Jerusalem, where Jesus' close friends Lazarus, Mary, and Martha lived. Lazarus had fallen seriously ill, and his sisters sent word to Jesus, hoping He would come quickly and heal him (John 11:1–3). But Jesus delayed, and by the time He arrived, Lazarus had been dead for four days (John 11:17). In Jewish tradition, the soul was believed to linger near the body for three days - so by day four, death was considered final. Hope had run out.

Martha met Jesus outside the village and said, "*Lord, if You had been here, my brother would not have died*" (John 11:21). In this moment of raw grief, Jesus did not just offer comfort - He made a radical claim: "*I am the resurrection and the life.*" He was not pointing to a future event or offering a theological idea. He was saying, "I am the source of resurrection. I am the power of life itself.

This promise has two parts. First, Jesus says, "*He who believes in Me will live even if he dies.*" This means that physical death is not the end for believers. Even if your body dies, you will live again - resurrected at the end of time. Second, He adds, "*Everyone who lives and believes in Me will never die.*" This refers to spiritual death. For those who trust in Jesus, eternal separation from God is impossible. Your soul is secure forever.

Then Jesus asks Martha, "*Do you believe this?*" It is a question that still echoes today. Do you trust Jesus to conquer death for you?

To prove His claim, Jesus went to Lazarus' tomb, prayed, and called out, "*Lazarus, come forth!*" (John 11:43). And Lazarus walked out, alive, still wrapped in burial cloths. This miracle caused many to glorify God, but it also alarmed the Pharisees, who began plotting to kill Jesus (John 11:45–53). The raising of Lazarus was not just a miracle - it was a preview of Jesus' own resurrection, a declaration that death does not have the final word.

Think of Jesus as the ultimate hero who defeats the darkest villain - death itself. Like a superhero who arrives when all hope seems lost, Jesus offers victory over death's grip. Whether you are facing fears about the future or mourning someone you have lost, Jesus promises that He is the Resurrection and the Life, and that eternal life is yours through Him.

A Miracle That Shakes Beliefs

The story of Lazarus in John 11 is one of the most dramatic miracles in Scripture, and it happens just before Jesus' own crucifixion. Bethany was only two miles from Jerusalem, and many Jews had come to mourn with Mary and Martha (John 11:19). Among them were religious leaders who opposed Jesus. By raising Lazarus in front of this crowd, Jesus provided undeniable evidence of His divine power, fulfilling Old Testament prophecies about the Messiah who would bring life.

The reaction of the Pharisees reveals the tension. In John 11:47–48, we read: *"The chief priests and the Pharisees convened a council, and were saying, 'What are we doing? For this man is performing many signs. If we let Him go on like this, all men will believe in Him.'"*

Instead of celebrating the miracle, they feared losing their influence and plotted to kill Jesus. This moment marked a turning point, setting the stage for Jesus' death and resurrection - His ultimate victory over death.

The Old Testament had long foretold this hope. Isaiah 25:8 proclaims: *"He will swallow up death for all time, and the Lord God will wipe tears away from all faces."*

Jesus fulfills this prophecy, showing that His power as the Resurrection and the Life brings comfort, hope, and eternal life to all who grieve.

Life Beyond the Grave

The truth of Jesus' resurrection is not just about the future - it transforms how we live today. Colossians 3:1–2 connects this reality to our daily mindset: *"Therefore if you have been raised up with Christ, keep seeking the things above, where Christ is, seated at the right hand of God. Set your mind on the things above, not on the things that are on earth."*

Because Jesus rose from the dead, believers are spiritually raised with Him. This means living with eternal priorities - focusing on God's kingdom rather than temporary things like popularity or possessions. This is a call to live with purpose, knowing your life matters forever.

The phrase *"no second death"* refers to Revelation 21:8, which warns: *"But for the cowardly and unbelieving and abominable... their part will be in the lake that burns with fire and brimstone, which is the second death."*

This "*second death*" is eternal separation from God for those who reject Jesus. But for believers, Jesus' promise ensures that they "*will never die*" spiritually - they are safe from this judgment.

Here are additional scriptures to deepen this truth

1 Corinthians 15:20-22 - "*But now Christ has been raised from the dead, the first fruits of those who are asleep. For since by a man came death, by a man also came the resurrection of the dead. For as in Adam all die, so also in Christ all will be made alive.*" Jesus' resurrection guarantees that believers will rise, undoing the death brought by Adam's sin.

John 5:24 - "*Truly, truly, I say to you, he who hears My word, and believes Him who sent Me, has eternal life, and does not come into judgment, but has passed out of death into life.*" Faith in Jesus moves you from spiritual death to eternal life, free from judgment.

Romans 6:4-5 - "*Therefore, we have been buried with Him through baptism into death, so that as Christ was raised from the dead through the glory of the Father, so we too might walk in newness of life. For if we have become united with Him in the likeness of His death, certainly we shall also be in the likeness of His resurrection.*" This connects our spiritual rebirth to Jesus' resurrection, promising a new life now and a future resurrection.

Living with Jesus as the Resurrection and the Life

So how do you live with Jesus as the Resurrection and the Life - not just as a theological truth, but as a daily reality? It begins with letting His victory over death reshape how you face grief, how you make decisions, and how you share hope with others.

One way to live this truth is by finding hope in grief. Losing someone you love is deeply painful, and death can feel overwhelming or final. But Jesus' promise means that death is not the end for those who believe in Him. If you are grieving, you can pray and trust Jesus to comfort you. 2 Corinthians 1:3–4 offers this assurance: "*Blessed be the God and Father of our Lord Jesus Christ, the Father of mercies and God of all comfort, who comforts us in all our affliction.*"

Jesus does not just offer sympathy - He offers supernatural comfort. Lean on Him in tough times, knowing that He walks with you through sorrow and promises eternal reunion with those who belong to Him. Another way to live with Jesus as the Resurrection and the Life is by choosing to live with eternal perspective.

Colossians 3:1–2 encourages: *"Therefore if you have been raised up with Christ, keep seeking the things above… Set your mind on the things above, not on the things that are on earth."*

This means shifting your focus from temporary to what truly lasts: your relationship with Jesus and your impact for His kingdom. For example, instead of chasing popularity, choose kindness. Instead of stressing over perfection, pursue integrity. These choices reflect a heart set on eternity.

You can also live this truth by trusting Jesus' power in your everyday challenges. The same power that raised Lazarus from the dead is available to you. Whether you are facing stress, fear, or uncertainty about the future, Jesus has authority over it all.

Philippians 4:13 reminds us: *"I can do all things through Him who strengthens me."* This is not just a motivational slogan - **it is a promise**. Jesus strengthens you to face what feels impossible, whether it is a difficult test, a broken friendship, or a season of anxiety. Trust that He is with you, empowering you to overcome.

Finally, living with Jesus as the Resurrection and the Life means sharing that hope with others. If a friend is struggling with fear, loss, or questions about life after death, do not be afraid to speak up. Share how Jesus has given you peace and purpose.

1 Peter 3:15 encourages: *"Always being ready to make a defense to everyone who asks you to give an account for the hope that is in you."*

Jesus, the Way, the Truth, the Life, - and the Vine

Life can often feel like "walking through a maze of high corn on a very hazy day," with countless paths promising many things. But in the midst of this noise, Jesus makes a bold and clarifying claim: He is *"the Way, the Truth, and the Life,"* and He is *"the Vine."* These declarations are not just inspirational - **they are foundational**. They reveal Jesus as the only path to God and the source of a fruitful, meaningful life.

In John 14:6, Jesus says: *"I am the way, and the truth, and the life; no one comes to the Father but through Me."*

This statement was spoken on the night before Jesus' crucifixion, in an upper room in Jerusalem where Jesus and His disciples were sharing the Last Supper. The atmosphere was tense - Jesus had just told His disciples that He was going away, and they were confused and anxious.

Earlier, in John 14:1–3, He had comforted them with these words: *"Do not let your heart be troubled; believe in God, believe also in Me. In My Father's house are many dwelling places... I am going to prepare a place for you... I will come again and receive you to Myself, that where I am, there you may be also."*

When Thomas asked, *"Lord, we do not know where You are going, how do we know the way?"* (John 14:5), Jesus responded with this profound declaration. He was not just offering reassurance - He was revealing His divine identity and exclusive role in salvation.

Jesus' statement has three parts, each rich with meaning.

First, He says, "I am the way." Jesus does not merely point to a path - He is the path. Imagine trying to enter an exclusive event with only one entrance and one valid ticket. Jesus is both the gate and the ticket. No other route can bring you into God's presence.

Second, He says, "I am the truth." In a world flooded with opinions, misinformation, and shifting values, Jesus stands as the ultimate source of truth. His teachings, His life, and His resurrection reveal the reality of God's love and justice. He does not just speak truth - He embodies it.

Third, He says, "I am the life." Jesus offers more than existence - He offers eternal life. He frees us from spiritual death caused by sin and invites us into a relationship that begins now and lasts forever.

The phrase *"no one comes to the Father but through Me"* is exclusive and essential. It challenges the idea that all spiritual paths lead to God. In Jesus' time, this claim confronted religious leaders who relied on laws and rituals. Today, it pushes back against the notion of relative truth.

Acts 4:12 reinforces this: *"And there is salvation in no one else; for there is no other name under heaven that has been given among men by which we must be saved."* Spoken by Peter after Jesus' resurrection, this verse confirms that salvation is found only in Jesus. His death and resurrection proved His claim, making Him the only bridge between humanity and God.

The Vine: Jesus as the Source of Fruitful Living

In John 15:5, Jesus says: *"I am the vine, you are the branches; he who abides in Me and I in him, he bears much fruit, for apart from Me you can do nothing."*

This statement was also spoken on the night before Jesus' crucifixion. After the Last Supper, Jesus and His disciples left the upper room and walked toward the Garden of Gethsemane. As they passed through the city - perhaps near a vineyard or a vine-covered gate - Jesus used a familiar image to teach a vital truth. He said He is the Vine, God the Father is the vinedresser (the gardener), and His followers are the branches.

In ancient Israel, vineyards were everywhere, and everyone understood that branches must stay connected to the vine to produce grapes. A branch cut off from the vine withers and dies. Jesus uses this image to show that staying connected to Him through faith, prayer, and obedience is essential for a fruitful life.

The Greek word for "abide" (*meno*) means **to remain, dwell,** or **stay connected.** Jesus is telling His disciples - and us - that spiritual growth, good works, and a life that glorifies God all depend on staying rooted in Him. The phrase *"apart from Me you can do nothing"* is a sobering reminder that without Jesus, our efforts for God's kingdom are empty.

Colossians 2:6–7 connects beautifully to this truth: *"Therefore as you have received Christ Jesus the Lord, so walk in Him, having been firmly rooted and now being built up in Him and established in your faith... and overflowing with gratitude."*

This verse encourages believers to stay rooted in Jesus, growing stronger in faith and overflowing with gratitude. Like a branch drawing life from the vine, we thrive by staying connected to Christ.

Imagine your life as a phone that needs to stay plugged into a power source. Jesus is the Vine - the source of your spiritual energy. When you are connected to Him, you produce fruit like love, kindness, and courage. But if you unplug - relying on yourself or the world - you will run out of power and wither.

The Exclusivity and Intimacy of Jesus

The declarations in John 14:6 and John 15:5 are profound theological truths that reveal both the exclusivity and intimacy of Jesus. As *"the Way, the Truth, and the Life,"* Jesus does not offer one option among many; He offers Himself as the only bridge to God.

His resurrection is the ultimate validation of this claim. As Paul writes in 1 Corinthians 15:17 - *"If Christ has not been raised, your faith is worthless; you are still in your sins."* Without the resurrection, Jesus' words would be empty. But because He conquered death, His promise of eternal life is trustworthy. No other spiritual leader has done this. Jesus stands alone.

And yet, this exclusivity does not lead to distance - it leads to intimacy. In John 15:5, Jesus calls Himself "the Vine," inviting us into a relationship that is not transactional but transformational. He does not just want to save us - He wants to live in us. This is not a one-time decision but a daily rhythm of abiding.

John 15:4 captures this beautifully: *"Abide in Me, and I in you. As the branch cannot bear fruit of itself unless it abides in the vine, so neither can you unless you abide in Me."* Jesus is not a distant deity - He is a present companion. Think of Him like a best friend who is always there, whispering truth when you are confused, offering strength when you are weak, and celebrating with you when you grow.

Additional scriptures:

John 6:44 - "No one can come to Me unless the Father who sent Me draws him; and I will raise him up on the last day." This supports Jesus as the only Way, showing that God draws people to Him through Jesus.

Galatians 5:22-23 - "But the fruit of the Spirit is love, joy, peace, patience, kindness, goodness, faithfulness, gentleness, self-control; against such things there is no law." This describes the "fruit" we bear when connected to 'The Vine'.

Living with Jesus as the Way, the Truth, the Life, and the Vine

So how do you live this out? How do you walk with Jesus in the everyday ups and downs of life? Here are four practical ways to apply these truths:

1. Trust Jesus as Your Only Way. It is easy to believe that good grades, popularity, or being "good enough" will earn God's favor. But Jesus says otherwise. Remember, salvation is not a reward - it is a gift. Ephesians 2:8–9 makes this clear: *"For by grace you have been saved through faith; and that not of yourselves, it is the gift of God; not as a result of works."* When you feel pressure to perform or prove yourself, remember: Jesus already did the work. Trust Him as your only way to God.

2. Seek His Truth. In a world full of conflicting messages - about identity, success, and morality - Jesus' truth is your anchor. When you are making decisions, like choosing friends or responding to peer pressure, let His Word guide you. The Sermon on the Mount (Matthew 5–7) is a great place to start. God's truth does not just inform - **it illuminates**.

3. Abide in Him Daily. Staying connected to Jesus is not a Sunday-only thing - it is a daily rhythm. Start your morning with a simple prayer: "Jesus, help me stay connected to You today." Read a short passage from the Gospels. Listen to worship music. Talk to Him throughout your day. Contemplate daily John 15:7 - *"If you abide in Me, and My words abide in you, ask whatever you wish, and it will be done for you."* Abiding is like plugging into a power source. Stay connected, and you will stay strong.

4. *Bear Fruit for Others*. Jesus does not just change you - He uses you to bless others. Let His life flow through you in love, kindness, and courage. Share your faith when the moment feels right. Matthew 5:16 says: *"Let your light shine before men in such a way that they may see your good works, and glorify your Father who is in heaven."* Your fruit is not just for you - it is for the world.

Jesus, the Alpha and the Omega—Eternal King and Creator

Imagine standing at the edge of the universe, staring into the night sky, wondering how everything began and where it is all heading. The stars stretch endlessly above you, and time itself feels like a mystery too vast to grasp. In that moment, Jesus steps forward with a declaration that anchors everything: *"I am the Alpha and the Omega."* This is not just poetic language - it is a cosmic claim. Jesus is the beginning and the end of all things, the eternal God who created the universe and the King who will bring it to completion.

This title, part of Jesus' divine self-revelation in the Book of Revelation, reveals His authority over all creation and His promise to include His followers in His eternal reign. In a world that often feels chaotic and uncertain, this truth offers hope, stability, and purpose.

Jesus' Eternal Sovereignty

In Revelation 1:8, Jesus proclaims: *"I am the Alpha and the Omega," says the Lord God, "who is and who was and who is to come, the Almighty."*

Later, in Revelation 22:13, He declares: *"I am the Alpha and the Omega, the first and the last, the beginning and the end."*

To understand these verses, picture the Apostle John – (now elderly and exiled on the island of Patmos around 95 A.D.). He has been imprisoned for his faith, and the early church is suffering under Roman persecution. In this dark moment, Jesus appears to John in a vision, radiant with glory, revealing the future of God's kingdom. The Book of Revelation is filled with dramatic imagery - angels, thrones, cosmic battles - but at its center is Jesus, the triumphant King.

The phrase *"Alpha and Omega"* comes from the first and last letters of the Greek alphabet. **It is a symbol of totality** - Jesus encompasses all of time and existence. He is the Alpha, the Creator who spoke the universe into being, and He is the Omega, the Lord who will bring history to its final, glorious chapter. The phrase *"who is and who was and who is to come"* emphasizes His eternal nature - Jesus exists now, has always existed, and will return in power.

Revelation 22:13 reinforces this truth in the final chapter of the Bible, where Jesus speaks as the risen Lord, preparing to return and establish His eternal kingdom. His additional titles - "the first and the last, the beginning and the end" - mirror Isaiah 44:6: *"Thus says the Lord, the King of Israel and his Redeemer, the Lord of hosts: 'I am the first and I am the last, and there is no God besides Me.'"*

For Jesus to take this title is a bold claim of equality with God, confirming His role as Creator and Ruler over all. Think of Jesus as the author of a cosmic story. He wrote the first chapter - creation. He is guiding the plot - your life, history, and the world. And He will write the final chapter - His return and eternal reign. No matter how confusing or overwhelming life feels, Jesus is in control, from start to finish.

Jesus' Glory in a Time of Persecution

The Book of Revelation (in part) was written to encourage Christians who were suffering for their faith during the age it was penned. In Revelation 1:9–18, John describes seeing Jesus in a vision - His eyes like flames of fire, His voice like rushing waters, His face shining like the sun. This was not a gentle image - it was a vision of power, majesty, and holiness. Jesus appeared not as a humble carpenter, but as the exalted King of the universe.

This vision was meant to inspire awe and hope. It reminded believers that Jesus is the Almighty, far above any earthly ruler - including the

Roman emperor who claimed divine status. Revelation 19:16 captures this truth: *"And on His robe and on His thigh, He has a name written: 'KING OF KINGS, AND LORD OF LORDS.'"*

This title appears during a vision of Jesus' return, riding a white horse to defeat evil and establish His kingdom (Revelation 19:11–16). For early Christians facing death, this was a powerful promise: Jesus will win. It is a reminder that Jesus is bigger than any challenge - stress, family struggles, or global chaos.

Jesus as Creator and Sustainer

Again, turn to Colossians 1:15–17 which ties directly to Jesus' role as Creator: *"He is the image of the invisible God, the firstborn of all creation. For by Him all things were created, both in the heavens and on earth... all things have been created through Him and for Him. He is before all things, and in Him all things hold together."*

This passage reveals that Jesus did not just show up in Bethlehem - He was present at creation. Everything in the universe was made through Him and for Him. He is the Alpha. John 1:1–3 echoes this truth: *"In the beginning was the Word, and the Word was with God, and the Word was God... All things came into being through Him, and apart from Him not even one thing came into being that has come into being."*

Jesus is the Word - the divine expression of God - who created all things. As the Omega, He holds everything together and will bring creation to its intended purpose. This means Jesus is not just a historical figure or a religious symbol. He is the eternal God who knows you, who made you, and who has a plan for your life. When you feel small or uncertain, remember: the One who created galaxies also created you - and He is writing your story with love and purpose.

Living with Jesus as the Alpha and Omega

So how do you live with Jesus as your Alpha and Omega? How do you let this truth shape your everyday choices, especially in the whirlwind of high school life?

Here are four practical ways to apply this truth:

1. Trust His Sovereignty. When life feels chaotic - whether it is stress about college applications, family tensions, or global uncertainty - remember that Jesus is in control. He is the beginning and the end of your story.

Romans 8:28 offers comfort: *"And we know that God causes all things to work together for good to those who love God, to those who are called according to His purpose."* Even when things do not make sense, Jesus is weaving your life into His greater plan. Trust Him to guide your story.

2. Focus on Eternity. It is easy to get caught up in temporary things, but Jesus calls us to lift our eyes. Colossians 3:2 says: *"Set your minds on the things that are above, not on the things that are on earth."* When you focus on eternity, your priorities shift. You begin to value kindness over popularity, truth over trends, and faith over fear.

3. Live with Purpose. Knowing that Jesus is the Creator and King gives your life meaning. Every choice you make - whether helping a friend, standing up for justice, or sharing your faith - can reflect His glory. 1 Corinthians 10:31 reminds us: *"Whether, then, you eat or drink or whatever you do, do all to the glory of God." Your life is not random. It is a canvas for God's glory."*

4. Share His Hope. Jesus, the Alpha and Omega, offers eternal life - and That is news worth sharing. You do not need a sermon - just a conversation. Tell a friend how Jesus gives you peace or how He is helped you through a tough time. 1 Peter 3:15 encourages: *"But sanctify Christ as Lord in your hearts, always being ready to make a defense to everyone who asks you to give an account for the hope that is in you, but with gentleness and respect."*

12

Your Certificate of Debt Canceled

Imagine you have racked up a massive credit card bill - thousands of dollars you can never repay. Every wrong choice, every mistake, adds to the debt, and the interest keeps piling up. You are trapped, with no way out. Then someone steps in, pays the entire bill in full, and tears up the statement, freeing you completely. That is what Jesus did for you on the cross. His death was not just a noble act or a symbolic gesture - it was the ultimate payment for your sins, canceling the "certificate of debt" that stood against you. This act of love, known as substitutionary atonement, means Jesus took your place, paying the penalty for your sins so you could be reconciled to God.

The Bible teaches that Jesus' sacrifice was sufficient - complete and final - for everyone who trusts in Him. Unlike other spiritual paths that demand you earn forgiveness through good deeds or rituals, Jesus offers a gift of grace that changes everything. Let us explore the scriptures that reveal the power of His sacrifice and how it can transform your life.

Jesus' Complete Payment

In 1 Peter 3:18, the Apostle Peter writes: *"For Christ also died for sins once for all, the just for the unjust, so that He might bring us to God, having been put to death in the flesh, but made alive in the spirit."*

This verse captures the heart of Jesus' mission. Written around 64 A.D. to encourage persecuted Christians, Peter reminds them that Jesus - the "just," sinless one - died for the "unjust," sinners like us. The phrase "once for all" is crucial. It means Jesus' death was a one-time, complete payment for all sins - past, present, and future. Unlike the Old Testament system, where priests offered animal sacrifices repeatedly to temporarily cover sins (see Hebrews 10:11), Jesus' sacrifice was perfect and final. It fully satisfied God's justice and opened the way to reconciliation.

Paul expands this truth in Colossians 2:13–14 : *"When you were dead in your transgressions and the uncircumcision of your flesh, He made you alive together with Him, having forgiven us all our transgressions, having canceled out the certificate of debt consisting of decrees against* us, which was hostile to us; and He has taken it out of the way, having nailed it to the cross."

This passage uses a vivid image: a "certificate of debt" - a legal document listing our sins and their penalties. It was "hostile" to us because we couldn't pay it. Sin makes us spiritually dead, separated from God (see Ephesians 2:1). But Jesus canceled this debt by nailing it to the cross. **He did not just erase the record - He paid it in full.**

Imagine a report card filled with failing grades for every mistake you have ever made. Jesus takes that report, tears it up, and gives you a perfect score - not because you earned it, but because He paid the price for you.

Peter continues this theme in 1 Peter 2:24–25 - *"He Himself bore our sins in His body on the cross, so that we might die to sin and live to righteousness; for by His wounds you were healed. For you were continually straying like sheep, but now you have returned to the Shepherd and Guardian of your souls."*

Here, Jesus' sacrifice is connected to His role as the Good Shepherd (John 10:11). By bearing our sins on the cross, He healed us spiritually and restored us to God. The imagery of straying sheep reminds us of our tendency to wander into sin, but Jesus - the Shepherd - brings us back to safety, guiding us into righteousness.

Peter also emphasizes the value of Jesus' sacrifice in 1 Peter 1:18–19, 23 : *"You were not redeemed with perishable things like silver or gold from your futile way of life inherited from your forefathers, but with precious blood, as of a lamb unblemished and spotless, the blood of Christ... for you have been born again not of seed which is perishable but imperishable, that is, through the living and enduring word of God."*

Jesus is compared to a perfect sacrificial lamb, fulfilling Old Testament imagery like the Passover lamb (Exodus 12:5–13). His "precious blood" paid a price far greater than money, redeeming us from slavery to sin and giving us a new, imperishable life through faith.

Paul explains the freedom we gain in Romans 6:6–7, 10–11, 17–18, 22:

"Knowing this, that our old self was crucified with Him, in order that our body of sin might be done away with, so that we would no longer be slaves to sin; for the one who has died is freed from sin... The death that He died, He died to sin once for all time; but the life that He lives, He lives to God. So you too, consider yourselves to be dead to sin, but alive to God in Christ Jesus... But thanks be to God that though you were slaves of sin, you became obedient from the heart to that form of teaching to which you were entrusted, and after being freed from sin, you became slaves to righteousness... But now, having been freed from sin and enslaved to God, you derive your benefit, resulting in sanctification, and the outcome, eternal life."

This passage shows that Jesus' death breaks sin's power over us. Our "old self" - the part controlled by sin - dies with Christ, freeing us to live for God. This process of sanctification means growing in holiness, with the ultimate outcome of eternal life.

Think of sin as a heavy chain binding you to guilt, shame, or destructive habits. Jesus' death on the cross shatters that chain, setting you free to live a new life powered by His Spirit. You are no longer a slave to sin's demands - you are free to follow Jesus and live with purpose.

Jesus' Sacrifice in God's Plan

To truly grasp the power of Jesus' death and resurrection, we must first understand the ancient framework it fulfills. In the Old Testament, God's people offered animal sacrifices to atone for their sins. These rituals - repeated year after year - were never meant to be permanent solutions. As Hebrews 10:4 declares: *"For it is impossible for the blood of bulls and goats to take away sins."*

These sacrifices pointed forward to a greater, perfect offering. That fulfillment came in Jesus, the Lamb of God. The prophet Isaiah, writing centuries before Jesus' birth, foresaw this in Isaiah 53:5 - *"But He was pierced through for our transgressions, He was crushed for our iniquities; the chastisement for our well-being fell upon Him, and by His scourging we are healed."*

This verse is a prophetic portrait of substitutionary suffering. Jesus was *"pierced"* and *"crushed"* - not for His own wrongdoing, but for ours. The punishment that brought us peace fell on Him, and His wounds became the source of our healing. This was not a tragic accident - it was God's deliberate plan to rescue humanity.

Jesus' death on a Roman cross was not random or merely political. It was the centerpiece of God's redemptive plan. Even the religious leaders and Roman officials who condemned Him were unknowingly fulfilling divine prophecy. As Peter boldly proclaimed in Acts 2:23 - *"This Man, delivered over by the predetermined plan and foreknowledge of God, you nailed to a cross by the hands of godless men and put Him to death."*

Three days later, Jesus rose from the dead, proving His victory over sin and death. His resurrection confirmed that His sacrifice was sufficient - no further payment was needed. This truth became the foundation of the early church's teaching, especially in the face of persecution and temptation. Peter and Paul emphasized that believers did not need to add rituals or good deeds to earn God's favor. Jesus' blood covered it all.

This message remains just as relevant today. In a world that often teaches you must earn love, approval, or forgiveness, the gospel offers something radically different: grace. Jesus paid the debt you could not pay. You do not have to perform to be accepted - you simply receive.

Freedom from Sin's Dominion

Jesus' sacrifice does not just cancel a legal debt - it breaks the power of sin itself. This victory over death also means a transfer of spiritual authority. Colossians 1:13 explains: *"For He rescued us from the domain of darkness and transferred us to the kingdom of His beloved Son."*

Before Jesus, we were trapped under sin's dominion - enslaved to guilt, fear, and spiritual death. But through His death and resurrection, we have been rescued and relocated. We now belong to a new kingdom, ruled by grace and truth.

This does not mean we will never struggle with sin. But it does mean sin no longer has the final say. Its power is broken. The Holy Spirit now empowers us to live victoriously, growing in holiness through daily surrender.

Hebrews 10:12–14 reinforces this truth: *"But He, having offered one sacrifice for sins for all time, sat down at the right hand of God... For by one offering He has perfected for all time those who are sanctified."*

Jesus' sacrifice was so complete that He sat down - His work was finished. And through that one offering, He perfected believers forever. Sanctification - the process of becoming more like Jesus - is now possible because of His finished work.

John the Baptist recognized this when he saw Jesus approaching. In John 1:29, he exclaimed: *"Behold, the Lamb of God who takes away the sin of the world!"* Jesus was not just a teacher or prophet - He was the Lamb, the ultimate sacrifice who removes sin's penalty for all who believe.

Applying the 'Payment Paid in Full'

So how can you live with your "certificate of debt" canceled? Here are four practical ways to apply this truth in your daily life:

1. Accept Jesus' payment. If you feel weighed down by guilt or think you need to earn God's love, remember that Jesus already paid for all your sins. 1 John 1:9 offers this promise: *"If we confess our sins, He is faithful and righteous, so that He will forgive us our sins and cleanse us from all unrighteousness."* Confession is not about shame - **it is about freedom**. When you bring your sins to Jesus, He does not condemn you. He forgives and cleanses you.

2. Live free from sin's control. When you are tempted - whether it is lying, cheating, gossiping, or giving in to peer pressure - remember that sin no longer owns you. You have the power to choose righteousness. Galatians 5:16 says: *"But I say, walk by the Spirit, and you will not carry out the desire of the flesh."* Walking by the Spirit means staying close to Jesus - through prayer, Scripture, and community. He gives you strength to resist temptation and live with integrity.

3. *Grow in sanctification.* Sanctification is the journey of becoming more like Jesus. **It is not about perfection - it is about progress.** Start by reading the Bible daily (the Gospel of John is a great place to begin), praying honestly, and reflecting Jesus' love in your actions. Philippians 1:6 encourages: *"For I am confident of this very thing, that He who began a good work among you will complete it by the day of Christ Jesus."* God is not finished with you. He is shaping you, day by day, into someone who reflects His beauty and truth.

By Faith It is Calvary Plus Nothing

Imagine you are drowning in a stormy sea, unable to swim to shore. You are helpless, flailing, with no way to save yourself. Then, a lifeguard dives in, pulls you to safety, and gives you a new chance at life - all without you earning it. That is what Jesus did on the cross. His death and resurrection paid the full price for your sins, offering you salvation as a free gift. The Bible calls this "justification by faith" -you are made right with God not by your own efforts, but by trusting in Jesus' sacrifice alone. The phrase "Calvary plus nothing" captures this truth: Jesus' work on the cross is enough. Nothing more is needed for you to be reconciled to God.

In a world that constantly tells you to earn your worth, Jesus offers a radically different way. His sacrifice at Calvary, where He shed His blood and rose again, is the complete payment for your sins. By faith, you can accept this gift and live in peace with God. Let us explore the scriptures that reveal this truth and see how "Calvary plus nothing" can transform your life, giving you confidence, freedom, and a secure hope in eternity.

Justification by Faith: The Heart of Salvation

The Apostle Paul, writing to the church in Rome around 57 A.D., opens Romans 5:1–2 with this declaration: *"Therefore, having been justified by faith, we have peace with God through our Lord Jesus Christ, through whom also we have obtained our introduction by faith into this grace in which we stand; and we exult in hope of the glory of God."*

Here, *"justified by faith"* means **being declared righteous** in God's sight - not because of what we have done, but because of what Jesus has done. Sin makes us guilty before a holy God, but faith in Jesus' death and resurrection makes us right with Him. This brings *"peace with God,"* ending the hostility caused by sin and giving us access to His grace - a gift we do not earn. Imagine being in trouble with a teacher for breaking a rule. Jesus steps in, takes the blame, and restores your relationship with the teacher. That is what justification does with God.

Paul continues in Romans 5:8–10: *"But God demonstrates His own love toward us, in that while we were still sinners, Christ died for us. Much more then, having now been justified by His blood, we shall be saved from the wrath of God through Him. For if while we were enemies we were reconciled to God through the death of His Son, much more, having been reconciled, we shall be saved by His life."*

This passage highlights the depth of God's love. Jesus did not wait for us to clean up our act - He died for us while we were still sinners, still His enemies. His blood justifies us, saving us from God's righteous judgment against sin. And His resurrection - *"saved by His life"* - secures our ongoing salvation. This means you do not have to be perfect before coming to Jesus. He loves you as you are and paid the price to bring you home.

Romans 3:23–25, 28 clarifies this even further: *"For all have sinned and fall short of the glory of God, being justified as a gift by His grace through the redemption which is in Christ Jesus, whom God displayed publicly as a propitiation in His blood through faith... For we maintain that a person is justified by faith apart from works of the Law."*

Paul makes it clear: everyone has sinned. No one meets God's perfect standard. But God offers justification as a gift. This gift comes through faith, not through rule-following or good deeds.

Galatians 2:16 reinforces this truth: *"Nevertheless, knowing that a person is not justified by works of the Law but through faith in Christ Jesus, even we have believed in Christ Jesus so that we may be justified by faith in Christ and not by works of the Law; since by works of the Law no flesh will be justified."* Written to churches in Galatia, this verse addresses Christians tempted to rely on religious rules - like circumcision or temple rituals - for salvation. Paul insists that no one can earn justification through works. Only faith in Jesus saves.

Galatians 3:11, 13, 24–26 adds layers of meaning: *"Now that no one is justified by the Law before God is evident; for, 'The righteous one will live by faith.' Christ redeemed us from the curse of the Law, having become a curse for us... Therefore, the Law has become our guardian to lead us to Christ, so that we may be justified by faith. But now that faith has come, we are no longer under a guardian. For you are all sons and daughters of God through faith in Christ Jesus."*

The Law was like a tutor - it showed people their sin, but it could not save. Jesus took the curse of sin upon Himself on the cross, freeing us to become sons and daughters of God through faith. This means you are not just forgiven - **you are adopted**. You belong to God's family, loved and accepted because of Jesus.

Hebrews 11:6 ties it all together: *"And without faith it is impossible to please Him, for the one who comes to God must believe that He exists, and that He proves to be One who rewards those who seek Him."* Faith is the key to pleasing God - not performance, not perfection. Believing in Jesus' finished work at Calvary is what opens the door to relationship, reward, and eternal life. His sacrifice is sufficient. Nothing needs to be added.

Jesus' Finished Work at Calvary

To understand the power of these scriptures, we need to step back into the ancient world of the Old Testament. God's people lived under the Law of Moses, which included a system of animal sacrifices to temporarily cover their sins. These rituals were repeated year after year, especially on the Day of Atonement, when the high priest would offer blood for the sins of the people. Leviticus 16:15–16 describes this practice: *"Then he shall slaughter the goat of the sin offering, which is for the people, and bring its blood inside the veil... and he shall make atonement for the holy place... because of the sins of the sons of Israel."*

But these sacrifices were never meant to be permanent. They pointed forward to a greater solution. As Hebrews 10:4 declares: *"For it is impossible for the blood of bulls and goats to take away sins."* Animal blood could only cover sin - it couldn't remove it. That is why Jesus came. His death on the cross fulfilled this entire system. Unlike the animals, Jesus was sinless. As Paul writes in 2 Corinthians 5:21 - *"He made Him who knew no sin to be sin on our behalf, so that we might become the righteousness of God in Him."* Jesus took our sin upon Himself, though He had never sinned. His resurrection proved His victory over sin and death, validating His claim to be "the resurrection and the life.

The early Christians, facing pressure from groups like the Judaizers - who insisted on following the Law for salvation - needed to hear that Jesus' work was enough. Paul and Peter wrote passionately to counter these false teachings.

The phrase "Calvary plus nothing" emphasizes that Jesus' death is sufficient. Adding requirements - like good deeds, rituals, or religious performance - implies His sacrifice was not enough, which contradicts scripture. Hebrews 10:12 affirms this: *"But He, having offered one sacrifice for sins for all time, sat down at the right hand of God."*

Jesus' act of sitting down signifies completion. In the temple, priests never sat - because their work was never finished. But Jesus sat down, declaring that the payment was made in full.

Faith in Christ's Sufficient Sacrifice

Scripture stresses that if Jesus' death is not enough, then His sacrifice was in vain. Paul echoes this in Galatians 2:21 - *"I do not nullify the grace of God, for if righteousness comes through the Law, then Christ died needlessly."* This verse is a bold defense of grace. If we could earn righteousness through rules or rituals, then Jesus' death was pointless. But we cannot. His sacrifice is the cornerstone of salvation.

Faith in Jesus means trusting that His blood paid for all sins. 1 John 2:2 declares: *"And He Himself is the propitiation for our sins; and not for ours only, but also for the sins of the whole world."*

"Propitiation" means Jesus satisfied God's justice. His death was not just symbolic - **it was substitutionary.** He took the punishment we deserved. And this offer is universal. Anyone - no matter their past - can be saved by faith. Romans 5:9 confirms the result: *"Much more then, having now been justified by His blood, we shall be saved from the wrath of God through Him."*

Jesus' resurrection proves His victory. Believers are justified - declared righteous - and freed from God's wrath. We are no longer condemned. Another passage I suggest memorizing that reinforces this truth is Ephesians 2:8-9 - *"For by grace you have been saved through faith; and this is not of yourselves, it is the gift of God; not a result of works, so that no one may boast."*

Salvation is a gift. You do not earn it. You receive it by faith. This ensures that all glory goes to God - not to us. Faith in Jesus is the only requirement for eternal life. Not religion. Not performance. Just belief. The Holy Spirit transforms us - not because we are good, but because God is merciful. Salvation is by faith alone in Christ's finished work, freeing us from the exhausting burden of trying to earn God's favor.

Living by Faith

So how can you live by faith in "Calvary plus nothing"? Let us explore four practical ways to apply this truth in your daily life.

First, trust Jesus' finished work. If you feel unworthy or think you need to earn God's love, rest in Jesus' complete payment. When guilt creeps in, pray and claim 1 John 1:9 - *"If we confess our sins, He is faithful and righteous, so that He will forgive us our sins and cleanse us from all unrighteousness."* Confession is not about earning forgiveness - it is about receiving it. Jesus is faithful. He forgives and cleanses.

Second, find peace in God. Romans 5:1 promises: *"Therefore, having been justified by faith, we have peace with God through our Lord Jesus Christ."* When you are stressed about school, relationships, or the future, trust Jesus to give you peace. Philippians 4:6–7 encourages: *"Do not be anxious about anything, but in everything by prayer and pleading with thanksgiving let your requests be made known to God. And the peace of God, which surpasses all comprehension, will guard your hearts and minds in Christ Jesus."* God's peace is not shallow - it is deep, guarding your heart like armor.

Third, live by faith, not by works. Resist the pressure to prove your worth through achievements or behavior. Instead, live to honor Jesus, knowing your salvation is secure. Galatians 5:22–23 describes the fruit of faith: *"But the fruit of the Spirit is love, joy, peace, patience, kindness, goodness, faithfulness, gentleness, self-control; against such things there is no law."* These qualities flow from faith - not effort. They are signs of a life rooted in Jesus.

The Free Gift of Grace

Imagine you are handed a beautifully wrapped present on your birthday - completely free, with no strings attached. You did not earn it, you did not pay for it - it is simply a gift from someone who loves you. Now imagine that gift is eternal life with God, offered through Jesus' death and resurrection. The Bible calls this the *"free gift of grace,"* meaning salvation is something God gives you, not something you can achieve through good deeds, church attendance, or personal effort. Trying to add your own efforts to Jesus' work is like trying to pay for a gift you have already been given - it dishonors the giver and misunderstands the nature of grace.

Let us explore the scriptures that reveal this truth and see how the free gift of God's grace can transform your life, giving you freedom, hope, and a secure future with God.

Salvation Through Faith Alone

Paul, writing to the church in Rome, makes a powerful contrast in Romans 6:23 - *"For the wages of sin is death, but the gracious gift of God is eternal life in Christ Jesus our Lord."*

Sin earns wages - death, both physical and spiritual. It is what we deserve. But God offers a *"gracious gift"* - eternal life through Jesus. This gift is not earned; it is received. Jesus paid the penalty for sin on the cross, and anyone who trusts in Him receives life, not death.

Paul elaborates on this in Ephesians 2:4–6, 8–9 : *"But God, being rich in mercy, because of His great love with which He loved us, even when we were dead in our wrongdoings, made us alive together with Christ (by grace you have been saved), and raised us up with Him, and seated us with Him in the heavenly places in Christ Jesus... For by grace you have been saved through faith; and this is not of yourselves, it is the gift of God; not a result of works, so that no one may boast."*

This passage emphasizes God's mercy and love. We were spiritually dead - unable to save ourselves - but God made us alive in Christ. Salvation is a gift received through faith, not something we earn. The image of being *"seated with Him in the heavenly places"* shows that believers are already secure in God's kingdom. This means your identity is not based on performance - it is rooted in grace.

Paul continues this theme in Romans 5:15, 17 - *"But the gracious gift is not like the offense. For if by the offense of the one the many died, much more did the grace of God and the gift by the grace of the one Man, Jesus Christ, overflow to the many... For if by the offense of the one, death reigned through the one, much more will those who receive the abundance of grace and of the gift of righteousness reign in life through the One, Jesus Christ."*

Here, Paul compares Adam's sin, which brought death to all, with Jesus' grace, which brings life to many. Jesus' gift of righteousness - being made right with God - far surpasses the effects of sin. It does not just cancel death; it empowers believers to *"reign in life,"* living with purpose and confidence.

Titus 3:5–7 reinforces this truth: *"He saved us, not on the basis of deeds which we did in righteousness, but in accordance with His mercy, by the washing of regeneration and renewing by the Holy Spirit, whom He richly poured out upon us through Jesus Christ our Savior, so that being justified by His grace we would be made heirs according to the hope of eternal life."*

Written around 62–64 A.D., this passage shows that salvation comes through God's mercy, not our deeds. The Holy Spirit regenerates us - makes us new - and we become heirs of eternal life. This means you are not just forgiven - **you are family**. You belong to God, and your future is secure.

Paul echoes this in 2 Timothy 1:8–9 - *"Therefore do not be ashamed of the testimony of our Lord... but join with me in suffering for the gospel, according to the power of God, who has saved us and called us with a holy calling, not according to our works, but according to His own purpose and grace, which was granted to us in Christ Jesus from all eternity."*

Here, Paul encourages bold faith. Salvation is not based on works - it is rooted in God's eternal purpose. Grace was God's plan from the beginning, not a backup strategy. You were chosen, called, and saved by grace.

Finally, Colossians 3:1–4 connects this grace to our new life: *"Therefore, if you have been raised with Christ, keep seeking the things that are above, where Christ is, seated at the right hand of God. Set your minds on the things that are above, not on the things that are on earth. For you have died, and your life is hidden with Christ in God. When Christ, who is our life, is revealed, then you also will be revealed with Him in glory."*

This passage urges believers to live with an eternal perspective. Your old self died with Christ, and your new life is secure in Him. For students, this means your worth is not tied to earthly success - it is anchored in heavenly truth.

Grace vs. Human Effort

From the beginning, the human heart has wrestled with the desire to earn approval through visible action or material proof. In the first century, many Jews believed that following the Law of Moses - through circumcision, sacrifices, and rituals - was the way to earn God's favor. Gentiles, too, were shaped by pagan religions that demanded offerings and acts of devotion to appease their gods. Into this world of performance and pressure, Paul wrote his letters to the Romans, Galatians, and Ephesians, proclaiming a radical truth: salvation is by grace through faith, not by works. This message challenged both Jewish legalism and human pride.

The Old Testament foreshadowed this grace. During the first Passover, God instructed His people to mark their doorposts with the blood of a lamb. Exodus 12:5–13 describes this moment: *"Your lamb shall be an unblemished male... And the blood shall be a sign for you on the houses where you live; and when I see the blood I will pass over you... so that no plague will come upon you to destroy you."*

This lamb pointed forward to Jesus, the true Lamb of God. In John 1:29, John the Baptist declares: *"Behold, the Lamb of God who takes away the sin of the world!"*

The Law revealed humanity's sinfulness, acting as a tutor to lead us to Christ. Galatians 3:24 explains: *"Therefore the Law has become our guardian to lead us to Christ, so that we may be justified by faith."*

Jesus' perfect life and sacrificial death fulfilled the Law, making salvation a free gift. Isaiah 55:1 prophesied this invitation centuries earlier: *"Ho! Everyone who thirsts, come to the waters; and you who have no money come, buy and eat. Come, buy wine and milk without money and without cost."*

Grace is for the thirsty, the empty-handed, the humble. It is not earned - it is received.

Grace Over Pride

Trying to earn salvation fosters pride - the very root of humanity's fall. In Genesis 3:5–6, the serpent tempts Eve: *"'For God knows that on the day you eat from it your eyes will be opened, and you will become like God, knowing good and evil.' When the woman saw that the tree was good for food... she took some of its fruit and ate."*

The desire to "be like God" led to rebellion. Pride says, "I can do this myself." Grace says, "I need a Savior." Ephesians 2:9 makes this clear: *"Not a result of works, so that no one may boast."* Salvation is designed to eliminate boasting. It ensures that all glory goes to God.

Adding works to Jesus' sacrifice insults His grace. Galatians 2:21 warns: *"I do not nullify the grace of God, for if righteousness comes through the Law, then Christ died needlessly."* If we could earn salvation, the cross was unnecessary. But we cannot. Jesus' death was essential - and sufficient. Paul celebrates this in 2 Corinthians 9:15 - *"Thanks be to God for His indescribable gift!"*

Grace makes us new. It replaces guilt with joy, striving with peace, and pride with worship.

Additional scriptures to deepen this truth:

John 3:16 - "For *God so loved the world, that He gave His only begotten Son, that whoever believes in Him shall not perish, but have eternal life.*" Salvation is a gift for all who believe.

Romans 11:16 - "*But it is by grace, it is no longer on the basis of works, otherwise grace is no longer grace.*" Grace and works cannot mix – salvation is entirely God's gift.

1 John 5:11-12 - "*God has given us eternal life, and this life is in His Son. He who has the Son has the life.*"

The Freedom of God's Grace

So how can you live in the freedom of God's grace? Let us explore three practical ways to apply this truth in your daily life.

First, accept the gift by faith. If you feel unworthy or think you need to earn God's love, trust that Jesus' sacrifice is enough. 1 John 1:9 offers this promise: *"If we confess our sins, He is faithful and righteous, so that He will forgive us our sins and cleanse us from all unrighteousness."* Confession is not about proving yourself - it is about receiving grace. Jesus is faithful. He forgives and cleanses.

Second, let go of pride. Humble yourself by admitting you cannot save yourself. When tempted to rely on good grades, popularity, or good deeds, remember that only Jesus saves. James 4:6 reminds us: "*But He gives a greater grace. Therefore, it says, 'God is opposed to the proud, but gives grace to the humble.'*" Grace flows to the humble. Pride blocks it.

Third, live with gratitude. Thank God daily for His free gift. Start your day with a simple prayer: "Thank You, Jesus, for saving me by Your grace." Colossians 3:17 encourages: "*Whatever you do in word or deed, do everything in the name of the Lord Jesus, giving thanks through Him to God the Father.*" Gratitude fuels joy. It reminds you that you are loved, not because of what you do, but because of who Jesus is.

13

The Early Church and the Question of Salvation

Imagine a bustling marketplace in a first-century city, where people from every corner of the Roman Empire - Jews, Gentiles, merchants, and travelers - exchange goods, ideas, and beliefs. In this vibrant setting, a new message spreads like wildfire: the gospel of Jesus Christ, proclaiming salvation through faith. Yet, even in this exciting time, a heated debate emerges among the early Christians. The question at the heart of the conflict is profound yet simple: What does it take to be saved? Is faith in Jesus enough, or must believers also follow the ancient rituals of the Law of Moses, such as circumcision?

This issue, which sparked disagreement among the first-century Christians, is not merely a historical curiosity. It reflects a timeless tension in human nature: the temptation to add human effort to God's gift of grace. This offers a powerful lesson about the nature of salvation, the freedom found in Christ, and the dangers of relying on our own works to earn God's favor.

In the early days of the Christian church, the gospel was spreading rapidly beyond the Jewish communities where it began. Gentiles - non-Jews from diverse backgrounds - were embracing faith in Jesus, drawn by the message of a Savior who died for all people. However, this influx of Gentile believers created a challenge for some Jewish Christians who had grown up under the Law of Moses.

For centuries, circumcision had been a sacred sign of God's covenant with Israel, a physical mark distinguishing God's chosen people (Genesis 17:10-14 - *"This is My covenant, which you shall keep, between Me and you and your descendants after you: every male among you shall be circumcised"*). To these Jewish believers, circumcision was not just a ritual but a badge of identity, a tangible link to their heritage and faith.

As Gentiles joined the church, some Jewish Christians insisted that these new converts must be circumcised to be fully saved. They argued that faith in Jesus was incomplete without adhering to the Law of Moses. This belief was not rooted in malice but in a deep-seated conviction that God's covenant required certain actions. It is like a high school student thinking they need to earn straight A's, join every club, and volunteer endlessly to "prove" they are worthy of college admission. The Jewish

Christians were adding a checklist to salvation, believing that faith alone was not enough.

The disagreement over circumcision was not a minor squabble - it was a theological crisis that could fracture the church. Acts 15:1-2 captures the intensity of the debate: *"Some men came down from Judea and began teaching the brethren, 'Unless you are circumcised according to the custom of Moses, you cannot be saved.' And when Paul and Barnabas had great dissension and debate with them, the brethren determined that Paul and Barnabas and certain others of them should go up to Jerusalem to the apostles and elders concerning this issue."*

Picture Paul and Barnabas, passionate missionaries who had seen God's Spirit move powerfully among the Gentiles, standing toe-to-toe with these teachers from Judea. The stakes were high: if circumcision was required, the gospel's message of universal grace would be restricted, creating a two-tier system of salvation - Jews who followed the Law and Gentiles who had to conform to Jewish customs. To resolve this, Paul and Barnabas traveled to Jerusalem, the heart of the early church, to enter into counsel with the apostles and elders.

In Jerusalem, the debate continued. Acts 15:4-5 records: *"When they arrived at Jerusalem, they were received by the church and the apostles and the elders, and they reported all that God had done with them. But certain ones of the sect of the Pharisees who had believed stood up, saying, 'It is necessary to circumcise them and to direct them to observe the Law of Moses.'"* These Pharisees, though believers in Jesus, clung to their tradition, insisting that Gentile converts adopt the full weight of the Mosaic Law. It is as if they were saying, "You can join our club, but only if you follow our rules as we do."

God's Grace Knows No Boundaries

The Jerusalem Council was a pivotal moment, and Peter's speech was a turning point. He reminded the assembly of God's clear revelation through his own experience with Cornelius, a Gentile, in Acts 10. Peter recounted how God had shown him that no one is unclean in His sight and that salvation is for all who believe.

Acts 15:7-11 captures his powerful words*: "Brethren, you know that in the early days God made a choice among you, that by my mouth the Gentiles should hear the word of the gospel and believe. And God, who knows the heart, bore witness to them, giving them the Holy Spirit, just* *as He also did to us; and He made no distinction between us and them, cleansing their hearts by faith. Now therefore why do you put God to the test by placing upon the neck of the disciples a yoke which neither our fathers nor we have been able to bear? But we believe that we are saved through the grace of the Lord Jesus, in the same way as they also are".*

Peter's argument is profound: God Himself had validated the Gentiles' faith by giving them the Holy Spirit, just as He had done for Jewish believers. If God made no distinction, why should the church? Peter compared the Law to a "yoke" that was too heavy to bear, a vivid metaphor for the burden of trying to earn salvation through human effort.

Imagine trying to carry a backpack filled with rocks up a steep mountain - each rock representing a rule or ritual you must perfectly follow to reach the top. Peter's point is that no one, not even the Jews, could carry that weight. Instead, Jesus offers a lighter path: salvation through grace, received by faith.

After much debate, the Jerusalem Council affirmed that salvation comes through faith alone, not through works of the Law. They sent a letter to the Gentile believers, reassuring them that they were not required to be circumcised or follow the Mosaic Law to be saved (Acts 15:23-29). This decision was a landmark in church history, preserving the gospel's simplicity and universality. It was like tearing down a wall that separated people from God, declaring that all - Jew or Gentile - could approach Him through faith in Jesus.

A Deeper Defense of Grace

The issue of circumcision did not end in Jerusalem. In Galatia, false teachers continued to confuse Gentile converts, insisting that circumcision was necessary for salvation. Paul, deeply concerned, wrote his Epistle to the Galatians to address this error head-on. His words are both a passionate defense of the gospel and a warning against legalism - the belief that human works can earn God's favor.

In Galatians 2:19-21, Paul writes: *"For through the Law I died to the Law, so that I might live to God. I have been crucified with Christ; and it is no longer I who live, but Christ lives in me; and the life which I now live in the flesh I live by faith in the Son of God, who loved me and gave Himself up for me. I do not nullify the grace of God, for if righteousness comes through the Law, then Christ died needlessly."*

Paul's imagery is striking. He describes being *"crucified with Christ,"* as if his old self, bound to the Law, was nailed to the cross alongside Jesus. The life he now lives is powered by faith, not by rituals. If righteousness could be earned through the Law, Paul argues, then Jesus' death was pointless - a sobering thought that underscores the sufficiency of Christ's sacrifice.

In Galatians 3:1-3, 5-9, Paul challenges the Galatians' confusion: *"You foolish Galatians, who has bewitched you, before whose eyes Jesus Christ was publicly portrayed as crucified? This is the only thing I want to find out from you: did you receive the Spirit by the works of the Law, or by hearing with faith? Are you so foolish? Having begun by the Spirit, are you now being perfected by the flesh? ... Does He who provides you with the Spirit and works miracles among you, do it by the works of the Law, or by hearing with faith? Even so Abraham believed God, and it was reckoned to him as righteousness. Therefore, be sure that it is those who are of faith who are sons of Abraham. And the Scripture, foreseeing that God would justify the Gentiles by faith, preached the gospel beforehand to Abraham, saying, 'All the nations shall be blessed in you.' So, then those who are of faith are blessed with Abraham, the believer."*

Paul reminds the Galatians that they received the Holy Spirit through faith, not through circumcision or any other work. He points to Abraham, the father of faith, who was justified not by rituals but by believing God's promise (Genesis 15:6 - *"Then he believed in the Lord; and He reckoned it to him as righteousness"*). Abraham's faith is like a seed planted long ago, sprouting into a gospel that embraces all nations through faith, not works.

Paul paints a picture of a heavy burden, like a wooden yoke placed on oxen to pull a plow. The Law was a constant reminder of human sinfulness and the impossibility of perfect obedience. Trying to earn salvation through works is like trying to climb a ladder to heaven with each rung representing a rule you must perfectly keep. One slip, and you fall.

Jesus, however, offers a different yoke*: "Come to Me, all who are weary and heavy laden, and I will give you rest. Take My yoke upon you and learn from Me, for I am gentle and humble in heart, and you* *will find rest for your souls. For My yoke is easy and My burden is light"* (Matthew 11:28-30). Faith in Christ replaces the crushing weight of the Law with the freedom of grace.

The Seed of Faith: Paul's reference to Abraham's faith (Galatians 3:6-9) is like a seed that grows into a mighty tree. Abraham believed God's promise, and that faith was credited to him as righteousness. This seed of faith, planted in Abraham, blossomed into the gospel, which promises blessing to all nations. This is a reminder that faith is not about earning God's love but trusting His promises, just as a seed trusts the soil to nourish it. When we believe in Jesus, we become part of Abraham's family, grafted into the tree of God's covenant.

The Jerusalem Council's decision was like opening a door that had been locked to the Gentiles. By affirming that salvation comes through faith alone, the apostles ensured that no one - Jew or Gentile - had to earn their way into God's kingdom.

Imagine a grand banquet hall where everyone is invited, regardless of their background, as long as they accept the host's invitation. Grace is the invitation, and faith is the act of walking through the door.

The Danger of Legalism

The debate over circumcision may seem distant to modern readers, but its lessons are timeless. Legalism - the tendency to add human works to God's grace - still creeps into our lives. This might look like believing they need to be "good enough" to earn God's love, whether through perfect behavior, attending church, or doing good deeds. While these actions are valuable, they do not save us. Salvation is a gift, received through faith, not a paycheck earned through effort.

Think of it like a scholarship to a prestigious university. If the scholarship is a gift based on someone else's generosity, you do not need to "pay" for it by working extra jobs. You simply accept it with gratitude. Similarly, Jesus' sacrifice on the cross is the payment for our salvation. Trying to add our own works is like telling the university, "Thanks for the scholarship, but I'm going to work three jobs to prove I deserve it." It misses the point of the gift.

The early church's struggle over circumcision teaches us that salvation is not about what we do but about what Christ has done. The Jerusalem Council and Paul's letter to the Galatians remind us that God's grace is sufficient, and faith is the key that unlocks it. Navigating a world full of pressures to perform and prove themselves, this message is liberating. You do not need to earn God's love - He already loves you and offers salvation as a free gift. Like Abraham, we are called to trust God's promises. Like Peter, we are invited to lay down the heavy yoke of legalism and embrace the light yoke of Christ's grace. And like the early church, we are challenged to share this good news with everyone, knowing that God makes no distinction between us and them.

Abraham and Faith

In his letter to the Romans, the Apostle Paul masterfully constructs a logical argument in Chapters 2 and 3, demonstrating that both Jews and Gentiles are saved not through rituals or strict adherence to the law, but by the transformative power of grace through faith. In Chapter 4, Paul uses Abraham, a foundational figure in Judaism, as a compelling example to illustrate that true justification comes through faith alone. He emphasizes that the only authentic descendants of Abraham are those who place their trust in Jesus Christ as their Savior, regardless of their ethnic or religious background.

Paul's argument delves into the heart of Old Testament theology, revealing that salvation has always been rooted in faith, not works. Abraham and other Old Testament saints were justified by looking forward in faith to the promised Messiah and His redemptive work, just as believers today look back to the cross and resurrection of Jesus. This continuity of faith across time is beautifully captured in Jesus' words to the Jewish leaders: *"Your father Abraham rejoiced to see My day; and he saw it, and was glad"* (John 8:56). In this verse, Jesus suggests that Abraham, through divine revelation, glimpsed the coming of the Messiah and rejoiced in the hope of salvation - a hope fulfilled in Christ.

To deepen this point, Paul highlights that God declared Abraham righteous <u>before</u> he was circumcised, and even before God introduced the covenant of circumcision (Genesis 15:6, 17:10-14). Circumcision was a physical sign of the covenant, but it was Abraham's faith - his heartfelt trust in God's promise - that justified him.

This distinction is critical: it was not the external act of circumcision that made Abraham right with God, but the internal posture of his heart, which expressed itself in unwavering belief. This challenges the notion that religious rituals or good deeds alone can earn salvation. Instead,

Paul underscores that faith is the foundation of a right relationship with God.

This truth carries profound implications for today. People may outwardly appear to follow God, attending religious services or performing good deeds, but God sees beyond appearances to the depths of the heart. As the Bible reminds us, *"The Lord looks at the heart"* (1 Samuel 16:7). Those who rely on external actions without genuine faith in Christ are deceiving themselves. Paul's message is a call to authenticity: to stop hiding behind superficial displays of spirituality and to embrace Jesus as Savior with true faith.

The Bible warns that rejecting Christ leads to ultimate folly, as true wisdom begins with acknowledging Him as Lord. *"The fool has said in his heart, "There is no God." They are corrupt, they have committed abominable deeds; There is no one who does good."* (Psalm 14:1).

Paul reinforces this with powerful scripture: *"For if Abraham was justified by works, he has something to boast about; but not before God. For what does the Scripture say? 'And Abraham believed God, and it was reckoned to him as righteousness.' Now to the one who works, his wage is not reckoned as a favor, but as what is due. But to the one who does not work, but believes in Him who justifies the ungodly, his faith is reckoned as righteousness"* (Romans 4:2-5).

Here, he quotes Genesis 15:6 to show that Abraham's righteousness came from faith, not from earning it through deeds. The term "reckoned" (*logizomai*) means God credited righteousness to Abraham's account, not because of his actions but because of **his trust in God's promise**.

Paul continues, *"For we say, 'Faith was reckoned to Abraham as righteousness.' How then was it reckoned? While he was circumcised, or uncircumcised? Not while circumcised, but while uncircumcised; and he received the sign of circumcision, a seal of the righteousness of the faith which he had while uncircumcised, that he might be the father of all who believe without being circumcised"* (Romans 4:9-11).

This passage emphasizes that Abraham's faith preceded the ritual of circumcision, making him the spiritual father of all believers - Jews and Gentiles alike - who share his faith. Circumcision was a "seal," a visible confirmation of the righteousness Abraham already possessed through faith, not a prerequisite for it. Paul presents Abraham as a model of faith for all people, uniting believers across cultural and ethnic divides under the banner of trust in God.

The message of Abraham's faith challenges us to examine our own hearts. Are we relying on religious routines, good behavior, or cultural identity to earn God's favor? Or are we, like Abraham, trusting wholly in God's promise of salvation through Jesus Christ?

The Works of Faith

In the book of James, the apostle confronts believers who claim to have faith but show no evidence of it in their daily lives. He boldly declares that faith without works is "dead" and useless, challenging Christians to demonstrate their faith through their actions (James 2:17). This passage does not contradict the doctrine of salvation by faith; rather, it clarifies that **true faith naturally produces good works** as evidence of a living relationship with Christ.

In James 2, written to believers who have already accepted Jesus as Savior, James addresses a problem in the early church: some Christians were claiming faith but living in ways that showed no change or commitment to God's will. To illustrate the inseparable link between faith and works, James uses two powerful examples - Abraham and Rahab - to show that authentic faith always results in obedient action.

<u>Abraham's Example</u>. James points to the moment when God tested Abraham by asking him to sacrifice his son Isaac (Genesis 22:1-18). Abraham's response was extraordinary: he obeyed immediately, trusting that God could raise Isaac from the dead if necessary (Hebrews 11:17-19).

As Abraham prepared to offer Isaac on the altar, God intervened, stopping him and affirming his faith. This act of obedience, James explains, was not what saved Abraham - his faith had already justified him decades earlier (Genesis 15:6). Instead, his willingness to act demonstrated the reality of his faith.

James writes, *"You see that faith was working with his works, and as a result of the works, faith was perfected"* (James 2:22). In other words, Abraham's actions completed or matured his faith, showing the world and God that his trust in God was genuine. This synergy of faith and works made Abraham not only righteous but also *"the friend of God"* (James 2:23).

Rahab's Example: James also highlights Rahab, a Gentile prostitute in Jericho, whose story is found in Joshua 2. When Hebrew spies entered Jericho, Rahab risked her life to hide them from the authorities. Her decision was not random; she had come to believe in the God of Israel, declaring, *"The Lord your God, He is God in heaven above and on earth beneath"* (Joshua 2:11).

Her faith in God prompted her to act courageously, protecting the spies and aiding God's people. Rahab's actions were the fruit of her newfound faith, proving that even someone new to faith - a "babe in Christ" - can demonstrate trust in God through bold obedience. Her story shows that faith transcends cultural, social, or moral backgrounds; what matters is a heart that trusts God and acts accordingly.

James addresses the practical outworking of faith in a believer's life. In the early church, some Jewish Christians emphasized external rituals, while others, perhaps influenced by a misunderstanding of grace, neglected holy living. James counters this by showing that **true faith is dynamic - it transforms** the believer and produces visible fruit.

Abraham's obedience decades after his justification shows a mature faith in action, while Rahab's immediate response reflects the power of even new faith to produce works. Together, these examples illustrate that faith, whether longstanding or newly formed, must express itself in actions that align with God's will.

James drives his point home with a series of rhetorical questions and examples: *"What use is it, my brethren, if someone says he has faith, but he has no works? Can that faith save him?... Even so faith, if it has no works, is dead, being by itself. But someone may say, 'You have faith, and I have works; show me your faith without the works, and I will show you my faith by my works.'... But are you willing to recognize, you foolish fellow, that faith without works is useless? Was not Abraham our father justified by works, when he offered up Isaac his son on the altar? You see that faith was working with his works, and as a result of the works, faith was perfected; and the Scripture was fulfilled which says, 'And Abraham believed God, and it was reckoned to him as righteousness,' and he was called the friend of God. You see that a man is justified by works, and not by faith alone. And in the same way was not Rahab the harlot also justified by works, when she received the messengers and sent them out by another way? For just as the body without the spirit is dead, so also faith without works is dead"* (James 2:14, 17-18, 20-26).

James' use of the term "justified" in relation to works does not mean earning salvation but rather being vindicated or proven genuine in one's faith. Abraham's willingness to sacrifice Isaac and Rahab's protection of the spies were public demonstrations of their inner trust in God. These acts were not the source of their righteousness but the evidence of it.

James compares faith without works to a lifeless body without a spirit - a powerful metaphor illustrating that faith, without action, lacks vitality and purpose (James 2:26). For believers today, this challenges us to live in a way that reflects Christ's transformative presence. If our lives show no evidence of love, generosity, or obedience to God's call, we must question whether our faith is alive

The examples of Abraham and Rahab also highlight the universal nature of faith. Abraham, a revered patriarch, and Rahab, a marginalized Gentile, both demonstrated faith through actions, showing that God values the heart's response over social status or religious pedigree. This was especially relevant in the early church, where Jewish and Gentile believers needed to understand their unity in Christ. James' message bridges the theological insights of Paul in Romans 4 - salvation by faith alone - with the practical reality that faith must be lived out to be authentic.

James' teaching urges believers to examine their lives. Are we actively responding to God's call, whether in small acts of kindness or bold steps of obedience? God often tests our faith through opportunities to act, just as He did with Abraham and Rahab. For mature believers, this might mean stepping out in faith during challenging circumstances, trusting God's provision. For new believers, it could involve simple acts of courage, like sharing their faith or serving others. As we grow in Christ, the Holy Spirit molds us to reflect God's character, fulfilling the Great Commission to make disciples (Matthew 28:19-20). If our actions do not reflect Christ, we must seek reconciliation with God, asking Him to renew our faith and empower us to live for Him.

James wrote to Jewish Christians scattered across the Roman Empire, many of whom faced persecution and social pressures. His emphasis on works was a call to live out their faith visibly in a world that often opposed them. By referencing Abraham and Rahab, he bridges the divide between Jewish and Gentile believers, reinforcing that faith in action unites all Christians. This message was vital in a church navigating cultural tensions and the temptation to compartmentalize faith as mere intellectual belief.

The message of James 2 is a clarion call to authentic Christianity. **Faith is not a private sentiment but a living force** that transforms how we live, love, and serve. Abraham and Rahab exemplify this truth: their faith led to actions that glorified God and blessed others. As believers, we are called to let the Holy Spirit shape us into Christ's likeness, producing works that testify to our faith. If our lives lack such evidence, we must turn to God, seeking His grace to revive our faith and align our actions with His will. True faith, as James reminds us, is never alone - it is always accompanied by works that reflect the heart of God.

The Definition of Faith

Hebrews 11 opens with a profound and timeless definition of faith: *"Now faith is the assurance of things hoped for, the conviction of things not seen"* (Hebrews 11:1). This verse serves as the cornerstone for the entire chapter, often called the "*Faith Hall of Fame*," setting the stage for a parade of biblical heroes whose lives embody this principle. For the original audience - Jewish Christians in the first century facing persecution - this definition was more than a theological statement; it was a lifeline, urging them to trust in God's promises despite visible hardships. For us today, this verse offers a blueprint for navigating life's uncertainties, inviting us to anchor our hope in God's unseen reality rather than the shifting sands of the world around us.

The phrase *"assurance of things hoped for"* (Hebrews 11:1) translates from the Greek word *hypostasis*, which carries the idea of a firm foundation or confident expectation. It is not wishful thinking but a deep-seated trust that what God has promised - salvation, eternal life, His kingdom - will come to pass, even if it lies beyond the horizon of our current experience.

The second part, "*the conviction of things not seen*," uses the Greek term *elenchos*, implying a **certainty** or **proof in the heart**, even without physical evidence. Together, these phrases paint faith as a dynamic force: it is both a forward-looking hope and an inner certainty that God's reality is more real than what our eyes can see.

This definition was revolutionary for the original readers. Written around A.D. 60–70, likely during or just before the intense persecution under Emperor Nero or Domitian, Hebrews addressed Jewish Christians tempted to abandon their faith under pressure from Roman authorities and Jewish communities who rejected Jesus as the Messiah. Social ostracism, imprisonment, and even martyrdom were real threats (Hebrews 10:32–34). In this context, faith meant trusting in God's unseen kingdom - a heavenly Jerusalem (Hebrews 12:22) - over the tangible but fleeting security of conforming to societal norms. The author of Hebrews used this definition to bridge the Old Testament's examples of faith with the new reality of Christ's fulfillment.

In the first-century Mediterranean world, faith was not a common concept in pagan religions, which often focused on rituals to appease gods rather than trust in their promises. For Jews, however, faith was rooted in their covenant with God, seen in figures like Abraham who trusted God's call (Genesis 15:6). Hebrews draws on this heritage, showing that faith has always been the hallmark of God's people. The Roman Empire's emphasis on visible power equals grand temples, military might, and emperor worship - clashed with the Christian call to trust in an invisible God. For these believers, faith was a radical act of defiance, choosing God's unseen promises over the empire's immediate rewards or threats.

The Jewish context is equally important. The readers, likely familiar with the Septuagint (the Greek translation of the Old Testament), would have recognized echoes of Old Testament faith in Hebrews 11:1. For example, Habakkuk 2:4 - *"the righteous will live by his faith"* - resonates with this definition, emphasizing trust in God amid uncertainty. The persecution faced by these Christians mirrored the trials of Old Testament heroes, making the chapter's examples a powerful reminder that faith endures across generations.

Theologically, Hebrews 11:1 positions faith as the bridge between the present and God's future. It is not blind optimism **but a reasoned trust** based on God's character and past faithfulness. The *"things hoped for"* include the ultimate fulfillment of God's promises - eternal life, the return of Christ, and the new creation (Hebrews 11:13–16). The *"things not seen"* encompass spiritual realities: God's existence, His sovereignty, and His redemptive plan through Jesus, *"the author and perfecter of faith"* (Hebrews 12:2).

Faith, then, is both **active and relational** - it involves trusting a personal God who has proven Himself reliable, as seen in the lives of the heroes that follow in Hebrews 11. The verse also implies a tension: faith requires waiting. The heroes of Hebrews 11 "*did not receive what was promised*" in their lifetimes (Hebrews 11:39), yet they trusted God anyway. This points to Jesus as the ultimate fulfillment of God's promises, making faith not just a historical act but a forward-looking hope in Christ's completed work. For the original audience, this was a call to persevere, knowing their faith was part of a larger story culminating in Jesus.

For modern readers, Hebrews 11:1 is a compass for navigating a world full of uncertainty, skepticism, and instant gratification. Faith is a GPS in "foggy times": Imagine driving through thick fog, unable to see the road ahead. Your GPS, though, assures you the path is there, guiding you turn by turn. Faith is like that GPS - when life's uncertainties (job loss, family struggles, or crises) cloud your vision, faith trusts God's direction, even when the destination is not visible. In a culture obsessed with instant answers, faith calls us to follow God's route patiently, trusting He knows the way.

Hebrews 11:1 challenges us to live differently in a world that prioritizes what is seen - wealth, status, or social media likes. Faith might mean trusting God's plan when peer pressure pushes you to compromise your values, like cheating on a test or chasing popularity. It could mean holding onto hope in God's provision during financial struggles or standing firm in your beliefs despite workplace pushback. Faith is not passive; it is an active choice to trust God's promises over the world's noise, to live for His kingdom rather than temporary trends.

This definition sets the tone for Hebrews 11's examples - Abel, Enoch, Noah, Abraham, Moses, Rahab, and others - who lived out this assurance and conviction in tangible ways. Their stories, rooted in this verse, show that faith is not just believing but acting on that belief, even when the world calls it foolish. As we face our own trials - whether personal doubts, societal pressures, or global uncertainties - Hebrews 11:1 invites us to stand firm, trusting that God's unseen reality is the truest thing we can hold onto.

14
The Honor Roll of Faith

Hebrews 11 is often called the "*Faith Hall of Fame*," and is a powerful chapter in the New Testament that celebrates the enduring trust in God displayed by men and women throughout biblical history. Written to Jewish Christians facing persecution around A.D. 60–70, this chapter encouraged them to hold fast to their faith despite trials, reminding them of their spiritual ancestors who trusted God against all odds. For us today, Hebrews 11 is a timeless reminder that faith is a living commitment to God's promises, even when the world offers no guarantees. Let us explore key figures in this chapter, their historical context, the deeper meaning of their faith, and how their examples encourage. A total of sixteen Old Testament individuals are listed in this 'Honor Roll' of Hebrews chapter 11. We shall briefly examine some of them.

<u>Abel: Faith in Worship</u>

The chapter starts with Abel, whose story is found in Genesis 4. *"By faith Abel offered to God a better sacrifice than Cain, through which he obtained the testimony that he was righteous, God testifying about his gifts, and through faith, though he is dead, he still speaks"* (Hebrews 11:4).

Historically, Abel and Cain were the sons of Adam and Eve, living in a pre-flood world where offerings were a primary way to honor God. Abel's sacrifice - likely the best of his flock - reflected a heart of genuine devotion, while Cain's offering lacked such sincerity. God's acceptance of Abel's sacrifice led to Cain's jealousy and Abel's murder, making Abel the first martyr.

Abel's faith shows that true worship prioritizes God's desires over our own. His offering was not just about the gift but the heart behind it - a willingness to give God his best. His death underscores that faith can come at a cost, yet his legacy endures.

In today's world, Abel's faith is like choosing to give your best effort in a group project, possibly a workplace task, even when others cut corners, because you are committed to a higher standard. It is posting on social media with integrity, refusing to chase likes with half-hearted content, because you value authenticity over applause. Abel's example challenges us to **offer our time, talents, and resources to God wholeheartedly**, even when it is unpopular.

Noah: Faith in Obedience

Next, Hebrews highlights Noah: *"By faith Noah, being warned by God about things not yet seen, in reverence prepared an ark for the salvation of his household, by which he condemned the world, and became an heir of the righteousness which is according to faith"* (Hebrews 11:7).

Historically, Noah lived in a corrupt, pre-flood world (Genesis 6–9), likely around 3000– 2500 B.C., based on biblical genealogies. In a society marked by violence and moral decay (Genesis 6:11–13), God chose Noah, a *"righteous man, blameless in his time"* (Genesis 6:9), to preserve life through a global flood—a concept unimaginable in a world that may not have seen rain (Genesis 2:5–6). God instructed him to build an ark, a massive vessel requiring precise craftsmanship, using tools and methods of a preindustrial age. This task, spanning decades - possibly 120 years (Genesis 6:3) - demanded relentless commitment while Noah faced ridicule from a godless society that scoffed at his warnings.

His faith was rooted in trusting God's word about an unseen future. His obedience was not merely practical (constructing the ark) but prophetic, as his unwavering dedication *"condemned the world"* by exposing its unbelief and rebellion. Each plank he laid testified to his trust in God's judgment and mercy. His righteousness stemmed not from perfection but from faith-driven action, aligning his life with God's purpose despite overwhelming opposition. Noah's faith also preserved creation, as he safeguarded his family and animals, embodying stewardship over God's world. His endurance shows that faith is active, requiring persistence in the face of doubt and hostility.

Noah's faith mirrors preparing for a radical career shift when peers urge, "Stay safe, don't risk it." It is like a scientist pursuing a breakthrough theory, ridiculed by colleagues, yet pressing on with conviction. It is investing years in a community project - like building a school in an underserved area - when others see no immediate payoff. In a culture craving instant gratification, Noah teaches us to build our "ark" - our purpose, values, or calling - one faithful step at a time. Noah challenges us to **heed God's warnings, act with courage,** and trust

His plan, even when the world mocks our efforts or the outcome remains unseen.

Abraham (Yes, again): Faith in the Unknown

Abraham dominates Hebrews 11, with multiple verses dedicated to his faith. *"By faith Abraham, when he was called, obeyed by going out to a place which he was to receive for an inheritance; and he went out, not knowing where he was going"* (Hebrews 11:8). Around 2000 BC, Abraham (then Abram) lived in Ur, a prosperous Mesopotamian city with advanced culture and idolatry. God called him to leave for Canaan, a distant land, with no map or guarantee (Genesis 12:1–4). Later, *"By faith Abraham, when he was tested, offered up Isaac"* (Hebrews 11:17), willing to sacrifice his promised son, trusting God could raise him from the dead (Hebrews 11:19).

His faith was a journey of surrender - leaving comfort for the unknown and trusting God with his deepest hopes (Isaac). His obedience was not blind but rooted in God's covenant promises (Genesis 15). His willingness to sacrifice Isaac showed that faith trusts God's provision, even in impossible moments.

Abraham's journey is like moving to a new city for a job without knowing anyone, trusting that opportunities will unfold. Offering Isaac is like letting go of a dream - maybe a relationship or a goal - because you believe God has something better. In a culture that idolizes control, Abraham's faith invites us to **step into the unknown, trusting God's direction** over our own plans.

Joseph: Faith in Perseverance

Joseph, sold into slavery around 1900 B.C. (Genesis 37–50), endured a harrowing journey marked by betrayal, slavery, and imprisonment in Egypt before rising to power. Born the favored son of Jacob, Joseph's early dreams of greatness provoked his brothers' jealousy, leading to his sale to Ishmaelite traders at age seventeen (Genesis 37:2, 28). In Egypt, he served in the Pot Egyptian household, only to face false accusations and years in prison (Genesis 39). Yet, by faith, Joseph interpreted dreams with divine insight, trusted God's plan through relentless hardship, and ultimately rose to govern Egypt, saving nations from famine (Genesis 41).

Hebrews 11:22 highlights his enduring faith: *"By faith Joseph, when he was dying, made mention of the exodus of the sons of Israel, and gave orders concerning his bones"*, trusting God's promise to lead Israel to Canaan centuries later (Genesis 50:24–25). Joseph's faith transformed suffering into purpose. Each trial - betrayal by family, enslavement, imprisonment - tested his trust in God's sovereignty. Rather than succumbing to despair, he excelled in every role, from servant to prisoner to ruler, reflecting a faith that saw God's hand in every setback. His dream interpretations, like those for Pharaoh, were not mere skill but acts of reliance on divine revelation (Genesis 41:16). His final act - requesting his bones be carried to Canaan - demonstrated unwavering hope in God's covenant with Abraham, a promise he would not live to see fulfilled. This forward-looking faith showed trust in God's timing, turning personal trials into a legacy of redemption for Israel.

Joseph's journey mirrors enduring an unjust setback - like a job loss or betrayal - while trusting new doors will open. It is mentoring others through your own struggles, believing in a larger plan. His faith is like a single parent working tirelessly to provide, trusting their efforts will bear fruit. In a culture craving quick fixes and instant success, Joseph's story challenges us to persevere through uncertainty, holding fast to God's promises. It is building a career through years of overlooked effort or forgiving a deep hurt, trusting God redeems pain for purpose. Joseph reminds us that **faith weaves our trials into God's eternal narrative, crafting hope from hardship**.

Moses: Faith in Sacrifice

Moses' faith is celebrated in Hebrews 11:24–26: *"By faith Moses, when he had grown up, refused to be called the son of Pharaoh's daughter, choosing rather to endure ill-treatment with the people of God than to enjoy the passing pleasures of sin, considering the reproach of Christ greater riches than the treasures of Egypt; for he was looking to the reward"* .

Historically, Moses (c. 1400 B.C.) was raised in Egypt's royal court during the New Kingdom, a period of unparalleled wealth and power under pharaohs like Thutmose III or Amenhotep II. Rescued from the Nile as an infant, he was adopted by Pharaoh's daughter, enjoying the privileges of royalty - education, luxury, and status (Exodus 2:1–10). Yet, at around age forty, Moses rejected this identity, choosing to align with the enslaved Hebrews, his true people, despite their oppression under

Egypt's brutal regime (Exodus 2:11–15). This decision led to exile, but later, God called him to lead Israel to freedom through the Exodus (Exodus 3–4), a mission fraught with danger and resistance.

His faith prioritized eternal values over temporary comfort. The *"reproach of Christ"* suggests he glimpsed a messianic hope, valuing God's redemptive plan over Egypt's fleeting riches. His choice to embrace hardship with the Hebrews over palace pleasures reflects faith's courage to stand with the marginalized, even at great personal cost. Fleeing Egypt after defending a Hebrew slave, Moses traded security for uncertainty, trusting God's purpose (Acts 7:23–29). His leadership - confronting Pharaoh, enduring Israel's complaints, and interceding for them - showed a faith that persevered through sacrifice, always looking to God's promised reward, a hope beyond earthly wealth.

Moses' faith is like declining a lucrative job that conflicts with your ethics to pursue a path aligned with your purpose. In a world obsessed with status, wealth, and instant success, Moses challenges us to invest in what lasts - relationships, justice, and God's kingdom - even when it demands sacrifice. His story is like a teacher staying in a struggling school to uplift students, trusting their efforts align with a greater good. Moses reminds us that faith often means **forsaking comfort for conviction, choosing God's eternal promises** over the world's temporary treasures.

Hebrews 11:32–34 mentions Gideon, Samuel, and others, stating, *"And what more shall I say? For time will fail me if I tell of Gideon, Samuel... who by faith conquered kingdoms, performed acts of righteousness, obtained promises"*. These figures, though briefly noted, exemplify faith's transformative power, each digging deeper into trust in God through distinct journeys.

<u>Gideon: Faith in Courage</u>

Historically, Gideon lived during the period of the Judges (c. 1200–1100 B.C.), when Israel faced relentless oppression by the Midianites, a nomadic people who ravaged their crops and livelihood (Judges 6–8). A farmer from the tribe of Manasseh, Gideon was threshing wheat in a winepress, hiding from Midianite raiders, when the angel of the Lord appeared, calling him a *"valiant warrior"* and commissioning him to deliver Israel (Judges 6:11–12).

Living in a time of spiritual and political chaos, with Israel's cyclic disobedience leading to divine discipline, Gideon's initial response was one of doubt. He questioned his worth, citing his lowly status as the least in his family and tribe (Judges 6:15). Seeking assurance, he requested signs - fleece tests - to confirm God's call (Judges 6:36–40), revealing a faith wrestling with uncertainty. Yet, by faith, Gideon obeyed, dismantling a Baal altar despite local outrage (Judges 6:25–27). God then reduced his army from 32,000 to a mere 300 men, ensuring victory would come through divine power, not human strength (Judges 7:2–7). Trusting God's unconventional strategy - using torches, jars, and trumpets - he led this small band against a vast Midianite army, securing a miraculous victory that shattered their oppression (Judges 7:19–22).

Gideon's faith grew from **hesitation to bold action**, a journey from fear to courage. His initial doubts reflect a relatable human struggle, yet his obedience shows that faith matures through trust in God's guidance. His victory "*conquered kingdoms*" (Hebrews 11:32–33) not by military might but by relying on God's plan, demonstrating that true strength lies in divine dependence. Gideon's story reveals that faith often starts small, grappling with insecurities, but blossoms through incremental steps of obedience, transforming weakness into triumph.

Today, Gideon's faith is like an entrepreneur launching a community initiative - like a food bank - when resources are scarce, relying on faith to bridge the gap. It is a young professional tackling a daunting work challenge, trusting in a vision others dismiss as impractical. In a world that celebrates self-reliance and instant results, Gideon's journey could mirror that a single, struggling, parent starting a small business, trusting each step will lead to stability despite skepticism. Gideon teaches us that faith transforms fear into courage, one obedient step at a time, empowering us to face overwhelming odds with trust in God's unconventional wisdom.

<u>Samuel: Faith in Listening</u>

Samuel, a prophet and judge (c. 1100–1000 B.C.), lived during Israel's turbulent transition from the era of judges to a monarchy (1 Samuel 1–16). Born to Hannah after her fervent prayers, Samuel was dedicated to God as a child and raised in the tabernacle at Shiloh under the priest Eli, in a time when "*the word of the Lord was rare*" (1 Samuel 3:1).

As a boy, Samuel's faith began with a transformative encounter: hearing God's voice calling him in the night, a rare occurrence in a spiritually stagnant Israel marked by corruption and idolatry (1 Samuel 3:2–10). Initially mistaking the voice for Eli's, Samuel learned to respond, *"Speak, Lord, for Your servant is listening,"* setting the foundation for a life of prophetic sensitivity.

By faith, he delivered God's judgment to Eli's corrupt household (1 Samuel 3:11–14), anointed Saul as Israel's first king (1 Samuel 10:1), and later David, shaping the nation's future (1 Samuel 16:13). Despite resistance, he spoke God's truth, confronting Saul's disobedience and mourning his failures (1 Samuel 15:26–35), yet obeyed God's call to anoint a new king (1 Samuel 16:1).

His faith was rooted in **listening to God and acting on His word**, even when it demanded courage. His sensitivity to God's voice required discernment in a culture deaf to divine guidance, and his obedience often meant delivering unpopular messages, like rebuking a king or lamenting Israel's demand for a monarchy (1 Samuel 8:6–22). His life shows that faith involves cultivating a heart attuned to God, paired with the resolve to follow through, even at personal cost. Samuel's role as prophet, priest, and judge bridged Israel's past and future, anchoring the nation in God's covenant through steadfast trust.

In modern terms, Samuel's faith is like tuning out the noise of social media to focus on core values, discerning truth amid endless opinions. In a world of constant distraction - scrolling feeds, competing voices - Samuel challenges us to carve out space for reflection, to hear and act on God's guidance. Samuel teaches us that faith requires both a listening ear and a courageous heart, acting with integrity when the world pulls us toward compromise.

In conclusion, Hebrews 11 was written during a time of intense pressure for early Christians. The author uses Jewish heroes to connect with the audience's heritage, showing that faith has always defined God's people. These examples - spanning from creation (Abel) to the conquest of Canaan (Rahab) - illustrate faith's diversity: worship, obedience, sacrifice, and redemption. The chapter's climax, *"And all these, having gained approval through their faith, did not receive what was promised"* (Hebrews 11:39), points to Jesus, *"the author and perfecter of faith"* (Hebrews 12:2), who fulfills God's promises.

Hebrews 11 challenges us to live with bold faith in a skeptical world. Like Abel, we offer our best to God, not just what's convenient. Like Noah, we prepare for God's future, even when it seems absurd. Like Abraham, we step into uncertainty, trusting God's direction. Like Moses, we choose purpose over popularity. Like Rahab, we embrace God's grace, no matter our past. Faith is our compass in a culture that often feels like a wilderness, pointing us to a hope that endures.

Wavering Faith, Restored by Grace

Hebrews 11 celebrates heroes of faith, but even the most devoted believers in Scripture had moments of doubt, disobedience, or fear. Their stories show that faith is a journey, often marked by stumbles yet redeemed by God's unwavering grace. The Bible assures us that wavering faith does not disqualify us; instead, God uses our failures to draw us closer to Him, restoring us to a deeper, unwavering trust. Below, we explore three figures - Jonah from the Old Testament, David from the Old Testament, and Peter from the New Testament - who faltered in their faith but were restored, offering hope for our own journeys in today's world.

<u>Jonah: Fleeing God's Call</u>

Jonah, a prophet in Israel during the 8th century B.C. (c. 780–750 B.C.), lived during the reign of Jeroboam II, a time of relative prosperity for the northern kingdom of Israel (2 Kings 14:23–25). The Assyrian Empire, including Nineveh, was a rising power known for its brutality, often threatening smaller nations like Israel. God called Jonah to preach repentance to Nineveh, a mission that challenged his nationalistic pride and fear of a hostile enemy (Jonah 1:1–2).

His faith **faltered due to fear and prejudice**. Instead of obeying God's command to go to Nineveh, he fled in the opposite direction, boarding a ship to Tarshish: *"But Jonah rose up to flee to Tarshish from the presence of the LORD"* (Jonah 1:3). Jonah's reluctance stemmed from his disdain for the Assyrians, whom he viewed as undeserving of God's mercy, and possibly fear of preaching to a dangerous, pagan city. His attempt to escape God's call showed a lack of trust in God's plan and sovereignty.

Jonah's **disobedience led to immediate consequences**. God sent a storm, endangering the ship and its crew. Jonah admitted his fault and was thrown overboard, only to be swallowed by a great fish: *"And* *the LORD appointed a great fish to swallow Jonah, and Jonah was in the stomach of the fish three days and three nights"* (Jonah 1:17). This divine discipline was both a consequence and a means of grace, protecting Jonah from death and giving him time to reflect.

In the fish's belly, Jonah repented and prayed: *"I called out of my distress to the LORD, and He answered me... I will sacrifice to You with the voice of thanksgiving"* (Jonah 2:2, 9). God delivered him, commanding the fish to vomit Jonah onto dry land (Jonah 2:10). Restored, Jonah obeyed God's renewed call, preaching to Nineveh: *"Yet forty days and Nineveh will be overthrown"* (Jonah 3:4).

His message led to the city's repentance, demonstrating God's mercy. Though Jonah initially struggled with God's compassion (Jonah 4:1–3), God used a plant and a worm to teach him about divine grace (Jonah 4:6–11), strengthening his faith in God's purposes. In a world divided by prejudice or fear, Jonah's story challenges us to embrace God's call to love others, even those we would rather avoid, trusting His plan over our biases.

David: Succumbing to Temptation

David, Israel's second king (c. 1010–970 B.C.), ruled during the United Monarchy, a period when Israel solidified its power against neighbors like the Philistines. Anointed as a young shepherd (1 Samuel 16), David was called *"a man after God's own heart"* (1 Samuel 13:14), yet his reign included significant failures. His era was characterized by tribal alliances, frequent warfare, and the establishment of Jerusalem as Israel's capital.

At the peak of his success, David's faith **faltered through idleness and lust**. Instead of leading his army, he stayed in Jerusalem and saw Bathsheba bathing: *"Then it happened in the spring, at the time when kings go out to battle... David stayed at Jerusalem... and from the roof he saw a woman bathing... and sent messengers and took her"* (2 Samuel 11:1–4). His sin of adultery, followed by orchestrating Uriah's murder (Bathsheba's husband), reflected pride and a lapse in devotion, prioritizing personal desire over his calling as a godly king.

His actions triggered severe consequences. The prophet Nathan confronted him, declaring, *"Why have you despised the word of the LORD by doing evil in His sight? ... Now therefore, the sword shall never depart from your house"* (2 Samuel 12:9–10). The death of David's child with Bathsheba, along with later family strife (Amnon's sin, Absalom's rebellion), showed how his wavering harmed others and his legacy.

David's repentance was swift and sincere: *"I have sinned against the LORD"* (2 Samuel 12:13). His prayer in Psalm 51 reflects deep contrition: *"Create in me a clean heart, O God, and renew a steadfast spirit within me"* (Psalm 51:10). God forgave David, restoring his relationship with Him, though consequences lingered. David's later psalms (e.g., 2 Samuel 22) and leadership reflect a renewed faith, trusting God's covenant promises (2 Samuel 7).

David's stumble is like getting caught up in a moment of weakness. His restoration is like owning your mistake and rebuilding trust with those you have let down. In a culture that often hides flaws, David's story shows that honest repentance opens the door to God's forgiveness, restoring our purpose.

Peter: Denying Under Pressure

Simon Peter, a Galilean fisherman, was a key disciple of all three years of Jesus' ministry. He witnessed the miracles, the teachings, and declared Jesus the Messiah (Matthew 16:16). But his faith was tested during Jesus' trial in Jerusalem.

His faith **crumbled under fear of persecution**. After Jesus' arrest, Peter followed but denied knowing Him when questioned: *"But he began to curse and swear, 'I do not know this man you are talking about!'"* (Mark 14:71). Despite vowing loyalty (Mark 14:29–31), Peter's fear of being linked to a condemned man overcame his faith, especially in the intimidating atmosphere of the high priest's courtyard.

Peter's denial led to immediate remorse: *"And he went out and wept bitterly"* (Luke 22:62). His failure caused emotional isolation and guilt, but it did not end his story. Jesus' resurrection provided the context for Peter's restoration, showing that God's plan outshines human weakness.

After His resurrection, Jesus restored Peter, asking three times, *"Do you love Me?"* (John 21:15–17), mirroring Peter's three denials. Jesus recommissioned him: *"Tend My lambs"* (John 21:15). Empowered by the Holy Spirit at Pentecost, Peter boldly preached, leading thousands to faith (Acts 2:14–41). His leadership in the early church and eventual martyrdom (traditionally under Nero, c. A.D. 64) reflect an unwavering faith rooted in Christ's forgiveness. In a world where fear of judgment can silence us, Peter's story shows that Jesus restores our courage, turning failures into opportunities for bold faith.

Pillars of Faith – Overcoming Wavering Faith

Even the most faithful Christians can falter, only to be restored by His grace. The stories of seven historical Christians - Martin Luther, John Newton, Corrie ten Boom, Samuel Ajayi Crowther, Pandita Ramabai, Watchman Nee, and Johnny Cash - show that faith is a journey, often marked by doubt, sin, or despair, yet redeemed by God's mercy. Spanning continents and centuries, their lives offer timeless lessons for navigating faith in today's complex world, proving that God transforms our weaknesses into powerful testimonies of His faithfulness.

Martin Luther: From Legalistic Despair to Reformation Faith

Martin Luther (1483–1546), a German monk and theologian, sparked the Protestant Reformation in 16th-century Europe. Born in Eisleben, Germany, during a time when the Catholic Church held immense power, Luther lived in a medieval world of feudalism and religious corruption, such as indulgences - payments to reduce punishment for sins. As an Augustinian monk, he sought to please God in a society where challenging Church authority risked excommunication or death.

Luther's early faith was driven by fear and legalism. Obsessed with his sinfulness, he confessed for hours and practiced extreme penances, yet felt God's wrath rather than love. He wrote, "I was exceedingly terrified at the wrath of God" (Luther's Works, Vol. 34). His wavering stemmed from a belief that salvation required perfect works, leading to despair that nearly drove him from faith.

His despair caused emotional and spiritual exhaustion, risking his withdrawal from religious life. His relentless efforts to earn salvation left him feeling unworthy, threatening to end his ministry before it began.

Studying Romans 1:17, - *"The just shall live by faith"* - Luther realized salvation comes through faith in Christ, not works. This insight, around 1515 - 1517, led him to post his 95 Theses in 1517, challenging indulgences and sparking the Reformation. Despite excommunication, Luther stood firm, declaring, "My conscience is captive to the Word of God... Here I stand" (Diet of Worms, 1521). His restored faith drove him to translate the Bible into German, making it accessible to all.

Luther's journey teaches that faith is trusting God's grace, not earning His favor. His despair mirrors our struggle with perfectionism, while his restoration shows that **Scripture can reframe our perspective**. His courage to reform a corrupt system inspires us to challenge injustice through faith.

His wavering is like being trapped in a cycle of overthinking, trying to "prove" your worth. His restoration is like finding a clear path through God's grace. In a world fixated on performance -Luther encourages us to rest in God's love, trusting faith over works.

<u>John Newton: From Slave Trader to Redeemed Hymn Writer</u>

John Newton (1725–1807), an English sailor and Anglican clergyman, lived during the British Empire's 18th-century maritime dominance. Born in London to a merchant father and devout Christian mother, he grew up in an era of naval rivalry, colonial expansion, and the transatlantic slave trade, a brutal system that enriched Europe's economy while dehumanizing millions.

Slavery was rarely questioned until later abolitionist movements, and Newton, as a young sailor, profited from this widely accepted practice, commanding slave ships in the 1740s. Newton rejected his mother's Christian teachings, embracing atheism, profanity, and immorality. He later described himself as "a wretch" in his Authentic Narrative (1764), admitting that pride, greed, and a culture that normalized slavery blinded him to God's truth.

His godless lifestyle led to reckless behavior, harming countless enslaved Africans through his role in their suffering. Near-death experiences - like a violent 1748 storm at sea and brief enslavement in West Africa by a slave trader's wife - exposed the emptiness of his rebellion, plunging him into despair and isolation from God.

The 1748 storm became a turning point, prompting Newton to cry out to God for mercy. Reading the Bible and *The Imitation of Christ* by Thomas à Kempis, he began a gradual conversion, wrestling with his past. By 1755, he left the slave trade, and in 1764, he became a pastor in Olney, England. His faith deepened, leading him to join the abolitionist movement, mentoring William Wilberforce and advocating for slavery's end. His hymn *"Amazing Grace,"* written in 1772, reflects his redemption: "I once was lost, but now am found, was blind, but now I see."

Newton's life proves that **no sin is beyond God's redemption**. His wavering shows how societal norms can dull our conscience, justifying evil until God's light pierces through. His restoration reveals God's power to transform even the hardest hearts, turning a slaver into an advocate for justice. In a modern world quick to cancel or condemn, Newton's life teaches that faith-driven repentance can heal personal failures and fuel societal good, offering hope that God's grace can redeem any past.

Corrie ten Boom: From Despair to Forgiveness

Corrie ten Boom (1892–1983), a Dutch Christian watchmaker, lived during World War II in Nazi-occupied Netherlands. The 1940s saw the Holocaust, with Nazi Germany systematically exterminating six million Jews and millions of others. In Haarlem, the ten Boom family, devout Calvinists, ran a watch shop that became a hub for the Dutch underground resistance. Motivated by their faith, they built a secret room in their home to hide Jews from deportation, risking their lives in a climate of fear, betrayal, and Nazi collaboration. Their network saved numerous lives, but informants exposed them, leading to their arrest in February 1944.

Corrie's faith faltered in Ravensbrück concentration camp, where she and her sister Betsie were imprisoned after their arrest. Facing starvation, brutal beatings, and dehumanizing conditions, Corrie witnessed Betsie's death in December 1944, a loss that deepened her anguish. The relentless cruelty of the camp - where over 50,000 women perished - tested her belief in God's goodness. Corrie grappled with despair and anger toward her captors, questioning how a loving God could allow such suffering. Her wavering stemmed from the trauma of loss, physical torment, and the temptation to let bitterness consume her heart.

Her despair risked hardening her spirit, potentially leading to lifelong resentment or loss of faith. In Ravensbrück's squalor, she struggled to pray or sense God's presence, moments that threatened to erode the courage that had driven her to hide Jews. This spiritual crisis could have left her embittered, undermining her earlier sacrificial love.

Betsie's unwavering faith, even in suffering, profoundly shaped Corrie. Betsie's vision of forgiveness and a post-war ministry to heal victims and perpetrators inspired Corrie to cling to hope. Miraculously released in December 1944 due to a clerical error, Corrie founded a rehabilitation center in the Netherlands to help war survivors rebuild. She traveled globally, sharing her story of forgiveness, most notably in 1947 when she forgave a former Ravensbrück guard who approached her after a talk, overcoming visceral revulsion through God's strength.

Her book The Hiding Place (1971) and its film adaptation (1975) chronicle this journey, inspiring millions to embrace forgiveness. Corrie's story shows that faith can falter under immense suffering but be restored through the transformative power of forgiveness. Her despair reflects the human struggle to trust God amid pain, while **her choice to forgive demonstrates faith's ability to overcome evil with good** (Romans 12:21). Her life illustrates that God can use our deepest wounds to bring healing to others, turning personal trauma into a beacon of hope and reconciliation.

Corrie's wavering is like being lost in a dark storm, doubting the light will ever return. Her restoration is like finding the sun through the act of forgiveness, illuminating a path forward. One of her most favorite quotes, (spoken many times by her sister Betsie) was "No pit is so deep – that He is not deeper still," and has been the text on many posters worldwide. In a world rife with deep grudges - Corrie's example urges us to release bitterness, trusting God to heal brokenness.

Samuel Ajayi Crowther: From Fear to Pioneering Faith

Samuel Ajayi Crowther (c. 1807–1891), a Yoruba man from Osogun, Nigeria, became the first African Anglican bishop, a monumental figure in 19th-century Christianity. Born during the height of the transatlantic slave trade, he was captured at age 12 by slave raiders in 1821, enduring the horrors of a slave ship before British naval forces liberated him in 1822. Resettled in Sierra Leone, a haven for freed slaves, Crowther was educated at a Church Missionary Society (CMS) school, where he embraced Christianity and trained as a teacher.

The 19th century saw European missionary expansion in Africa, often intertwined with colonial ambitions, creating complex tensions for African Christians navigating cultural identity and European skepticism. Crowther's ministry unfolded in this fraught context, as he sought to establish an indigenous African church.

Crowther's faith wavered under intense fear and cultural pressure. As a missionary along the Niger River in the 1860s–70s, he faced hostility from European missionaries who doubted African leadership, viewing them as inferior due to racist colonial attitudes. Local African communities, wary of Christianity's association with European imperialism, often resisted his message. Caught between these worlds, Crowther feared he was unfit to bridge the cultural divide, questioning his ability to lead. His self-doubt was compounded by personal losses, including the death of his son in 1864, and professional setbacks, such as the CMS's scrutiny of his missions. This hesitation threatened to paralyze his calling and slowed the progress of his mission to build an African-led church.

Crowther's faith was **restored through perseverance, prayer, and trust in God's calling.** Supported by African converts who shared his vision, he leaned on Scripture, finding strength in passages like Isaiah 41:10 *("Do not fear, for I am with you")*.

In 1864, he was consecrated as the first African bishop of Western Africa, a historic affirmation of his leadership. His translation of the Bible into Yoruba, completed in the 1880s, empowered African Christians to worship in their language, fostering a vibrant, culturally rooted church. His schools and missions along the Niger River laid foundations for African-led Christianity, proving God's faithfulness despite doubts.

His journey shows that faith can falter under external pressures - cultural rejection, systemic bias, or personal inadequacy - but be restored through God's affirmation. His fear reflects the challenge of living out faith in divided contexts, where identity and calling are questioned. His restoration demonstrates that God equips those He calls, using their unique cultural identity to advance His kingdom. Crowther's work bridged African and European Christian worlds, showing that faith can transcend cultural barriers. He inspires us to trust God's calling, persevering through opposition to create lasting change, confident that our identity is a gift for His purpose.

Pandita Ramabai: From Doubt to Transformative Ministry

Pandita Ramabai (1858–1922), an Indian Christian reformer, lived during British colonial rule in India, a period marked by social reform, religious tension, and the struggle for Indian identity. Born into a scholarly Brahmin family in Maharashtra, Ramabai was uniquely educated in Sanskrit by her father, defying norms that restricted women's learning. Orphaned young, she faced widowhood and poverty after her husband's death in 1882, navigating a society bound by rigid caste systems and gender inequality.

The late 19th century saw India grappling with British missionary influence, which sparked resistance from Hindu reformers and traditionalists alike. Ramabai's journey unfolded in this complex landscape, as she sought to reconcile her intellectual heritage with her newfound Christian faith.

After converting to Christianity in 1883 while studying in England, Ramabai grappled with doubts about its compatibility with Indian culture. Hindu communities branded her a traitor for abandoning her Brahmin identity, while European missionaries criticized her independence and refusal to fully adopt Western Christian norms. Caught in this cultural crossfire, Ramabai questioned whether God could use her as an Indian Christian woman to bridge these worlds, wrestling with feelings of inadequacy and isolation in her calling.

Ramabai's doubts led to personal isolation and slowed her early efforts to serve India's marginalized, particularly widows. Her skepticism about Christianity's cultural fit risked alienating her from both Christian and Hindu communities, threatening to limit her influence. This period of uncertainty could have derailed her vision, leaving her ministry fragmented and her impact diminished.

Through fervent prayer and immersion in Scripture, particularly passages like Galatians 3:28, *"There is neither Jew nor Greek, there is neither slave nor free man, there is neither male nor female; for you are all one in Christ Jesus"*, that affirm equality in Christ, Ramabai found a vision for a Christianity that honored her Indian identity. In 1889, she founded the Mukti Mission in Kedgaon, Maharashtra, a sanctuary for widows and orphans, offering education, vocational training, and spiritual care.

By integrating Indian cultural practices - such as using Marathi (her local language) in worship - she made Christianity accessible to her people. Her translation of the Bible into Marathi empowered Indian Christians to engage with Scripture in their language, fostering an indigenous church. Ramabai's restoration affirmed God's call to use her unique perspective to advance His kingdom. Her story illustrates that faith can waver amid cultural conflict but be restored through God's inclusive love.

Her doubts reflect the universal struggle to reconcile faith with cultural identity, especially in contexts of societal division. Her restoration demonstrates that **God equips those He calls**, using their unique backgrounds to bridge divides and effect change. Her work teaches that faith can confront systemic injustice - caste, gender oppression, or colonial legacies - creating lasting hope.

Ramabai's wavering is like standing at a crossroads, unsure which path honors your roots while embracing new convictions. Her restoration is like building a bridge between worlds, blending heritage with purpose. In a present globalized world of identity clashes - racial, cultural, or ideological - Ramabai's example is like an immigrant weaving their heritage into a new community, Ramabai inspires us to trust God to use our unique voice, and overcoming opposition to create transformative change for His glory.

Watchman Nee: From Compromise to Steadfast Witness

Watchman Nee (1903–1972), born Ni Shu-tsu in Fujian, China, was a pivotal Christian leader who founded the Little Flock movement, a network of indigenous house churches that profoundly shaped China's underground Christian community. Living through China's tumultuous 20th century, Nee witnessed the fall of the Qing dynasty, the instability of the Republic of China, and the rise of Communist rule under Mao Zedong.

The 1940s–50s brought severe persecution, as Mao's regime targeted Christians, viewing religion as a threat to state ideology. Churches were shut down, pastors imprisoned, and believers forced underground. In this hostile climate, Nee's ministry emerged, emphasizing autonomous local churches free from foreign missionary control, rooted in deep biblical teaching and communal faith.

In the 1930s, Nee's faith wavered under intense personal and external pressures. Criticism from Western missionaries and rival Chinese Christian groups, who questioned his independent approach, sowed discouragement. Personal struggles, including financial strain and family responsibilities, compounded his doubts. Feeling overwhelmed, Nee briefly stepped back from ministry around 1934, focusing on a family pharmaceutical business in Shanghai and distancing himself from his calling. This compromise stemmed from a temptation to avoid conflict and seek stability in a turbulent era marked by political upheaval and economic hardship. His hesitation reflected a human struggle to trust God amid criticism and uncertainty.

Nee's temporary retreat weakened his early influence, causing confusion among his followers in the Little Flock movement. His withdrawal slowed the momentum of his ministry, delaying the spread of his vision for indigenous, biblically grounded churches. This period of disengagement risked undermining his role as a leader, potentially diminishing his impact on China's growing Christian community at a critical time.

His **faith was restored through renewed commitment to God's call**, fueled by prayer and reflection on Scriptures like Philippians 1:6, which promises God's completion of His work. By the late 1930s, he returned to full-time ministry with vigor, refining his teachings on spiritual maturity and local church autonomy. His writings, including The Spiritual Man (1928), gained widespread influence.

Arrested in 1952 under Communist persecution, Nee faced false charges of financial misconduct, yet his faith remained unshaken. From prison, he smuggled out writings that became books like The Normal Christian Life, offering profound insights on living for Christ. Despite 20 years of imprisonment, harsh labor, and isolation until his death in 1972, Nee's steadfast witness inspired China's house churches, which grew under persecution, numbering millions today.

Nee's story illustrates that faith can falter under discouragement or societal pressure but be restored through recommitment to God's purpose. His compromise reflects our tendency to retreat when criticism, hardship, or fear overwhelms us. His restoration shows that God strengthens those who return to Him, using trials to deepen faith and amplify impact. Nee's endurance in prison transformed his personal struggle into a global legacy, proving that faith, refined in suffering, can inspire generations. He inspires us to press on, trusting God to sustain us through trials, turning fleeting setbacks into enduring testimonies of His faithfulness.

Johnny Cash: From Darkness to Redemptive Song

Johnny Cash (1932–2003), known as the "Man in Black," was an American singer songwriter whose music blended country, gospel, rock, and folk, resonating with millions across generations. Born J.R. Cash in Kingsland, Arkansas, during the Great Depression, he grew up in a poor cotton-farming family in Dyess, Arkansas, steeped in Southern Baptist traditions. The mid-20th century saw the United States grappling with cultural shifts: the rise of rock 'n' roll, civil rights struggles, and the countercultural movements of the 1960s–70s.

Cash's career, spanning the 1950s to his death, unfolded against this backdrop, marked by economic hardship, social change, and his own battles with addiction. His gospel music and prison concerts, like those at Folsom Prison in 1968, reflected his empathy for the marginalized and his deep, yet turbulent, Christian faith.

Raised on gospel hymns and baptized at age 12, Cash made an early commitment to Christ, influenced by his mother, Carrie, and his devout brother Jack, whose tragic death in a sawmill accident at age 14 left Cash guilt-ridden and spiritually shaken. As his fame grew with hits like "Folsom Prison Blues" and "I Walk the Line," the pressures of stardom - endless touring, media scrutiny, and access to drugs - led him astray.

In the 1960s, Cash's addiction to amphetamines and barbiturates spiraled, fueling reckless behavior, arrests, and strained relationships, including his failing marriage to Vivian Liberto. He later admitted to singing gospel songs like "Were You There When They Crucified My Lord" while under the influence, feeling the duplicity of his actions. His wavering stemmed from guilt, the lure of fame, and a culture that glamorized rebellion, causing him to drift from the faith of his youth. By 1967, at the height of his addiction, he crawled into Nickajack Cave in Tennessee, intending to die, overwhelmed by despair and spiritual emptiness.

Cash's wavering led to profound personal and professional consequences. His addiction contributed to the collapse of his first marriage, leaving four daughters and a fractured family. Legal troubles, including arrests for drug possession, tarnished his public image, and his erratic behavior alienated colleagues and fans. His spiritual disconnection left him isolated, as he later described to Rolling Stone in 2000: "To put myself in such a low state that I couldn't communicate with God, there's no lonelier place to be".

This period of darkness slowed his career, with fewer hits in the early 1960s, and risked derailing his calling to share God's grace through music. His internal conflict - between the "Johnny" who sought faith and the "Cash" who courted trouble - threatened to define him as a cautionary tale rather than a redemptive one.

Cash's restoration began in 1967 in Nickajack Cave, where, intending to end his life, he felt God's presence, hearing a quiet voice say, "I am still here, and I'm still waiting. I still love you".

Emerging from the cave, he committed to sobriety with the help of June Carter, a fellow musician whose steadfast faith and love became his anchor. They married in 1968, and her influence, alongside his renewed study of Scripture, guided him back to Christ. Cash's recommitment was marked by public acts of faith: he produced Gospel Road: A Story of Jesus (1973), a film about Christ shot in Israel, wrote Man in White (1986), a novel about the Apostle Paul, and recorded gospel albums like My Mother's Hymn Book.

His friendship with evangelist Billy Graham, whom he joined at over 30 crusades, reinforced his witness, as he shared his testimony of redemption to audiences worldwide. Despite relapses into addiction in the 1970s and 1980s, requiring treatment at the Betty Ford Clinic and other facilities, Cash always returned to his faith, declaring in his later years an "unshakable faith" in Christ. His final recording, a haunting cover of "Hurt" in 2003, reflected his lifelong journey of sin, grace, and redemption, with imagery of Jesus' cross in its video.

Cash's story, rooted in 1 Timothy 1:15 - *"Christ Jesus came into the world to save sinners, among whom I am foremost"*- shows that faith can falter under the weight of temptation but be restored through God's relentless grace. His struggles with addiction and fame mirror our own battles with worldly pressures that pull us from God.

His restoration, **fueled by love, Scripture, and community, reveals that God pursues even the "greatest sinners"**, using their brokenness to proclaim His mercy. Cash's music, from "Ring of Fire" to "Peace in the Valley," became a testimony, blending raw honesty with hope, reaching sinners and saints alike. His life teaches that faith, though tested, can grow stronger through trials, turning personal pain into a universal message of redemption.

Cash's wavering is like a ship lost in a storm, drifting from the harbor of faith under the pull of turbulent waves. His restoration is like finding the North Star, guided back by God's light and the anchor of loved ones.

His life urges us to return to faith, using our stories to shine God's hope in a broken world.

Martin Luther, John Newton, Corrie ten Boom, Samuel Ajayi Crowther, Pandita Ramabai, Watchman Nee, and Johnny Cash faced diverse trials - legalism, sin, despair, fear, cultural doubt, compromise , and addiction - yet were restored by God's grace. Their contexts, from medieval Europe to colonial Africa, Asia, and Communist China, to Hollywood mirror modern struggles: perfectionism, ethical failures, trauma, prejudice, identity conflicts, and persecution. Luther found freedom in Scripture, Newton in repentance, Corrie in forgiveness, Crowther in perseverance, Ramabai in contextualized faith, Cash in a returning prodigal, and Nee in endurance, echoing Hebrews 11's trust in *"things not seen"* (Hebrews 11:1). Their lives show that faith grows through trials, turning weakness into strength.

Wavering faith is like a flickering candle in a storm - dim but not out. God's grace is the shelter that steadies the flame, making it shine brighter. In a society quick to judge or divide, these stories remind us that no failure is final. Whether we are battling doubt, sin, or opposition, God invites us to trust His mercy, restoring our faith to light the way for others.

15
Salvation and the Holy Spirit

The Holy Spirit, the third person of the Trinity, plays an essential role in the process of salvation. Salvation, the act of being saved from sin and reconciled to God, is not merely a human decision but a divine work initiated, sustained, and completed by God's Spirit. The Holy Spirit is God Himself, equal with the Father and the Son, and His involvement in salvation reveals His power, love, and transformative presence in the life of a believer.

The Holy Spirit is not an impersonal force but a divine person with intellect, emotions, and will. He is fully God, co-equal with the Father and Son. The Bible affirms His deity in passages like Acts 5:3-4, where Peter confronts Ananias: *"Why has Satan filled your heart to lie to the Holy Spirit? ... You have not lied to men, but to God."* This verse equates lying to the Holy Spirit with lying to God, confirming His divine nature.

The Holy Spirit is eternal (Hebrews 9:14), omnipresent (Psalm 139:7-8), and the source of life and power (John 6:63). Understanding His divine nature is crucial because it underscores His authority and ability to accomplish the work of salvation in human hearts.

Salvation begins with the Holy Spirit's **work of conviction**, where He reveals to individuals their sinfulness and need for a Savior. John 16:8-11 is a powerful example of this. Jesus says of the Holy Spirit, *"And He, when He comes, will convict the world regarding sin, and righteousness, and judgment: regarding sin, because they do not believe in Me; and regarding righteousness, because I go to the Father ... and regarding judgment, because the ruler of this world has been judged."*

This conviction is not mere guilt but a divine awakening, showing people their separation from God and pointing them to Christ. Once convicted, the Holy Spirit regenerates, or gives new life to, those who repent and believe. This is often called being "born again,"

In John 3:5-6, Jesus tells Nicodemus, *"Truly, truly, I say to you, unless someone is born of water and the Spirit, he cannot enter the kingdom of God. That which has been born of the flesh is flesh, and that which has been born of the Spirit is spirit."* The Holy Spirit transforms a person's heart, making them a new creation (2 Corinthians 5:17).

This regeneration is entirely God's work, as Titus 3:5 explains: *"He saved us, not on the basis of deeds which we did in righteousness, but in accordance with His mercy, by the washing of regeneration and renewing by the Holy Spirit."*

The Holy Spirit enables faith, which is essential for salvation. Ephesians 2:8-9 states, *"For by grace you have been saved through faith; and this is not of yourselves, it is the gift of God; not a result of works, so that no one may boast."* The ability to trust in Christ is a gift facilitated by the Spirit, who opens hearts to receive the gospel (Acts 16:14).

Upon faith, the Holy Spirit applies Christ's righteousness to believers, a process (mentioned in a previous chapter) called justification. Romans 8:1-2 declares, *"Therefore there is now no condemnation at all for those who are in Christ Jesus. For the law of the Spirit of life in Christ Jesus has set you free from the law of sin and of death."* The Spirit **assures believers** of their right standing with God, freeing them from guilt and condemnation.

Salvation is not only a one-time event but an ongoing process of becoming more like Christ. The Holy Spirit indwells believers, empowering them to grow in holiness. In 2 Corinthians 3:18, Paul writes, *"But we all, with unveiled faces, looking as in a mirror at the glory of the Lord, are being transformed into the same image from glory to glory, just as from the Lord, the Spirit."* This transformation is the Spirit's work, shaping believers' character to reflect Jesus.

The Spirit also produces spiritual fruit, such *as "love, joy, peace, patience, kindness, goodness, faithfulness, gentleness, self-control"* (Galatians 5:22-23). These qualities demonstrate the Spirit's active presence, enabling believers to live out their faith in practical ways. Additionally, the Spirit empowers believers to overcome sin, as Romans 8:13 states: *"For if you are living in accord with the flesh, you are going to die; but if by the Spirit you are putting to death the deeds of the body, you will live."*

The Holy Spirit as the Seal and Guarantee of Salvation

The Holy Spirit serves as the **seal and guarantor of a believer's salvation**, ensuring their eternal security. Ephesians 1:13-14 explains, *"In Him, you also, after listening to the message of truth, the gospel of your salvation - having also believed, you were sealed in Him with the*

Holy Spirit of the promise, who is a first installment of our inheritance, in regard to the redemption of God's own possession, to the praise of His glory." The Spirit's presence in a believer's life is like a divine stamp, marking them as God's own and guaranteeing their future redemption.

This sealing also brings assurance. Romans 8:16 says, *"The Spirit Himself testifies with our spirit that we are children of God."* The Holy Spirit provides inner confirmation of a believer's relationship with God, fostering confidence in their salvation.

The Holy Spirit and the Completion of Salvation.

The Holy Spirit's work extends to the final stage of salvation, known as glorification, when believers are fully transformed into Christ's likeness at His return. Philippians 1:6 assures, *"For I am confident of this very thing, that He who began a good work among you will complete it by the day of Christ Jesus."* The Spirit, who began the work of salvation, will bring it to completion, ensuring believers' resurrection and eternal life (Romans 8:11).

The Holy Spirit's role in salvation reveals God's intimate involvement in human redemption. His work is not distant or mechanical but deeply personal, touching every aspect of a believer's life. The Spirit convicts to draw people to God, regenerates to give new life, empowers faith and obedience, and guarantees eternal hope. This underscores God's grace, as salvation is entirely His work, not human effort.

Moreover, the Holy Spirit's presence unites believers with Christ and one another. In 1 Corinthians 12:13, Paul writes, *"For by one Spirit we were all baptized into one body, whether Jews or Greeks, whether slaves or free, and we were all made to drink of one Spirit."* The Spirit creates a spiritual community, the Church, where believers live out their salvation together.

Understanding the Holy Spirit's role in salvation should inspire awe, gratitude, and dependence on God. Believers are called to *"walk by the Spirit"* (Galatians 5:16), living in reliance on His guidance and power. This involves prayer, studying Scripture, and yielding to the Spirit's leading in daily life. It also means trusting in the Spirit's work to sustain faith, even in trials, knowing that He who began the work will complete it.

The Holy Spirit is the divine agent of salvation, working from conviction to glorification. He reveals sin, grants new life, enables faith, transforms character, and secures believers for eternity. Through His presence, believers experience God's love and power, fulfilling the promise of John 14:16-17 - *"I will ask the Father, and He will give you another Helper, so that He may be with you forever; the Spirit of truth ... He remains with you and will be in you."* The Holy Spirit's work in salvation is a testament to God's grace, ensuring that all who trust in Christ are saved, sanctified, and secured for eternity.

The Choices of Life

Life for all of us is a life of constant choosing. Every day we have to make choices that will affect our lives tomorrow, next week, next year, and eternity. We have the choice to share Christ with others just as we have the choice to break the law. Some of our choosing has resulted in success while others have resulted in pain and sorrow.

Certain choices have made us happy and some have made us sad. Yes, to live in this life means to choose. But of all the choices we will be required to make in this life, there is none more important than the rejection or acceptance of Jesus Christ as Lord and Savior. No decision will have the awesome magnitude of that choice. It will determine your eternal future.

The Certainty of Judgment

We have a future appointment and it will be one of standing before Christ. 2 Corinthians 5:10 states: *"For we must all appear before the judgment seat of Christ, so that each one may be recompensed for his deeds in the body, according to what he has done, whether good or bad."* This verse is a sobering reminder of a universal truth: every person will one day stand before Jesus Christ **to give an account** of their life.

The phrase *"we must all appear"* underscores the inevitability of this divine appointment. No one is exempt - neither the rich nor the poor, the young nor the old, the believer nor the unbeliever. This universal accountability is rooted in God's justice and holiness. Hebrews 9:27 reinforces this: *"And inasmuch as it is appointed for men to die once and after this comes judgment."* The Bible reminds us that life is fleeting, and our choices now shape our eternal future.

The "*judgment seat of Christ*," known as the Bema seat in Greek, was a term familiar to the Corinthians, evoking the image of a raised platform where rewards were given to victorious athletes. For believers, this judgment is not about determining salvation - that is secured through faith in Christ (Ephesians 2:8–9) - but about evaluating their works and faithfulness.

1 Corinthians 3:12–15 explains: *"Now if anyone builds on the foundation with gold, silver, precious stones, wood, hay, or straw, each one's work will become evident; for the day will show it because it is to be revealed with fire, and the fire itself will test the quality of each one's work."* This imagery can resonate with teens who are familiar with being evaluated - whether in sports, academics, or personal achievements. The question is: Are we building with materials that last for eternity, or with those that will burn away?

For those who reject Christ, the judgment takes a different form, known as the Great White Throne Judgment, described in Revelation 20:11–15: *"Then I saw a great white throne and Him who sat upon it... And I saw the dead, the great and the small, standing before the throne, and books were opened... and the dead were judged from the things which were written in the books, according to their deeds."*

This judgment determines eternal separation from God for those who have not accepted Christ's atoning sacrifice. The contrast between these two judgments highlights the critical choice each person faces: to accept or reject Jesus as Savior.

For those who have accepted Christ, the judgment seat of Christ is an opportunity to receive rewards for faithful service. This is not about earning salvation but about living out the faith we profess. Romans 14:10–12 echoes this: *"For we will all stand before the judgment seat of God... So then each one of us will give an account of himself to God."* This raises practical questions: How are we using our time, talents, and resources? Are we living for God's glory or for temporary pleasures?

Consider the parable of the talents in Matthew 25:14–30, where servants are entrusted with resources to steward for their master. The faithful servants, who invested wisely, are rewarded with the words, *"Well done, good and faithful servant!"* (v. 21). This parable encourages us to think about their unique gifts - whether in academics, athletics, creativity, or relationships - and how they can use them to honor God.

Small acts, like showing kindness or standing up for truth, can be "gold, silver, and precious stones" that endure the test of fire.

However, the warning in 2 Corinthians 5:10 about "good or bad" deeds reminds us that not all actions please God. For believers, "bad" deeds do not result in loss of salvation but may lead to a loss of rewards. This can be a motivating concept. Choosing to follow Christ in a world that often mocks faith requires courage, but the promise of eternal rewards can inspire perseverance.

The Parable of the Talents: Stewarding God's Gifts with Purpose

The parable of the talents, found in Matthew 25:14–30, offers a powerful illustration of the responsibility we have to use our God-given resources wisely. In this story, Jesus describes a master who entrusts his servants with talents - significant sums of money - before going on a journey. To one servant, he gives five talents; to another, two; and to the third, one, *"each according to his own ability"* (v. 15). The first two servants invest their talents diligently, doubling what they were given, and are rewarded with the master's commendation: *"Well done, good and faithful servant! You were faithful with a few things, I will put you in charge of many things; enter into the joy of your master"* (vv. 21, 23). The third servant, however, buries his talent out of fear, producing nothing, and is rebuked for his unfaithfulness.

This parable is a vivid call to action, inviting you to consider how you steward the unique gifts God has entrusted to you - whether in academics, athletics, creativity, relationships, or even your time and influence. These gifts are not yours to hoard or waste; they are opportunities to honor God and build something eternal.

The choices you make today - how you use your talents - will be tested at the judgment seat of Christ (2 Corinthians 5:10). Will your actions produce *"gold, silver, and precious stones"* that withstand the fire, or will they burn away like *"wood, hay, or straw"*?

Understanding Your Talents

The word "talent" in the parable refers to a unit of currency, but for us, it symbolizes the unique abilities, opportunities, and resources God has given each person. Ephesians 2:10 declares, *"For we are His workmanship, created in Christ Jesus for good works, which God prepared beforehand so that we would walk in them."* This verse assures us that God has intentionally designed each of you with specific purposes in mind.

Your talents might include a knack for solving math problems, a gift for encouraging others, a passion for music or art, or the ability to lead a team on the field or in a business project. Even your personality traits - like compassion, humor, or perseverance - are gifts from God to be used for His glory.

It is easy to compare your talents to others' and feel either inferior or superior. The servant with one talent in the parable may have felt insignificant compared to the others, but the master did not expect him to produce five talents - only to be faithful with what he was given. Similarly, God **does not compare you to others**.

As 1 Peter 4:10 instructs, *"As each one has received a special gift, employ it in serving one another, as good stewards of the multifaceted grace of God."* Whether you have many talents or a few, the call is the same: use them faithfully to serve God and others.

What does it look like to be a *"good and faithful servant"*?

The parable shows that faithfulness is not about achieving grand results but about being intentional with what you have been given. Small acts of obedience can have eternal impact. For example, choosing to show kindness can reflect God's love, building "gold" that lasts. Standing up for truth - whether by defending a peer against gossip or sharing your faith in a respectful way - can be a precious stone in God's eyes. Even using your academic or professional skills can be an act of stewardship that honors God.

Consider the story of David in 1 Samuel 17:34–37, where he describes how he faithfully tended his father's sheep, protecting them from lions and bears. This seemingly small task prepared him to face Goliath, showing that God values faithfulness in the "little things." For you, this might mean being diligent in your schoolwork, practicing your sport or instrument with integrity, or investing time in prayer and reading God's Word.

Luke 16:10 reinforces this: *"The one who is faithful in a very little thing is also faithful in much; and the one who is unrighteous in a very little thing is also unrighteous in much."* Every choice you make now is practice for the greater responsibilities God may entrust to you later.

The Danger of Fear and Inaction

The third servant in the parable buried his talent out of fear, saying, *"Master, I knew you to be a hard man... and I was afraid, and went away and hid your talent in the ground"* (Matthew 25:24–25). His fear led to inaction, and his inaction led to loss. Fear can take many forms: fear of failure, fear of rejection, or fear of standing out. You might hesitate to share your faith because you're worried about what friends will think or avoid using your talents because you doubt your abilities. But burying your talents - whether by neglecting them, hiding them, or using them selfishly - robs God of the glory He deserves and limits your own growth.

Proverbs 3:5–6 offers a remedy for fear: *"Trust in the Lord with all your heart and do not lean on your own understanding. In all your ways acknowledge Him, and He will make your paths straight."* Instead of letting fear paralyze you, trust God to guide your steps as you use your gifts. For example, if you are gifted in writing, start a blog or journal to share encouraging words or if you are a natural leader, organize a service project for your church. These steps of faith, no matter how small, align with God's call to be faithful stewards.

The faithful servants in the parable did not just receive rewards; they were invited to *"enter into the joy of your master"* (Matthew 25:21). This phrase points to the ultimate reward: fellowship with God and the joy of knowing you have pleased Him. For believers, the judgment seat of Christ is **not a place of condemnation but of celebration**, where faithful service is rewarded with eternal significance.

Revelation 22:12 echoes this promise: *"Behold, I am coming quickly, and My reward is with Me, to render to every man according to what he has done."*

This can be a motivating vision. Investing your talents for God's kingdom offers rewards that last forever. Imagine hearing Jesus say, *"Well done, good and faithful servant!"* because you chose to use your gifts to love others and glorify Him. That moment will far outweigh any earthly achievement.

To bring this parable to life, consider these questions and action steps:

Identify Your Talents: Reflect on what God has given you. Are you skilled in music, sports, or problem-solving? Do you have a heart for helping others? Write down one or two gifts you can use to serve God this week.

Take Small Steps: You do not need to do something big to be faithful. Volunteer to lead a prayer in youth group, help a younger sibling or encourage a friend. These acts are "gold" in God's eyes.

Overcome Fear with Faith: If fear holds you back, pray for courage. Philippians 4:13 says, "*I can do all things through Him who strengthens me.*" Ask God to help you step out in faith.

Seek Accountability: Share your goals with a trusted friend, parent, youth leader or pastor. They can encourage you to stay faithful in using your talents.

The parable of the talents challenges you to see your life as a stewardship opportunity. Every gift, every moment, is a chance to honor God and prepare for the day you'll stand before Christ. By choosing faithfulness over fear, you can build a life of "*gold, silver, and precious stones*" that will shine for eternity. As you navigate life, let the promise of God's joy and approval inspire you to invest your talents wisely, knowing that even the smallest acts of obedience can have an eternal impact.

The Consequences of Rejecting Christ

There are tragic consequences of rejecting Christ, a decision with eternal ramifications. To reject the gift of salvation is to reject God's love and truth, effectively calling Jesus a liar, as 1 John 5:10 states: "*The one who does not believe God has made Him a liar, because he has not believed in the testimony that God has given concerning His Son.*"

This can be a challenging but vital truth. The decision to reject Christ is not always a dramatic, conscious act; it can be a gradual drift, a refusal to engage with God's truth, or a choice to prioritize worldly values. Yet, the Bible is clear about the outcome. John 3:36 warns: "*The one who believes in the Son has eternal life; but the one who does not obey the Son will not see life, but the wrath of God remains on him.*" Without

Christ's atoning blood, a person stands before a holy God with no defense against their sin, leading to condemnation.

The imagery of *"torment, weeping, and gnashing of teeth"* (Luke 16:23; Matthew 8:12) paints a vivid picture of the eternal separation from God.

In the parable of the rich man and Lazarus (Luke 16:19–31), the rich man, who lived for himself, finds himself in torment, longing for relief but separated from God's mercy. This is not meant to scare people into faith but to underscore the gravity of their choices. God desires all to come to repentance (2 Peter 3:9), but He honors human freedom to choose or reject Him.

The Parable of the Rich Man and Lazarus: The Weight of Our Choices

The parable of the rich man and Lazarus, found in Luke 16:19–31, is a sobering story that illustrates the eternal consequences of how we live our lives. Jesus describes two men: a rich man who lives in luxury, clothed in fine garments and feasting daily, and Lazarus, a poor beggar covered in sores, longing for scraps from the rich man's table.

After their deaths, their fates are reversed: Lazarus is carried by angels to Abraham's side, a place of comfort and fellowship with God, while the rich man finds himself in Hades, in torment, longing for even a drop of water to ease his suffering (v. 23). Separated by a great chasm, he pleads for relief, but Abraham explains that his choices in life have fixed his eternal state: *"Child, remember that during your life you received your good things, and likewise Lazarus bad things; but now he is being comforted here, and you are in agony"* (v. 25). This vivid imagery underscores the irreversible consequences of living for self rather than for God and others.

The rich man's downfall was not his wealth but his heart - his indifference to Lazarus's suffering and his failure to live for God's purposes. You face countless decisions: how to treat others, what to prioritize, and whether to follow Christ. The parable reminds us that these choices matter, not just for today but for eternity.

Yet, it also points to God's heart of love and mercy, as 2 Peter 3:9 assures us: *"The Lord is not slow about His promise, as some count slowness, but is patient toward you, not willing for any to perish, but for all to come to repentance."* God honors our freedom to choose or reject Him, but His deepest desire is for every person to turn to Him and find life.

The rich man's life was marked by self-centeredness. He had every opportunity to help Lazarus, who lay at his gate, but chose to ignore him. His wealth could have been a tool for blessing others, but he used it only for his own comfort. This reflects a broader biblical warning about the dangers of living for self. Jesus teaches in Luke 12:15, *"Beware, and be on your guard against every form of greed; for not even when one is affluent does his life consist of his possessions."*

This might not mean literal wealth but the temptation to prioritize popularity, social media likes, or personal success over loving God and others. The rich man's story challenges you to ask: Am I noticing the "Lazarus's" in my life - those who are hurting, overlooked, or in need? Am I using my resources - time, talents, or influence - to make a difference?

The rich man's torment in Hades reveals the gravity of his choices. Luke 16:24 describes him crying out, *"Father Abraham, have mercy on me, and send Lazarus so that he may dip the tip of his finger in water and cool off my tongue, for I am in agony in this flame."* This vivid picture of suffering is to awaken us to the reality of eternal separation from God. The *"great chasm"* (v. 26) symbolizes the finality of our choices in this life.

Hebrews 9:27 reinforces this: *"And inasmuch as it is appointed for men to die once and after this comes judgment."* This can feel distant, but it is a reminder that life is fleeting, and the way you live now shapes your eternal future.

In contrast, Lazarus's story offers hope. Despite his earthly suffering - poverty, illness, and rejection - he is comforted in eternity, resting at Abraham's side. This reversal reflects God's heart for the marginalized and His promise to lift up those who trust in Him.

Psalm 34:18 declares, *"The Lord is near to the brokenhearted and saves those who are crushed in spirit."* Lazarus's faith, though not explicitly described, is implied by his eternal reward. This is a powerful reminder that God sees your struggles - whether it is feeling left out, facing family challenges, or dealing with daily pressure. Your faithfulness to God, even in hardship, is never overlooked.

Lazarus's story also challenges us to see others through God's eyes. The rich man ignored Lazarus, but Jesus calls us to love our neighbors actively. Matthew 25:40 says, *"Truly I say to you, to the extent that you did it for one of the least of these brothers or sisters of Mine, you did it for Me."* This might mean befriending someone who is lonely, volunteering at a local shelter, or simply listening to someone who is struggling. These acts of love reflect God's heart and store up eternal treasure.

God's Heart: Mercy and the Call to Repentance

The parable ends with a poignant moment: the rich man, now aware of his mistake, begs Abraham to send Lazarus to warn his brothers, saying, *"If someone goes to them from the dead, they will repent!"* (Luke 16:30).

Abraham's response is striking: *"If they do not listen to Moses and the Prophets, they will not be persuaded even if someone rises from the dead"* (v. 31). This points to the sufficiency of God's Word to guide us to repentance. This is a reminder that God has given you everything you need to make the right choice - His Word, His Spirit, and the testimony of Jesus' life, death, and resurrection.

God's desire is not for anyone to face the rich man's fate. Ezekiel 33:11 captures His heart: *"Say to them, 'As I live!' declares the Lord God, 'I take no pleasure in the death of the wicked, but rather that the wicked turn from his way and live. Turn back, turn back from your evil ways!"*

God's patience and love are boundless, but **He respects our freedom to choose**. This is both a privilege and a responsibility. Navigating a world of competing voices - social media, peers, culture - the parable urges you to listen to God's Word and respond to His call to repentance and faith.

This parable invites you to reflect on your choices and their eternal impact. Here are some ways to apply its lessons:

Notice the Overlooked: Look for those who feel invisible or left out. A kind word, a shared lunch, or an invitation to hang out can reflect God's love.

Prioritize Eternal Values: Ask yourself: Am I chasing temporary things like *popularity or grades, or am I living for God's kingdom?*

Colossians 3:2 encourages, "Set your mind on the things above, not on the things that are on earth."

Share God's Truth: The rich man wanted his brothers warned, but it was too late. You have the opportunity now to share the gospel with friends or family. Be an ambassador for Christ (2 Corinthians 5:20).

Trust God's Mercy: If you are wrestling with doubts or past mistakes, remember that God is patient and ready to forgive. 1 John 1:9 promises, *"If we confess our sins, He is faithful and righteous, so that He will forgive us our sins and cleanse us from all unrighteousness."*

Choosing Life Over Regret

The truth of 2 Corinthians 5:10 is both a warning and a promise. For believers, it is a call to live faithfully, knowing that their works will be evaluated by a loving Savior who rewards obedience. For those who reject Christ, it's a sobering reminder of the consequences of their choice - eternal separation from God. This passage is an invitation to reflect on their faith, make intentional choices, and share the hope of the gospel with others. As they navigate the challenges of adolescence, may they anchor their lives in the truth of John 10:10, where Jesus promises: *"I came that they may have life, and have it abundantly."* The choice is theirs, and the stakes are eternal.

The apostle Paul writes in Philippians 1:6, "For I am confident of this very thing, that He who began a good work in you will perfect it until the day of Christ Jesus." This verse is a powerful promise for every Christian, assuring us that God is actively at work in our lives, shaping us into the image of His Son, Jesus Christ.

Navigating the complexities of life, this truth offers hope and purpose. God has begun a good work in you, and He is committed to completing it. However, this process requires your active participation, as you face daily choices to yield to His transforming power or to follow your own desires. These choices, though often small, carry eternal weight, shaping not only your character but also your future at the judgment seat of Christ.

God's Promise: A Work in Progress

Philippians 1:6 is a beacon of encouragement, reminding us that salvation is not a onetime event but the beginning of a lifelong journey of transformation. The phrase *"He who began a good work"* points to God as the initiator of our faith.

He continues to mold us, as a potter shapes clay, into vessels that reflect His holiness and love (Isaiah 64:8). The promise of *"perfecting it until the day of Christ Jesus"* assures us that this process will continue until Jesus returns or we meet Him in eternity.

This can be a comforting truth. You may not feel like 'a work in progress', wrestling with doubts, insecurities, or mistakes. But Philippians 1:6 reminds you that God is not finished with you yet. He sees your potential, even when you don't, and He is patiently working to bring out His best in you. Romans 8:29 reveals the goal: "*For those whom He foreknew, He also predestined to become conformed to the image of His Son.*" Every challenge, every decision, is an opportunity to grow closer to Christ's likeness.

The Choice to Yield or Resist

While God is faithful to complete His work, He does not force His will upon us. As Christians, you have the freedom to yield control of your life to Christ or to cling to your own plans and desires. This freedom is both a gift and a responsibility. Joshua 24:15 captures this choice: "*Choose for yourselves today whom you will serve... but as for me and my house, we will serve the Lord."*

This choice plays out in everyday moments: Will you honor God in how you treat your friends, respond to temptation, or prioritize your time? Will you trust His guidance, even when it is unpopular?

Yielding to Christ often requires courage, especially in a world that pulls you toward compromise. 1 John 2:15–17 warns, "*Do not love the world nor the things in the world... For all that is in the world, the lust of the flesh and the lust of the eyes and the boastful pride of life, is not from the Father, but is from the world. The world is passing away and also its lusts; but the one who does the will of God continues forever."* We face these temptations daily. Choosing God's way means anchoring your decisions in His Word, even when it feels countercultural.

Walking by the Spirit vs. the Flesh

Every day presents a choice between walking by the Spirit or returning to the deeds of our sinful nature. Galatians 5:16–17 explains,

*"*But I say, walk by the Spirit, and you will not carry out the desire of the flesh. For the flesh sets its desire against the Spirit, and the Spirit against the flesh; for these are in opposition to one another, so that you do not do what the flesh desires."*"

This internal battle is real for every Christian. The *"works of the flesh"* listed in Galatians 5:19–21 - such as jealousy, strife, and immorality - can be tempting. In contrast, the *"fruit of the Spirit"* (v. 22–23) - love, joy, peace, patience, kindness, goodness, faithfulness, gentleness, and self-control - reflect the character God is forming in you.

Romans 6:12–13 urges, *"Therefore do not let sin reign in your mortal body so that you obey its lusts... but present yourselves to God as those alive from the dead, and your members as instruments of righteousness to God."* Each decision to walk by the Spirit is a step toward becoming the person God created you to be.

The Fruit of Our Choices

The Bible teaches that our choices bear fruit, both in this life and eternity. Galatians 6:7–8 states, *"Do not be deceived, God is not mocked; for whatever a person sows, this he will also reap. For the one who sows to his own flesh will from the flesh reap corruption, but the one who sows to the Spirit will from the Spirit reap eternal life."*

As a Christian, the fruit you produce - your attitudes, actions, and impact on others - reveals what you are sowing. Are you cultivating love, kindness, and faithfulness, or are you stuck in stagnation, indifference, or selfishness?

This principle is practical. If you sow time into prayer and studying God's Word, you will grow in wisdom and peace (Psalm 119:165). If you sow kindness, you will build relationships that reflect Christ's love. Conversely, sowing to the flesh - through dishonesty, laziness, or pride - leads to consequences like broken trust or missed opportunities.

Jesus' words in Matthew 7:16–17 emphasize this: *"You will know them by their fruits... Every good tree produces good fruit, but the bad tree produces bad fruit."* Ask yourself: What kind of fruit am I producing in my school, family, job, or friendships? What does it reveal about my heart?

Taking Up Your Cross: The Cost of Discipleship

Jesus' call in Matthew 16:24 is both challenging and inspiring: *"If anyone wants to come after Me, he must deny himself, and take up his cross, and follow Me."* Taking up your cross means dying to selfish desires and living for God's purposes, even when it's difficult.

This might mean standing up for your faith, choosing purity in relationships, or prioritizing church over a busy schedule. These choices can feel like a cross - heavy and costly - but they lead to life. Jesus continues in verse 25, *"For whoever wants to save his life will lose it; but whoever loses his life for My sake will find it."*

Consider the example of Daniel, who resolved not to defile himself with the king's food (Daniel 1:8). As a young man in a foreign land, he faced pressure to conform, yet he chose obedience to God. His faithfulness led to God's favor and influence. Such choices shape your character and prepare you for God's greater plans.

Philippians 1:6 assures us that God is at work, but your choices matter. It is a promise that God is committed to perfecting you, but it is also a call to choose His way daily. You face countless decisions that shape your character and eternal future. Will you yield to the Spirit or follow the flesh? Will you sow seeds of faith or stagnation? Jesus' invitation to take up your cross is an opportunity to partner with God in His transformative work. By making choices rooted in His Word, you can produce fruit that lasts for eternity, confident that *"He who began a good work in you will perfect it until the day of Christ Jesus."*

Let this truth inspire you to live boldly for Christ, knowing that every step of obedience draws you closer to His perfect design for your life.

16

The Crowns, Rewards, and Heaven

The Crowns of Life

The Holy Spirit's work in salvation not only secures believers' eternal life but also prepares them for the crowns and rewards God promises to those who faithfully follow Christ. These rewards are not earned through human effort alone but are gracious gifts from God, made possible through the Spirit's empowerment and guidance.

The Bible speaks of specific crowns and rewards awaiting believers, each carrying profound spiritual significance and reflecting the culmination of a life transformed by the Holy Spirit.

The New Testament describes several "crowns" (in the Greek: *stephanos*, means **a victor's crown**) as rewards for faithful service. These crowns symbolize honor, victory, and God's approval of a believer's life. They are not given for salvation itself, which is a gift of grace (Ephesians 2:8-9), but for how believers live out their salvation through the Holy Spirit's enablement. Below are key crowns mentioned in Scripture:

The Crown of Life: This crown is promised to those who endure trials and remain faithful, even unto death. James 1:12 states, *"Blessed is a man who perseveres under trial; for once he has been approved, he will receive the crown of life which the Lord has promised to those who love Him."* Similarly, Revelation 2:10 encourages persecuted believers: *"Be faithful until death, and I will give you the crown of life."* This crown signifies eternal life and the joy of overcoming through the Spirit's strength, as the Holy Spirit sustains believers in trials (Romans 8:13).

The Crown of Righteousness: Awarded to those who long for Christ's return and live righteously, this crown reflects a life aligned with God's will. In 2 Timothy 4:7- 8, Paul writes, *"I have fought the good fight, I have finished the race, I have kept the faith; in the future there is reserved for me the crown of righteousness, which the Lord, the righteous Judge, will award to me on that day; and not only to me, but also to all who have loved His appearing."* The Holy Spirit fosters this longing for Christ's return, guiding believers to live in holiness (2 Corinthians 3:18).

The Crown of Glory: This crown is promised to faithful shepherds and leaders who serve God's people selflessly. 1 Peter 5:2-4 instructs elders to *"shepherd the flock of God among you ... not under compulsion, but voluntarily ... and when the Chief Shepherd appears, you will receive the unfading crown of glory."* This reward highlights the Spirit's work in equipping leaders to serve with humility and love, reflecting Christ's example (John 16:13-14).

The Crown of Rejoicing: This crown is associated with the joy of leading others to faith in Christ. In 1 Thessalonians 2:19-20, Paul asks, *"For who is our hope or joy or crown of exultation? Is it not even you, in the presence of our Lord Jesus at His coming? For you are our glory and joy."* The Holy Spirit empowers believers to share the gospel (Acts 1:8), and those won to Christ become a source of eternal joy, a reward for faithful witness.

The Imperishable Crown: This crown is given to those who exercise discipline in their 'Christian Walk', pursuing godliness with perseverance. In 1 Corinthians 9:24- 25, Paul compares the Christian life to a race: *"Run in such a way that you may win. Everyone who competes in the games exercises self-control in all things. They then do it to receive a perishable wreath, but we an imperishable."* The Holy Spirit enables this discipline, helping believers *"put to death the deeds of the body"* (Romans 8:13) to live for eternal purposes.

Treasures Beyond crowns

Scripture describes additional rewards for believers who faithfully serve God. These rewards are often linked to stewardship - how believers use their time, talents, and resources for God's kingdom. In Matthew 6:19-20, Jesus instructs, *"Do not store up for yourselves treasures on earth, where moth and rust destroy, and where thieves break in and steal. But store up for yourselves treasures in heaven, where neither moth nor rust destroys, and where thieves do not break in or steal."* These treasures are eternal rewards for acts of faith, generosity, and obedience, empowered by the Holy Spirit.

The parable of the talents (Matthew 25:14-30) as previously studied, illustrates this principle. This reward includes greater responsibility and intimacy with God in eternity, reflecting the Spirit's work in cultivating faithfulness (Galatians 5:22- 23).

The crowns and rewards awaiting believers are not about personal glory but about glorifying God. They reflect the Holy Spirit's transformative work, as He enables believers to live lives worthy of their calling (Ephesians 4:1). These rewards are rooted in God's grace, not human merit, as the Spirit equips believers to persevere, serve, and love. The crowns also point to the ultimate reward: eternal fellowship with Christ.

Revelation 22:12 records Jesus' words: *"Behold, I am coming quickly, and My reward is with Me, to render to every man according to what he has done."* This reward is ultimately Christ Himself, the source of all joy and fulfillment. Moreover, the act of receiving crowns and rewards is often depicted as an act of worship.

In Revelation 4:10-11, the twenty-four elders *"cast their crowns before the throne, saying, 'Worthy are You, our Lord and our God, to receive glory and honor and power.'"* This suggests that believers' rewards are not for personal boasting but for offering back to God, acknowledging that all they have accomplished is through the Spirit's power.

The promise of crowns and rewards motivates believers to live with eternal perspective, knowing their faithfulness matters. The Holy Spirit empowers them to persevere in trials, share the gospel, serve humbly, and long for Christ's return. Believers should rely on the Spirit through prayer and obedience, trusting Him to produce eternal fruit. At the same time, the focus remains on God's glory, not personal gain, as all rewards are ultimately a reflection of His grace.

Every crown, every treasure, points back to Him. The true reward, after all, is Christ Himself, as He declares, *"Behold, I am coming quickly, and My reward is with Me"* (Revelation 22:12).

If you have asked Jesus Christ to come into your life, to forgive you of your sins, and ask Him to make you the kind of person He wants you to be – you are part of the 'reward' coming back with Christ Himself. I very much look forward to meeting you and fellowshipping together – and all in the glory of His presence. Amen.

Heaven – What is it really like?

"Do not let your heart be troubled; believe in God, believe also in Me. In My Father's house are many dwelling places; if it were not so, I

would have told you; for I go to prepare a place for you. If I go and prepare a place for you, I will come again and receive you to Myself; that where I am, there you may be also." (John 14:1-3)

Heaven is the dwelling place of God, as well as myriads upon myriads of angels, and a host of countless other heavenly creatures. Sitting at the right-hand of the Father on the Throne is Jesus, who is interceding on behalf of those who are His followers. Our world is but a small glimpse (or hazy mirror) of what Heaven is truly like (1 Corinthians 2:9; 13:12).

Because of our limitations as humans we cannot (even with our wildest imaginations) fathom the depth of Heaven's beauty, glory, riches, emotions, relationships, and magnificence. The music, praise, aromas, colors, landscapes, among many other things are currently beyond our fullest comprehension.

The root meanings for the Biblical Greek word for Heaven *(ouranus)* literally means '**to cover**' and '**to encompass**.' Simply stated then, Heaven encompasses the intimate, personal presence of God; and will be an eternal, perfect, indescribable place bestowed upon us because we are 'covered' by the blood shed on the cross by Christ.

An important note to consider when discussing Heaven - is the resurrected Christ. Jesus was recognizable by His followers; He ate and cooked food; He instantly vanished from one place to another; He went through walls and into the presence of His Disciples; yet He also was flesh and bone and touched by the Disciples; He 'rose' in the air; and He will be riding a horse when He returns to the earth.

In Heaven there is no sickness, pain, death, cancer, blindness, turmoil, depression, anger, war, arguments, hate, lying, stealing, nightmares, accidents, divorce, sin, growing old, fear, loneliness, anxiety, hopelessness, boredom, traffic tickets, debts, and every other form of uncertainty and human weakness. In Heaven, there will be no banks or money. Even the streets you walk upon are paved with perfect gold. However, the Bible does give us a partial glimpse of what is in Heaven.

<u>In Heaven</u>:

Angels accompany the 'new arrivers' into God's presence (Luke 16:19-31)

God's people will receive an inheritance and treasures (Ephesians 1:18; John 1:12; Matthew 19:21; Luke 12:33; 18:22)

We are going to reign with Christ as Children of the King and serve Him simultaneously (Revelation 22:3; 2 Timothy 2:12; Romans 5:17)

Our bodies will be imperishable and immortal (1 Corinthians 15:52)

We will have an everlasting home, and our citizenship will be there (2 Cor 5:8; Philippians 3:20)

Christ Himself will fill us with joy and eternal pleasures (Psalms 16:11)

Christ Himself will reward His children with crowns (2 Tim 4:8; James 1:12; 1 Peter 5:4)

There will be an enormous City that is 1500 miles across, 1500 miles wide, and 1500 miles high. (Hebrews 11:6, Revelation 21:10-27)

A very comforting thought is that when we get to Heaven not only will we recognize and remember family members, friends, and other acquaintances; we will also recognize (and get to know) Bible characters in Heaven you have read about, as well as other 'saints' who have gone before you into God's presence throughout human history (Matthew 17: 1-9). And the best part about Heaven will be seeing, conversing, and enjoying Jesus Christ face-to-face.

Additional Scripture passages:

"And it will be said in that day, "Behold, this is our God for whom we have waited that He might save us. This the Lord for whom we have waited; Let us rejoice and be glad in His salvation." (Isaiah 25:9)

"And He will reign over the house of Jacob forever, and His Kingdom will have no end." (Luke 1:33)

"Things which eye has not seen and ear has not heard, and which have not entered the heart of man, all that God has prepared for those who love Him." (1 Cor 2:9)

"But store up for yourselves treasures in heaven, where neither moth nor rust destroys, and where thieves do not break in and steal." (Matthew 6:20)

"And He will wipe away every tear from their eyes; and there will no longer be any death; there will no longer be any mourning, or crying, or pain; the first things have passed away." (Revelation 21:4)

"And I will dwell in the house of the Lord forever." (Psalms 23:6)

"There will no longer be any curse; and the throne of God and of the Lamb will be in it; and His bond-servants will serve Him." (Revelation 22:3)

Amen. So let it be so

About The Author

As the founder and president of *Layman Bible College Institute*, RW Nelson and a network of diligent pastors, provides structured Bible education courses (via online meeting resources) to Christians living in small remote villages and economically challenged areas from central Africa all the way to the Koreas.

In recent years, RW originated and coordinated three annual symposiums (attended by many global ministries) to plan and meet the needs of the people of North Korea and the global North Korean Diaspora. He is the co-founder of *'Hearts for North Koreans International'* a global North Korea educational and awareness program (hearts4northkorea.net), and the Executive Director of the *'Korea Unite International Honor Society'*.

Born in Texas, he received his Bachelor of Arts degree from Texas A&M University and Master of Arts degree in Communications (with a cognate in Media Management) from Regent University, and the Christian Broadcasting Network, Virginia Beach, VA.

RW is an ordained Baptist minister; and the former president of two Christian film distribution companies. For numerous years, he was also the creator and host of the radio program - *'Bible School of the Air'*, sharing God's Word to North America, South America and Africa. With the assistance of his daughter Ayu, RW created the online scripture memory course *'A-Z Scripture Memory'*, engaging many thousands of young Christian students and Christian schools from many parts of the world in the memorization of God's Word.

He is the writer of many Laymen Bible College courses such as *'The Minor Prophets, The Beatitudes, The Holy Spirit, Old Testament Survey, New Testament Survey, Romans, The Book of Luke, Spiritual Warfare*, (among others); and wrote his first historical fiction novel - <u>No Dark Clouds</u> while ministering in India for two and a half years (rwnelson-author.com).

Finally, RW holds two certified California special education teaching credentials, and is the recipient of two AFI/Digital Voices Awards for the video productions, *An Emerson to Einstein Silent Movie'* and *'Mummy Math.'*

www.ingramcontent.com/pod-product-compliance
Lightning Source LLC
LaVergne TN
LVHW020926090426
835512LV00020B/3231